Western Frontiersmen Series
XXXI

Asa Shinn Mercer as a young man.
Courtesy of Special Collections Division, University of Washington Libraries, Negative No. UW 3392.

Asa Shinn Mercer

Western Promoter and Newspaperman 1839-1917

by
Lawrence M. Woods

THE ARTHUR H. CLARK COMPANY
Spokane, Washington
2003

Arthur H. Clark Company
P.O. Box 14707
Spokane, WA 99214

Library of Congress Catalog Card Number 2002019279
ISBN-0-87062-315-X

Library of Congress Cataloging-in-Publication Data

Woods, L. Milton (Lawrence Milton), 1932–
Asa Shinn Mercer: western promoter and newspaperman / by Lawrence M. Woods.
p. cm.—(Western frontiersmen series; 30)
Includes bibliographical references and index.
ISBN 0-87062-315-X
1. Mercer, A.S. (Asa Shinn), 1839–1917. 2. Pioneers—West (U.S.)—Biography. 3. Adventure and adventurers—West (U.S.)—Biography. 4. Newspaper editors—West (U.S.)—Biography. 5. Businessmen—West (U.S.)—Biography. 6. Ranchers—West (U.S.)—Biography. 7. College teachers—Washington (State)—Biography. 8. West (U.S.)—Description and travel. 9. West (U.S.)—Biography. I. Title. II. Series.

F594.M52 W66 2002
978'.02'092—dc21
[B] 2002019279

Contents

Illustrations

INTRODUCTION

Asa Shinn Mercer finished his long life on the western slopes of the Big Horn Mountains, and for him to finish a lifetime of adventure in such a quiet place was almost anticlimactic. His neighbors there had only a hazy notion of the many things he had been involved with, and his own interviews pared the story down to the events that now seemed to him to matter most: teaching at the university of frontier Washington Territory, recruiting and transporting young women from the east, and publishing a newspaper in Cheyenne. There was not a word of a host of other activities, or of the controversy that seemed never far away from Asa Mercer, in New York, Massachusetts, Washington, D. C., Oregon, Maryland, Texas, and Wyoming.

At the outset, it is necessary to answer this question: Why should we chronicle the life of a man who lived and worked in more than seven American states and territories, engaging in as many occupations, to say nothing of additional money-making schemes, sometimes close to the outer edge of the law, only to finish his life in relative obscurity, never having tasted any sweet rewards for his work?

The answer lies, of course, in the remarkable tale of striving, the endless expenditure of energy, and not a little money (albeit mostly from the contributions of others). The boundless optimism he harbored seemingly knew little of depression or discouragement, and each of his unforgiving minutes was filled with sixty seconds of running. His was not distance running on the model Kipling urged, for sometimes Asa seemed only to be running in place, or even falling backward, but he was running, all the same. And most emphatically, he was never running away.

In this sense, perhaps Mercer even becomes some sort of psychological role model for losers, the Willie Lomans of the world, who often can't do anything right, but still need to learn to cope with the experiences of the lives they have been given.

Mercer's granddaughter assembled some of the details of his life, perhaps with the expectation that she would publish his story, but for some reason she did not continue this effort. We do not know why.

Anthony West, commenting on Rebecca West, who tended to rewrite her life story—sometimes very substantially—said, "Like George Sand before her, she thought of her life history as something that could easily be improved by editing." Asa Mercer had the same habit, and making sense out of the many comments he made about his life is often a difficult task, for he seems almost like an author who tries to improve the novel he has written by repeated editing. Perhaps this tendency can be excused in part because Mercer's story is at times truly remarkable, and not unlike a somewhat imaginative novel. Nevertheless, for our purposes, it is nearly always necessary to confirm Mercer statements from other sources, and in this work we have tried to do so, where possible. Although the reader must ultimately judge what effect these efforts to confine Asa to the facts have on the drama of his often frenetic life, we advance the tentative conclusion that the truth may well be as remarkable as the fictions were intended to be.[1]

[1]The quote is from Anthony West, *H. G. Wells: Aspects of a Life* (New York, 1984), 57.

Chapter I

The Mercers

Clarence Booth Bagley, who was married to Asa Mercer's niece, commented some nine years before Asa's death that except for Asa, all of the Mercer family were "eminently truthful." Ample testimony to the fairness of the majority judgment of Bagley's comment can be seen in the many places in Seattle, which are adorned with the Mercer name, in most cases honoring Asa's older brothers, Thomas and Aaron.[1]

As for Asa, he was never reticent about the genealogy of the Mercer family, and he made a long list of family connections, beginning with descent from King Humbert of Scotland. Supposedly every Mercer generation included at least one boy who was the exact likeness of the King, and Asa claimed that honor for his second son, Asa, Jr., who was six feet, three and a half inches tall, with Scotch hair on his legs.[2]

Asa believed that the American Mercers were descended from Edward Mercer, son of a Scottish Lord, who was said to have emigrated to New Amsterdam where he received a grant of 160 acres, half north and half south of Canal Street. Others identify the famous Mercer grant with the father of Edward, Gideon Mercer, who came to the colonies in 1730, and supposedly had a grant in New Jersey or New York, or both. This grant, which was sometimes in one location and sometimes in another, was supposed to have been leased out in 1768 or 1769 on a ninety-nine-year term when Gideon, or Edward, or both, left the north for Virginia.

[1]Clarence Bagley to Julia H. Emery, January 3, 1908, Clarence Bagley collection, University of Washington. A school in Seattle may have been named for Asa Mercer.

[2]Asa Mercer gave his version of the Mercer genealogy in a long letter to B. H. Tillotson, April 15, 1911. Wyoming State Archives.

In Asa's version of the Mercer grant story, he claimed that recovery of the property was hampered by the fact that the title records had been shipped to Albany for safekeeping during the Revolution, where they were kept in a big room that was opened only for an hour each day. The story of the New York land grant spawned an organization of Mercer heirs who hoped to realize on the expected windfall, and after Asa moved to Cheyenne the story was repeated by the Cheyenne newspapers. One might be inclined to dismiss this last bit of publicity as needling by journalistic competitors, but for the fact that communications from the Gideon Mercer "heirs" can be found among Asa's papers.[3]

Still another Mercer Scottish inheritance which Asa claimed involved a "very valuable" Scottish estate, which was not inheritable until the fourth generation. He blamed his difficulty in laying hold of his share of this estate on the fact that the papers were hard to decipher, and furthermore, "the courts are loath to let go of any money to people in other countries."

There was a tradition in the Mercer family that they were related to General Hugh Mercer, of Revolutionary War fame, and Asa apparently accepted that tradition, although he did not know what direct connection there was between his family and the general. General Mercer's place in history was real enough, for he had been elected a brigadier in the Continental Army in February, 1776, and died early the following year, from wounds suffered at the battle of Princeton.[4]

We recount these anecdotes which at worst are dubious and at best not capable of proof, to give a taste of Asa Mercer's fondness

[3]Asa said that all members of the family were asked to give a power of attorney to facilitate settlement of the claim in New York, but that he had refused to do so. He claimed that one of the Ohio heirs had suddenly come into $3 million, "unquestionably from the Mercer estate settlement in New York City." Gideon Mercer died in 1765, at Winchester, Virginia. His son, Edward, was born in 1730 and died in 1763; he was apparently the father of Aaron Mercer. In 1902, Asa placed Gideon's grant at the junction of Canal Street and Broadway, in Manhattan. The 1886 story in the Cheyenne papers gave the Mercer grantee's name as William. Asa S. Mercer to Clarence B. Bagley, March 3, 1902, and Mercer family Bible records, in the Dorothy Weintz collection, University of Washington, hereafter the Weintz collection, and *The Cheyenne Daily Sun*, April 23, 1886.

of a good tale. Throughout his life he would weave stories that departed widely from the facts, and he often did so without any obvious motive. He was, in short, a promoter, and one of his ongoing lifetime promotions was Asa Mercer, himself.

The Mercer family connections that can be verified begin with William Mercer, who was born in Winchester, Virginia. The oldest of his four children was Aaron Mercer, father of Asa, who was born in Virginia in 1792 and later moved to Ohio, where he learned the weaving business and later owned a woolen mill; he married Jane Dickerson when he was nineteen, and she was sixteen. It was there that Thomas Mercer, the eldest son in a large family, was born in 1813. The introduction of steam weaving machines destroyed Aaron's business, and in 1834 the family moved to Princeton, Illinois, where Aaron died in 1844, followed by his wife a year later.[5]

Asa Shinn Mercer, the youngest of thirteen children, was born in Princeton, Illinois, in 1839. Illinois was a frontier in those days, but just how primitive it was we do not know. Years later, Asa claimed that the Indian tribe was still in the neighborhood and the chief was often a visitor at their house. Our earliest description of young Asa is of a freckled-faced boy with curly auburn hair, and he was still a youngster when his father died. Asa said that he was ten at the time, but he may have erred in this recollection, since the available information suggests he was only five.[6]

Whatever the details of those early years may be, after their parents' deaths, Thomas, the oldest son, became the surrogate father to the two younger boys, Asa and his next older brother, Joshua

[4]Brig. Gen. Hugh Mercer of Virginia died of wounds received at the battle of Princeton, January 3, 1777. Congress voted $500 for a suitable monument to General Mercer in Fredericksburg, Virginia, and also agreed to educate his youngest son at the expense of the United States. Worthington Chauncey Ford, ed., *Journals of the Continental Congress*, (Washington, D. C., 1907), passim. Asa added his own colorful twist to the Hugh Mercer story, saying that Hugh Mercer had been a young lieutenant in the army of the Old Pretender, and escaped to the United States, where he settled in western New York.

[5]Aaron Mercer was born February 20, 1792, and died December 2, 1844; Jane Dickerson Mercer was born April 8, 1796. Thomas Mercer was born March 11, 1813. Weintz collection. Other sources give Aaron's death as October 6, 1845. H. C. Bradsby, ed., *History of Bureau County, Illinois* (Chicago, 1885), 173.

[6]A. S. Mercer, *The Pioneer* (Chicago, 1913), 11. Mercer identified the chief as "Shabona."

Dickerson Mercer. Asa was so much younger than Thomas that his nieces and nephews among Thomas' children were his contemporaries in age. Six years after his father's death the estate was divided among his children, and Asa thus received his inheritance. We do not know how much this windfall was, but by the time he was seventeen his needs had already outrun his resources, for he was borrowing money.[7]

Asa said that when he was five, he had sat on Abraham Lincoln's lap and listened to the future president's "funny stories," and we do know that when Asa was a child in Illinois, Lincoln was practicing law in Springfield in partnership with William Henry Herndon. Nevertheless, except for one occasion there is no record that Lincoln was ever in the town of Princeton, which was located some distance north of Lincoln's usual circuits. When Lincoln ran for the U. S. House of Representatives, his campaign took him to Princeton on the Fourth of July, 1856, where he drew one of the largest crowds the little town had ever seen. If Asa saw Lincoln on that occasion, it is most unlikely that he sat on the future President's lap, for young Mercer was then seventeen, not five.[8]

In the spring of 1852, Thomas Mercer and his brother Aaron sold their property in Princeton, Illinois, and began the long journey to the West Coast in a train of twenty wagons, with Thomas as captain. The Mercers stopped first in Oregon, and in 1853 Thomas made his way north to Seattle, where he was one of the pioneers of that settlement. The Seattle settlement was attacked by Indians near the end of January 1856, and there was considerable devastation of King County in the aftermath of that attack. As a result, growth in the area was virtually halted until the Civil War ended.[9]

7By 1911, Asa had revised his count on the number of children in his family from thirteen to fourteen. Asa Shinn Mercer was born June 6, 1839, and Joshua Dickerson Mercer was born July 17, 1836. There is a note dated May 12, 1857, for $200, due April 5, 1858, with interest at 10%. Weintz collection.

8George B. Harrington, *Past and Present of Bureau County, Illinois* (Chicago, 1906), 107.

9Aaron Mercer was born January 23, 1824. Clarence B. Bagley, *History of Seattle, From the Earliest Settlement to the Present Time*, 3 vol. (Chicago, 1916), *passim*, and Angie Burt Bowden, *Early Schools of Washington Territory* (Seattle, 1935), 183. Also, *Seattle Times*, April 4, 1966, and Arthur A. Denny, *Pioneer Days on Puget Sount* (Seattle, 1908), 90. A school in Seattle may have been named for Asa Mercer.

Asa remained behind in the East, and in June of 1860, he graduated from Franklin College, a Presbyterian school, in New Athens, Ohio, receiving the A. B. degree after completing the four years of required course work in a year and a half. His graduating class of sixteen was the largest for the school up to that point, and five of his fellow graduates became Presbyterian ministers.

His formal education completed, it was now time for Asa to be about the business of his life's work. The year of his graduation was that somber time when the Union was disintegrating, and for a young man of twenty-one years, the national events must have been of great concern, for after Abraham Lincoln took office in the spring of 1861, he called for 75,000 troops to put down the rebellious South. Many young men then flocked to the colors.[10]

The question naturally arises as to what young Asa was doing during this period of national crisis. Years later, Rev. Edward Everett Hale recalled a meeting at which Asa was sitting at his side, and another New Englander was sitting on the other side of Asa. The New Englander noted that a tenth of college graduates in New England had served in the war, and asked, "Mr. Mercer, did your western colleges make so good a showing?" According to Hale's recollection, Mercer replied, "I was in Lafayette College at the time. The whole college volunteered as a regiment and the President went as their colonel."[11]

While this snappy retort put an end to that line of questioning, there is absolutely no evidence that Asa ever attended Lafayette College; nor is there evidence of his service in the Union forces. Although he never discussed his reasons for leaving Illinois when

[10]Asa said he graduated from Franklin College on June 7, 1860. Asa S. Mercer to Clarence B. Bagley (from Chicago), February 1, 1912. Also, Asa S. Mercer to Linnie March, December 7, 1910, Weintz collection, Erving E. Beauregard, *Old Franklin: The Eternal Touch, A History of Franklin College, New Athens, Harrison County, Ohio*, 206, and *Franklin College Register: Biographical and Historical* (Wheeling, 1908), 122.

[11]The meeting to which Hale refers was to hear James Russell Lowell's "Commemoration Ode." Edward Everett Hale to Frank B. Cooper, November 16, 1903. Weintz collection. The quotas and numbers of men furnished under the draft calls are given in *War of the Rebellion: A Compilation of the Official Records of the Union and Confederate Armies, Series III, Volume IV* (Washington, D. C., 1900), 1265-69. There were a long list of acceptable reasons for exemption from the draft, including providing a substitute, or paying for one.

he did, it is at least interesting that he decided to go very soon after the firing on Fort Sumter (on April 12), and Lincoln's call for volunteers three days later. He was traveling away from the coming war, not toward it, and whatever his dreams for the future may have contained, they did not include any aspiration to become a military hero.[12]

[12]Prior to the effective date of the Civil War draft law, at the beginning of March 1863, Civil War military service was voluntary; thereafter, every able-bodied male citizen between the ages of twenty and forty-five was subject to the draft. Under the 1863 act, quotas were assigned to the states, and the act also provided for the assignment of quotas to the western territories, but apparently no such assignments were made, and Washington Territory did not furnish any soldiers under the several draft calls.

Chapter II

ACTING UNIVERSITY PRESIDENT

In 1861, Asa, then a young man of twenty-two with carrot-red hair and beard, followed his older brothers to Seattle, where he arrived on the last day of June, having traveled from New York by sea to the Isthmus of Panama and up the west coast.

Asa did not lack in energy, although his first jobs were not particularly auspicious. He helped dig the cellar of the house being built for the president of the territorial university and also helped to clear the site for the school. Then there was a stint at tallying lumber shipped from Yesler's mill, the major business in the area at the time, and Asa even tried his hand at farming, without success, as the land was too gravelly to grow crops. On Sundays he led the choir at the Methodist Church.[1]

Asa said that the man who had the government survey contract for the area had lost his crew, presumably because of the difficulty of surveying the heavily wooded hillsides, and that Asa took up the contract and surveyed nearly all of Seattle, over to the lakes. Actually, Edwin Richardson, who had the contract to survey the area where Seattle was located, did not lose the contract, although his crews suffered from considerable turnover in axmen, who were detailed to clear underbrush for the surveyors. However, the records for the survey do disclose the name of Asa Mercer, who was employed as a chainman in August 1861. The usual survey crew consisted of the surveyor, two chainmen, who measured distances using the surveyor's chain, and an axman.[2]

---

[1] *Seattle Post Intelligencer*, September 15, 1888, and Asa S. Mercer to Clarence B. Bagley, February 1, 1912, Weintz collection.

The territorial university, where Asa performed his first work in Washington Territory, was to figure largely in Asa's next efforts. The institution can be traced back to 1854, when the first territorial legislature asked Congress for the donation of two townships of land to support a territorial university. Congress obliged, granting two townships of land which the Washington legislature was to select from the public domain.[3]

Following the congressional action, the Washington territorial legislature authorized not one, but two institutions, and created a board of commissioners to select the land. Despite this optimistic beginning, no money was spent on the university, and as of the end of 1857 the land had not even been selected. The 1859 legislature reorganized the university land commissioners, reducing their number to three, and gave them instructions on selecting the university lands. Taken together, the terms made it clear that the lawmakers expected the land selection process to be accomplished slowly.[4]

Location of the university was complicated by the fact that the site of the capital of the territory had not finally been decided, and landowners in Seattle hoped to locate it there. It was the Rev. Daniel Bagley, who was also one of Asa Mercer's childhood friends, who convinced the Seattle delegation that the university would be of more value to Seattle than the capital would be. Bagley also asked to be appointed as one of the commissioners to locate the lands Congress had granted for the university.[5]

---

[2]The survey notes for the 1861 survey of Township 24 North, Range 4 East, are in the Portland Office of the Bureau of Land Management. The contract with Edwin Richardson to survey this township was dated May 25, 1861. Mercer, who called the surveyor "Edwin Smith," also claimed that under his own supervision, the surveyors discovered coal on the eastern shore of Lake Washington. It appears that Mercer served as chainman for approximately half a month. He also worked on the survey for the second addition to Seattle. *Seattle Post Intelligencer*, September 15, 1888, August 22, 1917.

[3]Oregon Territory had been granted two townships, one to be south of the Columbia, and one north thereof. The enactment of July 17, 1854, gave Washington Territory and Oregon each two townships, 10 *Statutes at Large* 305. Also, Charles M. Gates, *The First Century at the University of Washington, 1861–1961* (Seattle, 1961), 8.

[4]Only one-third of the grant was to be selected before the next session of the legislature, and the commissioners were limited to three meetings per year, with annual per diem payments not to exceed 90 days. Charles M. Gates, *The First Century*, 9.

When the legislature met in November 1860, the university was assigned to Seattle, on the condition that a ten-acre site could be donated. Another bill, passed early the following January, named Bagley as one of the three land commissioners. In an action which was of later importance to Asa Mercer, the land commissioners then chose Bagley to be president of the board and gave him full authority to act for it. Wielding this authority, Bagley single-handedly established the university, and selected and sold the lands reserved for that purpose by Congress.[6]

The 1854 act of Congress had only "reserved" the two sections of land for the university in Washington Territory, and the Federal officials expected that the Interior Department would approve the selections made by the territory before any patents were issued. However, Bagley read the law differently, and he at once set about selecting *and selling off* the land grant, actions which would cause him a great deal of embarrassment later, and require a subsequent act of Congress to straighten out.[7]

Bagley ultimately spent as much money on this project as the federal government was then spending on the territorial capital building in Olympia. By the end of 1861 Bagley had selected more than 29,000 acres and sold more than 20,000 at $1.50, yielding $30,000, all of which he had already spent to construct buildings on the university site.

In the summer of 1861, construction was proceeding apace, and, as we have already noted, Bagley gave young Asa Mercer a job working on the buildings. On the Fourth of July, territorial dignitaries came to Seattle to view the construction progress, and

---

[5]Bagley was a Methodist minister who had been a friend of the Mercers back in Illinois, and knew Asa Mercer from childhood. He came west to Oregon in 1852 with Thomas Mercer. With respect to the congressional grant, they were authorized to sell the two townships of land at not less than $1.50 per acre—a very considerable hurdle, since public lands were available at $1.25 per acre.

[6]To satisfy the legislative condition, the site in Seattle consisted of eight acres donated by Arthur Armstrong Denny, together with donations by two adjoining landowners.

[7]In 1864, after A. A. Denny was elected as Washington territorial delegate, Congress passed a law which had been introduced by Denny, who was more than casually involved in the matter; this law confirmed the Bagley sales as having been made in fee simple. 13 *Statutes at Large* 28, approved March 14, 1864.

Bagley's protégé was also given the privilege of addressing the gathering. Thereafter, Asa would always claim he had delivered the first Fourth of July oration in the area.[8]

The main university building was fifty feet by eighty feet and two stories high; the commodious president's house was also two stories, forty by fifty feet; and there was a boarding house twenty-four by forty-eight feet. When the main building was ready to be occupied by the late fall of 1861, Bagley hired Mercer as a teacher, and his compensation consisted of $200, plus all of the tuition received from students.

Since students were scarce, this latter compensation provided a clever incentive for the teacher to recruit them, and Asa at once set about to do so. He printed circulars which he circulated in the logging camps and mills around the Sound, promising men they could pay their way by chopping wood on Saturdays, at $1.50 per cord. These efforts attracted fifteen or twenty men, who were taught classes in mathematics, spelling, and grammar.[9]

The board elected Thomas Milton Gatch, who was then president of Willamette University, as university president, but he declined to serve. Mercer was therefore left as the senior member of the staff, and Bagley seems to have treated him as temporary president of the university. These arrangements were confirmed by the regents when they first met in November 1862, although they referred to Mercer as acting professor of the department of literature, science, and arts. In this fashion, Asa came to be known as first president of the University of Washington.[10]

During that first year, the university was not what we would now expect from such an institution. All the classes were conducted in one room in the southwest corner of the building, offer-

[8]Asa S. Mercer to Clarence B. Bagley, written from Omaha, March 3, 1902. Weintz collection.

[9]Delphine Henderson, "Asa Shinn Mercer, Northwest Publicity Agent," *Reed College Bulletin*, XXIII (January, 1945), 21.

[10]Mercer continued to direct the university until William E. Barnard arrived in 1863. Charles M. Gates, *The First Century*, 31, and Linnie March, "Presidents of the University," *The Washington Alumnus*, IV, No. 13 (December 17, 1910), 6.

ing university-level subjects, as well as grade school and high school classes. Organization of the institution was meager, and much dominated by the Mercer and Bagley families. Whenever Mercer was absent, which must have been frequently, considering the scope of his duties, the position of substitute principal was filled either by Dillis B. Ward, half-brother of Mrs. Thomas Mercer, or Clarence B. Bagley, who would marry Thomas Mercer's daughter Alice.[11]

The first year, classes were held for only five months, commencing November 4, 1861, and when that session ended, Mercer hired another teacher to conduct a primary school in the same building during May, June, and July, 1862. Mercer also arranged for housing for students who came some distance to go to school. He bought groceries wholesale in San Francisco, and hired a couple to operate a boarding house, where students were charged three dollars per week. As we have noted, the boys were able to earn money for their board by cutting wood. These arrangements continued for two years.[12]

When the first term ended, Mercer set out to recruit students. More circulars were printed, and after he spent two weeks, hiring two Indians and a canoe, traveling 400 miles to logging camps on the east side of Puget sound, about a dozen young men, ranging in age from twenty to thirty, enrolled for the second term.

The second term of the university opened at the end of October 1862, again as a private school headed by Mercer, with the assistance of Mrs. Virginia Calhoun. There were sixty students enrolled when the second term opened, but in the spring of 1863 there were only five enrolled, and the institution closed for lack of students. When the university did reopen in September 1863, it would be headed by a new president, William E. Barnard. For all the energy

[11]Angie Burt Bowden, *Early Schools*, 182, 206, 233.

[12]Angie Burt Bowden, *Early Schools*, 233.

[13]The university continued to have financial trouble after Mercer left, and closed again in the summer of 1867; the following year the campus was put up for lease, but no takers appeared. The school reopened again in 1869, but closed again for a time in 1874 and 1876. *Three-Quarters of a Century at Washington* (Seattle, 1941), 8-9, and Charles M. Gates, *The First Century*, 31.

he had expended, Asa Mercer's association with the institution had ended in failure.[13]

Mercer's energetic approach to the problem of organizing a territorial university apparently was well received in the community, and a contemporary said, "Mercer was a great fellow . . . he was always doing something and kept things moving." Although he may have been disappointed, Asa Mercer was not discouraged, and he was now ready to and venture forth in the interest of a different cause.

Chapter III

Immigration Commissioner

We do not know when Asa met the governor of Washington Territory, but certainly his mentor, the Rev. Daniel Bagley, was connected well enough to the small territorial power structure, and could have arranged the introductions. The work that Mercer would next undertake would thrust him into the public eye, and he would even be elected to public office, for the first and only time in his life.

The governor of Washington Territory was William Pickering, who had come to Illinois from England, had served in the Illinois legislature, and chaired the state's delegation to the 1860 Republican Convention in Chicago. In contrast to Mercer's assertions about Lincoln, there can be no doubt of Pickering's friendship with the President. It has been said that Lincoln offered Pickering the choice of the British embassy, or the governorship of Washington Territory, but the rationale for Pickering's choice of the territorial post has not survived.[1]

Pickering came to Olympia in the summer of 1862, when Asa Mercer was still teaching at the University of Washington. The following year, Pickering appointed Asa Mercer as commissioner of immigration, with responsibility for stimulating immigration to Washington Territory. Asa soon concentrated on one segment of the immigration problem, namely, the considerable shortage of marriageable women in the Northwest, where men outnumbered women nine to one. The acute nature of the problem was obvious, for early in 1860, ninety-six men in the Puget Sound

[1]Pickering was born in Yorkshire in 1798; he died April 22, 1873.

region had called a meeting of bachelors, "to devise ways and means to secure this much-needed and desirable emigration."[2]

Such a problem was not uncommon in frontier areas, and indeed, the French had been faced with just such a situation in Louisiana, early in the eighteenth century. In order to " anchor" the lawless *coureurs de bois* to the new colony, a shipment of twenty-three mostly Parisian girls was sent over in 1704, under the watchful eye of two nuns. Later, more young women were recruited, and they began arriving in 1727, carrying small chests to hold the allotments of personal items provided by the French government, giving them the nickname "casket girls" (*filles à la cassette*). To ensure propriety during the courtship period, a convent of Ursuline nuns was established in New Orleans, and given control of the women until they were married.[3]

Asa could not hope that the United States government would give him the support the French government had given Louisiana, but he had another idea. The Civil War was claiming the lives of many fathers and husbands, and Mercer reasoned that there would be large numbers of female orphans and widows in the East who would welcome the opportunity to move to Washington Territory. When his duties at the university ended in March 1863, Mercer solicited contributions to finance a trip to Boston, and then sailed for the East.[4]

Uncharacteristically, Mercer apparently did not tell anyone in Washington Territory what he was about, and indeed, we do not know where he was, or what he was doing during the next year. This is not the only gap in Mercer's time line, but there are not many of them, for Mercer was never reluctant to talk about himself. Although he later would write many letters to the press telling of his activities, there seem to have been none of these communi-

[2]Clarence B. Bagley, "'The Mercer Immigration:' Two Cargoes of Maidens for the Sound Country," *The Quarterly of the Oregon Historical Society* V, No. 1 (March, 1904), 6.

[3]The girls were unaccustomed to the New World diet, particularly the corn, and complained to the bishop who had recruited them. Grace Elizabeth King, *Jean Baptiste le Moyne, Sieur de Bienville* (New York, 1892), 137-38, 145.

[4]Clarence B. Batley, "The Mercer Immigration," 7.

cations during the 1863-64 period. This is particularly odd, considering that he had journeyed to the East to recruit immigrants, and he would be expected to enlist newspapers in this effort.

We can only speculate on the reasons for his reticence, but it is interesting that the summer of 1863 was the time of the draft riots in New York, and there was much public unrest about this means of raising troops for the war. Although non-residents were not supposed to be enrolled for the draft, the system did not always function as it should. Perhaps a young single man traveling about the northeast would have been uneasy about his relationship to the larger conflict, but we do not know that. Although these considerations might explain the lack of newspaper coverage, it still does not tell us how Asa made his living during that year.[5]

In his accounts of the first expedition, Asa simply emphasized that he raised the money for the trip, and then passed over the large time gap that followed. Flora Engle, whose father and sisters were in the first expedition, begins her story of the first expedition journey in Lowell, Massachusetts, in the spring of 1864. Consequently, the story of Mercer's first importation of women can be taken up only in the spring of the year following his departure from Seattle in 1863.[6]

At some point, Mercer found his way to Lowell, Massachusetts, which was to prove a fertile ground for recruiting women for the Pacific Northwest. Deprived of southern cotton, the New England mills had been hard hit by the Civil War, and many young women were unemployed. Moreover, the manpower needs of the war had siphoned off numbers of men, so that there was a large surplus of marriageable females in the population, and this fact had been mentioned in the local press.

[5]Considering the difficulties Mercer had in raising money a year later, it seems unlikely that he could have raised enough money in Seattle for his first expedition to finance his travel expenses, as well as his living expenses for a year. Clarence Bagley, who should have known more about the matter than any other source we have, does not offer any clues about Mercer's 1863-64 year, either.

[6]Flora Engle apparently did not have access to Mercer when she wrote her article, as she indicated she did not know his address. Flora A. P. Engle, "The Story of the Mercer Expeditions," *The Washington Historical Quarterly*, VI, No. 4 (October, 1915), 225-37.

It may be that Asa had more than one public meeting in Lowell, but considering the fact that he only recruited eight women from Lowell, perhaps Bagley was correct in his assertion that all of them were recruited as the result of that one meeting. In his presentation, Asa did not stress marriage opportunities in the West, but instead emphasized the financial advantage for the young women who would migrate to Washington Territory, where small fortunes might be made in teaching.[7]

In the middle of March, eight young ladies left Lowell with Mercer for New York, to make the long journey to Washington Territory. With this small group was the father of two of the women, who had been an overseer in the cotton mills before the war, but was now also unemployed and wanted to go west to sell women's shoes. Three other young women later joined the group, two from New Hampshire and one from Boston, so that the final total was eleven young women. While the word that reached the West Coast at the beginning of April spoke of fifty who were making journey, this number in all likelihood reflected Mercer optimism regarding additional recruiting possibilities, particularly in New York. Each member of the group paid $225 passage money.[8]

The little group left New York in March 1864, and made their way first to the Isthmus of Panama, and then up the west coast to San Francisco. From San Francisco, they boarded the bark *Torrent* for Port Gamble, and a sloop carried them on the final leg of the journey to Seattle, where they arrived at about midnight on May 16. Eight of these young women later married, and only three remained unmarried, one of whom died soon after arriving, and another returned East.[9]

---

[7]In a letter to Bagley in 1912, Asa emphasized that he did not go East in 1864 with backing from the Territory. Asa S. Mercer to Clarence B. Bagley, February 1, 1912. Weintz collection. Also, *The Lowell Daily Courier*, October 19, 1863.

[8]The presence of the New Hampshire and Boston recruits may indicate that Mercer had made a sweep of New England, but if so, the yield was sparse. Flora Engle's mother and two other sisters came to Seattle with Mercer's second expedition in 1866, making a total of six from that family who made the journey.

[9]Flora A. Pearson Engle, "The Story of the Mercer Expeditions," 228, Bagley, "The Mercer Immigration," 8, and *Seattle Weekly Gazette*, April 5, 1864.

When Mercer returned from the east he kept himself in the public eye by speaking at such events as the meeting of the King County Agricultural Society, of which he was secretary. He also learned that he had been nominated on the Union ticket for the Council of the territorial legislature. Unfortunately, the 1864 election in Washington Territory was unkind to Unionists, and the Council that was elected included six Democrats, and only three Union members, including Mercer.

We must assume that publicity attendant on his emigration venture propelled Mercer into the Council post, against the prevailing political tide in Washington Territory. Nevertheless, he soon found that his popularity did not extend inside the Council chambers, where the Democratic majority expected to carry the day. When the Council convened, Mercer rose to ask that the ministers of Olympia be asked to open each session with prayer; the opposition, contending that the ministers would not accept such an unpaid obligation, defeated the motion.[10]

The 1864-1865 legislative session seems not to have produced any memorable laws, and there were certainly none from Mercer's hand, although he did sponsor the bill to print the governor's message, and he became embroiled in debate on a county boundary line bill. When he asked the legislature to endorse him as immigration agent for the territory, the lawmakers refused to do so, which should have given him warning of trouble to come.[11]

The Democratic-controlled legislature did pass a bill that would cause Mercer grief in connection with his later immigration project. There were rumors that the Freedman's Bureau, which had the responsibility to provide food and clothing for destitute former slaves, and also to lease confiscated land to them, wanted to send

[10] *The Overland Press* (Olympia), December 10, 17, 1864, and *Seattle Weekly Gazette*, October 25, 1864.

[11] *The Overland Press* in Olympia noted on one occasion that it omitted the report on the proceedings, because there was no news of great interest to its readers. Also, *Seattle Weekly Gazette*, May 11, 1865. In 1912, Asa recounted an attempt by a ship captain to bribe him with $5,000 in gold. He did not explain why anyone would try to bribe a minority member of the council, with virtually no power to persuade the Democratic majority. Asa also had the dates wrong, saying he had served in the 1863 legislature, rather than that of 1864. Asa S. Mercer to Clarence B. Bagley, February 16, 1912. Weintz collection.

"several hundred" starving freedmen to the west coast. Reacting to these rumors, the Washington territorial legislature passed a bill to discourage importation of freedmen, and to punish those engaged in such activity. The acting governor refused to sign the bill, but this legislative foray roiled the upcoming campaign to elect the territorial delegate.[12]

Although Washington Territory did not pay Asa for his first expedition, somehow he had accumulated enough money to permit him to invest in land, for early in 1865 he paid $400 for a half-interest in 150 acres in King County. Of course, the money could have been borrowed from his family and friends, but the transaction seems to signal what was for him a rare period of comfortable financial security.[13]

After his first stint as a lawmaker, Asa turned once again to the matter of bringing single women to the west coast, for his small early success in the immigration business suggested that he should repeat the formula on a much larger scale. At the beginning of June, he wrote from Seattle to Governor Addison Gibbs, of Oregon, to try to broaden the appeal of his efforts in that direction. He announced that he was going back east in the coming winter, and suggested that he could induce New England teachers to come to Oregon, bringing "as many teachers from the east as you may wish." There is no indication that the Oregon governor replied to this letter.[14]

He judged that the field in the East was ripe for his recruiting efforts there, for the previous fall the Seattle *Gazette* had noted that Massachusetts led the list of those states where there were more females than males. The Massachusetts excess was 37,000 females,

[12]The Freedman's Bureau was created by Congress effective March 3, 1865; it was headed by General O. O. Howard. *Pacific Tribune* (Olympia), May 27, 1865, and J. G. Randall and David Donald, *The Civil War and Reconstruction* (Lexington, Massachusetts, 1969), 576. It seems unlikely that the management of the Freedman's Bureau was seriously contemplating any projects on the West Coast at this time, as it struggled to take possession of confiscated lands, and to set up its field operations in the former Confederacy.

[13]H. L. Yesler and S. B. Yesler to Asa S. Mercer and John Hornback, January 25, 1865. Book 1 Deeds, 244, King County Recorder, Seattle.

[14] A. S. Mercer to Addison Gibbs, June 2, 1864. Addison Gibbs collection, Oregon Historical Society.

and the editor opined that the war's drain on male population had probably raised the excess for that state to about 100,000. Mercer undoubtedly knew these statistics, for his first expedition had concentrated on Massachusetts, and he now was determined to do something considerably more audacious than his first expedition.[15]

[15] *Seattle Weekly Gazette*, November 28, 1864.

Chapter IV

Mercer's Belles

Mercer's plans for his second immigration expedition were very different than his first had been: for this time there would be no low-profile recruiting. He prepared to go east with the governor's encouragement, if not the territory's money, and his hopes were high, for he expected to enlist the help of the United States government. With luck, he expected to repeat his previous success several times over.

After the legislature adjourned in 1865, Mercer began laying the groundwork for his second immigration expedition. He contacted employers in the Puget Sound region, and asked them to guarantee employment for the immigrants he expected to bring to the territory. In these discussions, Mercer did not limit his immigration efforts to women, and at first, it appears that he intended to bring families to the Pacific Northwest. The managers of eight principal lumber mills agreed to offer employment to 100 married men, if Mercer could bring them to the west coast. Nevertheless, the importation of single women soon became a significant part of Mercer's objectives for the second expedition, as it had been in the first, but for a time his focus was not at all clear, at least in his publicity efforts.

Asa said he obtained about sixty assurances from employers, although we do not know how specific the guarantees were. Later, Asa often claimed that he could guarantee women a wage of four dollars in gold per week, plus board, and some of his Seattle employers may well have given him assurances of some such wage. He hoped to recruit a total of about 800 people, and he expected the so-called Opposition shipping lines would agree to carry them to the West, presumably at discounted fares.[1]

Mercer also resolved to undergird the financial viability of the expedition by drawing up contracts with the single young men of the region. These contracts obligated Mercer to bring each of these men a suitable wife of good moral character in exchange for the payment of $300 passage money, which included Mercer's fee (apparently expected to be $50). Roger Conant, the New York *Times* reporter who came west with the second expedition, later charged that Mercer was none too finicky in selecting the men with whom he signed these contracts. Conant listed names such as Humbolt Jack, apparently a sea captain, Lame Duck Bill, Whiskey Jim, White Pine Joe and Bobtailed and Yeke, among those who signed up with Asa.[2]

Mercer expected that his recruiting efforts would be concentrated in the Northeast, and especially in Massachusetts, where Governor John Albion Andrew had actually signified his sympathy with projects such as Mercer's. Andrew told the Massachusetts legislature that the surplus of unemployed women had given rise to "unnatural" competition for employment "fitted for men alone." He asked the lawmakers to assist these women to emigrate to Oregon, California, and other "remote" western regions, to take employment as teachers, and in "every other appropriate . . . employment." While the legislature declined to act as the governor recommended, Mercer could certainly expect that the Andrew would be receptive to his emigration work.[3]

Massachusetts already had an organization unit capable of

[1]The description of Mercer's pre-expedition negotiations is from a letter signed "T. M.," to the editor of the California *Alta*, dated March 9, 1865; the letter is quoted in the *Seattle Weekly Gazette*, April 27, 1865. For a number of years, so-called Opposition shipping lines sprang up to offer lower fares than the established carriers, but they generally enjoyed only brief existence.

[2]Apparently the contracts with Washington Territory men were signed about March 1, 1865, shortly before Mercer departed for New York. Charles W. Smith, "Asa Shinn Mercer, Pioneer in Western Publicity," *Pacific Northwest Quarterly*, XXVII (1936), 348, Angie Burt Bowden, *Early Schools*, 190, Clarence B. Bagley, "The Mercer Immigration," 13, and Roger Conant, in Lenna A. Deutsch, ed., *Mercer's Belles: The Journal of a Reporter, by Roger Conant* (Seattle, 1960), 130. Conant said that when the girls met these men, they often would not even speak to them.

[3]The governor's message was delivered January 6, 1865.

assisting Mercer's project, for the predecessor of the New England Emigrant Aid Company had been chartered by the legislature in 1854 to aid emigration, and this organization had been a key factor in directing New England emigration to Kansas. Indeed, the Emigrant Aid company had already indicated its sympathy with the plight of single women. The company suggested that women had not been treated fairly in emigration, since a man could go to the West Coast in steerage for $225, while a woman required better accommodations, which would cost her about $450.

Nevertheless, Mercer soon found that his promotional efforts were not the only ones in the field, for other regions were trying to attract settlers from the Northeast. The Denver *News* called for the immigration of single women to the Colorado mining regions, promising the "Utopia of their dreams," including wages thirty to fifty dollars per month, payable in gold, for household duties. As soon as the Civil War ended, there were also numerous articles calling attention to bargain-basement opportunities in the defeated South, which was reeling from the devastation of the war.[4]

In late February, Mercer headed east, carrying references from Governor Pickering, who also supported Mercer's efforts by personal visits in Washington and with letters of support. Asa later said that when he left the governor, Pickering said, "God bless you, Mercer, and make your undertaking a great success. If you get into financial trouble and need money, do not hesitate to wire me and I will give you help." If the governor did, in fact use such words, they would come back later to haunt him.[5]

As we have already inferred, the early newspaper references to the Mercer expedition did not speak of widows and orphans, but instead said that the emigrants would be families of "respectability and refinement." Indeed, Mercer said that he at first tried to recruit workers, such as brickmakers, blacksmiths, shoemakers, carpenters, and machinists, but the majority of those whom he attracted were unable to pay the $200 passage he requested. Asa

[4] *The Boston Herald*, May 24, June 30, 1865.

[5] Clarence B. Bagley, "The Mercer Immigration," 17.

then turned for help to Governor Andrews, and then went to Washington, D. C., where Governor Pickering was also in town from Washington Territory.[6]

Although Pickering favored the Mercer project, his support did not exempt Mercer from political opposition in Washington Territory. Rumors circulated that Mercer was in league with the Freedman's Bureau to send former slaves to work in the lumber mills of the Puget Sound area, and when the campaign began to elect the delegate to Congress, the Democrats opposed the Mercer scheme because of its perceived effect on white labor.[7]

The Unionist press immediately denied the Democrat charge, but the chief Democratic paper in Olympia slyly noted that Mercer had been in town when the story broke, and he did not deny the allegation. Finally, in an effort to end the public debate on the matter, the Seattle *Gazette* offered to bet $1,000 that no non-whites were to be with the Mercer expedition. The story only died away when the Union candidate won the election by a comfortable majority. It is interesting that throughout the fight, there was no direct response from Mercer's usually ready pen. There may even have been a reason for Asa's silence, for as we shall see, in the fall of 1865, Mercer told the New York *Times* that he had seen General Howard, who was then running the Freedman's Bureau.[8]

Mercer needed a ship to bring the emigrants back to Seattle, and he hoped to convince President Lincoln to provide such a suitable vessel. It was in connection with this matter that Asa later related the claim we have already mentioned, of sitting on the future president's lap when he was only five, and listening to Lincoln's "funny stories." Mercer said that if he had been able to ask

[6]This description was given by Mercer at his speech in Yesler Hall, May 23, 1866. *Puget Sound Weekly* (Seattle), May 28, 1866. *The Seattle Weekly Gazette* of March 4 said that Mercer had sailed from Victoria two weeks before. Also, *The Pacific Tribune* (Olympia), January 21, 1865. Pickering had sailed for Washington on January 16. William Pickering, who was born in 1798, was chairman of the Illinois delegation to the 1860 Republican convention, and was one of those behind the Lincoln nomination for president.

[7]*Pacific Tribune* (Olympia), May 20, 1865.

[8]Arthur A. Denny won the delegate's seat by a vote of 2,351 to 1,213. Also, *Seattle Weekly Gazette*, May 18, 1865.

the President's help, "not a shadow of doubt existed in my mind as to the outcome." We have already commented on this claim, and while Mercer probably did intend to receive help from Lincoln, it is more likely that Pickering's ties to the President would have been of more importance than his own childhood associations.

In any case, plans to make use of Lincoln's influence were doomed to failure, for the President was assassinated before Mercer even had the chance to begin work in the East. The first word Asa may have sent west from New York was a letter to his brother Thomas, written on April 17. In that letter, he claimed that he had been delayed ten days in the transit of the Isthmus, so that he only arrived in New York on the very day that Lincoln was assassinated. Referring to the effect of the assassination on his plans, Mercer said, "I was at sea without a compass."[9]

The truth was considerably less dramatic. Asa arrived in New York aboard the steamer *Golden Rule*, on April 2, not April 14. The ship was from San Juan del Norte, in Nicaragua, which implied that he had crossed the Nicaraguan isthmus, not the one in Panama. His route would have been down the west coast to San Juan del Sur, then across Lake Nicaragua to San Juan del Note, where he caught the steamer north to New York. We do not know what Mercer did in New York from April 2 until the 17th, when he wrote to Thomas, but he most assuredly did not spend that time in transit.[10]

Mercer said that after the disappointment presented by the Lincoln assassination, he then went to Kansas, to explore the possibility of organizing an overland expedition. The mysterious Kansas trip is another small unverifiable gap in Mercer's life, and Asa never said why he chose to go to Kansas, if indeed he made such a journey. In any case, Mercer also said that, on closer exam-

[9]Angie Burt Bowden, *Early Schools*, 191, and Clarence B. Bagley, "'The Mercer Immigration:' Two Cargoes of Maidens for the Sound Country," *The Quarterly of the Oregon Historical Society*, V, No. 1 (March, 1904), 13. Mercer wrote from New York to his brother Thomas on April 17, 1865. C. B. Bagley collection, University of Washington.

[10]San Juan del Norte was also called San Juan de Nicaragua, or Greytown.

ination, Kansas proved not to be a fertile prospect for his project, and he again returned to New York.[11]

In New York Mercer said that he then devised a plan to take 150 women and 150 families who could pay their own passage, to Washington Territory. This scheme, which introduced the first of many different estimates of numbers of emigrants, also failed to draw a sufficient number of passengers for the voyage.

Mercer next went to Massachusetts, the scene of his recruiting success a year earlier, and he had to wait three days to see Governor Andrew. Mercer said that the Governor gave him a letter to President Johnson, and another to the Secretary of War, but certainly the most important introduction from Andrew was to Rev. Edward Everett Hale, a Unitarian minister, who was interested in emigration, and readily agreed to help Mercer. Hale invited Mercer to his church on Sunday, and seated him in the chancel, while Hale spoke to the congregation on the "replenish the earth" text from Genesis. When the sermon was finished, Hale invited Mercer to make his own pitch for the emigration scheme.[12]

Hale readily lent his name to Mercer's project, and he signed Asa's promotional circulars as chairman of the Pacific committee of the New England Emigrant Company. Support from such a reputable source must have been very important at this stage of planning for the expedition. Mercer also wrote a more extensive piece of promotional material for the Mercer expedition, and this work may also have been his first publication.

Washington Territory: The Great North-West, Her Material Resources and Claims to Emigration was a small tract of some forty-two pages

[11]If Mercer went to Kansas, it is possible that the Rev. Edward Everett Hale suggested that destination, even though Mercer's account suggests that he met Hale only after returning from Kansas. Hale was involved with the Emigrant Aid company, and knew Charles Robinson, the first governor of the new state of Kansas, who had also been an agent for the Emigrant company. It would be logical that the devastation of "Bleeding Kansas" would have left many people in the mood to emigrate.

[12]Mercer's assertion that Andrew gave him two letters of introduction is difficult to square with his later action. There is no record of any visit with President Johnson, and when he finally did go to see the Secretary of War, one of the Oregon senators introduced him. Edward Everett Hale was born in 1822; he died June 10, 1909.

The Reverend Edward Everett Hale, who gave valuable assistance to Asa Mercer's efforts to recruit passengers for his expeditions from the Northeast to Washington Territory.
From the collections of the Library of Congress.

extolling the virtues of Washington Territory. This promotional work, which was published in Utica, New York, furnished a description of the territory, and when he dealt with the market for the territory's products, we see the promotional style that would characterize much of his later writing.

He contended that "Every stick, and every plank" of the territory's lumber was in demand in the Pacific Ocean region, from the Cape of Good Hope to the Bering Strait, and out across the Pacific islands. As for the fish of the Puget Sound region, he saw the principal market as encompassing the entire United States west of the Rocky Mountain, a region where he expected great economic development of its mineral wealth. Beyond the shores of the United States, he also foresaw a foreign market on both shores of the Pacific, where the people were "fish eating," because, he helpfully added, they were "generally [C]atholic."[13]

With the recruiting publicity underway, Mercer now had to give his attention to the unsolved logistical problems, and he could only do this in Washington. He needed a ship, and he undoubtedly reasoned that he should approach the Navy, whose mission involved ships, but a visit to the secretary of the Navy only produced the information that military transports were under the authority of the Secretary of War.

Asa then went to the War Department, and despite his supposed letter of introduction from Governor Andrew, he did not see the Secretary. Instead, he went to see Lt. Col. Theodore S. Bowers, who was the Assistant Adjutant General on General Grant's staff, and it was Bowers who got him an appointment with Grant. For young Asa to sit across the desk from Grant, then basking in the glory of having won the war for the North, must have been a heady experience, indeed. The two men found themselves on familiar ground, for Grant had been stationed at Vancouver, Washington, in 1852, and Mercer said that the general harbored fond memories of that area.[14]

In his conversation with Grant, Mercer did not mention that he wanted to bring families and craftsmen to the West Coast. Instead, he emphasized the object of transporting the widows and orphans of the Civil War, stressing the plight of those who had suffered from that conflict. Perhaps he chose this emphasis for his presentation because he felt it would have the greatest influence with the Grant. Nevertheless, when he returned to New England he again tried to recruit families and craftsmen, in the hope that these emigrants could pay for their passage.

The interview with Grant produced results, and on July 18, Grant

[13]Asa S. Mercer, *Washington Territory: The Great North-West, Her Material Resources, and Claims to Emigration. A Plain Statement of Things as They Exist* (Utica, N. Y., 1865), 38, 39.

[14]When Grant was stationed at Fort Vancouver, he lost money on several unsuccessful speculations, even leasing a farm, where he raised potatoes and oats, but these financial reverses apparently did not color his opinion of the area. Charles G. Ellington, *The Trial of U. S. Grant: The Pacific Coast Years, 1852-1854* (Glendale, California, 1987), 115, 122.

wrote to General Stewart Van Vliet, the New York quartermaster, and asked him to help Mercer in the "speedy" transportation of not more than 700 emigrants to San Francisco. If the government had vessels bound to Aspinwall, or to San Francisco via the Cape route, Van Vliet was to transport the women, and if not, Grant vaguely suggested that Van Vliet could make some sort of deal with the Panama Line to carry them. Clearly, any deal with the Panama line would cost money.[15]

Mercer's later recollection of these events reads more into the Grant letter than the words actually state, but we do not know what additional informal assurances the General might have given to this young man from Washington Territory, who had such a fantastic scheme. Mercer recalled that Grant's "order" required Van Vliet to turn over to him a steamship, large enough to carry 500 women to Seattle. With this assurance, Asa at once set out to see Van Vliet in New York, apparently carrying a copy of Grant's letter with him.

In New York, the first conversation with General Van Vliet also went well, and Van Vliet promised to help. Mercer agreed to furnish the food for the passengers, if the government would provide the vessel for the voyage, although there is no indication of where he hoped to get the money for food. Asa was then renting an office in New York, and he was spending money on rail fare back and forth to Washington, and also to and from New England, all of which must surely have strained his meager resources. Nevertheless, he did not hesitate to push forward.

With the assurance he thought he had from Van Vliet, Mercer went back to New England to finish his recruiting effort. There, local editors were stirring interest in his project, by quoting Western reports that women were much in demand out there; the *Rocky Mountain News* said of the Colorado region, "There is scarce one woman where six could find profitable employment." Asa said he visited 100 towns by the first of August, but since there were only two weeks between the date of Grant's letter and the end of July,

[15]Rufus Ingalls to Brigadier General Stewart Van Vliet, July 18, 1865.

the 100 towns must have been either a very round number, or a cumulative count for a considerably longer period. The *Times* reported that Mercer had contracts with 400 girls who would receive free passage to Washington Territory, and he was making preparations for departure.[16]

As we have already noted, when Asa spoke to audiences in the northeast, he actually downplayed his quest for young single female emigrants. At the end of July he was in Lowell, and there he gave a comprehensive list of the skills wanted in Washington Territory. He guaranteed "good wages" for 150 men, "constant" business at "fair" prices for shoe and bootmakers, first class blacksmiths, a brickmaker, a foundryman, a machinist, a sash and door maker. Obviously, such a specific list of skills must have reflected the requirements he had obtained from the Seattle businessmen he canvassed before setting out for the East.[17]

"Young ladies" were also on Mercer's list, but they were by no means in first position. They were not a majority of the passengers in the expedition, and their passage was not to be free. Mercer offered "constant" employment for 100 young ladies, at four dollars per week, payable in gold. Finally, he would take 300 war widows and their orphans for twenty-five dollars each, if they furnished their own bedding. In response to criticism that he was accepting prostitutes for the expedition, he added a requirement for "good references." The financial bombshell in his proposal was that, except for the war widows, everyone would have to pay the $200 fare for the journey from New York to Seattle. The steamer was expected to sail on or about August 20th.[18]

Mercer also wanted to make sure that all was in place in Seattle to receive the expedition, and on July 23, while he was still in Lowell, Mercer wrote to the editor of the *Seattle Gazette*, saying, "The 19th of August I sailed from New York with upwards of three hun-

---

[16]The comment from the Denver *News* was quoted in *The Lowell Daily Courier*, July 18, 1865.

[17]Mercer specified the need for six shoe and bootmakers, and four first-class blacksmiths, but only one of each of the other skills. *The Lowell Daily Courier*, July 24, 1865.

[18]*The Lowell Daily Courier*, July 24, 1865.

dred war orphans—. . . ." He added that he could "cheerfully" vouch for the intelligence and moral character of his passengers, and he asked each neighborhood to appoint a committee to meet the ship, and to welcome the women into their homes.

The Boston *Herald* gave additional details on the arrangements, under the headline, "A Chance for the Anxious and Aimless," identifying the ship as the steamer *de Molay*, which the *Herald* claimed had been made available by the government, at the urging of Governor Andrews. The 300 "lady" passengers were to go down the coast to Aspinwall, where they would cross the Isthmus and sail up the coast to Washington Territory, and the entire voyage was to be "entirely free." The *Herald* again noted that the women were assured of good wages, paid in gold, and there was also the prospect of "probable marriage within three months, if they wish."[19]

Governor Andrew wanted to help Mercer, but he was having a hard time keeping up with the changing requirements for the expedition. The governor's office was receiving inquiries about the Mercer project, both in person and by letter, "every day," and these were routinely referred to Asa for his response. Mercer gave the governor copies of at least some of his responses, but the cumulative effect was one of utter confusion. Early in August, Andrew's private secretary wrote to Mercer, asking him what fare was expected from women who were not widows, what provisions they should make for the voyage, and what sort of occupation awaited them in Washington Territory.[20]

Asa's supporters in Seattle at once responded to his request for help in receiving the women. A meeting, complete with brass band, was called to canvass the community for "food, shelter and rest," to use the words of Rev. Daniel Bagley, who addressed the group. Apparently, some criticism of Mercer arose during the meeting, and

[19] *The Boston Herald*, July 26, 1865.

[20] H. Ware to A. S. Mercer, August 4, 1865, Massachusetts State Archives. Mercer's response has apparently not survived. At this time, Governor Pickering from Washington Territory was in Washington, D. C., and Governor Andrew went down to meet him there, where they undoubtedly would have had occasion to discuss the Mercer project.

Bagley did not try to defend what Mercer was doing, but instead emphasized the emergency nature of the request to accommodate the women. He said, "We cannot stop to question the propriety of Mr. Mercer's actions." Ultimately, there was good response from those present. One man agreed on the spot to take thirty women, the committee for Olympia agreed to take eighty, and twenty-five other committees were appointed to find accommodations for the remainder. Acting Governor Evans also gave his support to the effort, by addressing the Olympia group.[21]

Elsewhere, press comments on the Mercer expedition were somewhat of a mixed bag. In San Francisco, the *Alta California*, which also identified the *de Molay* as the vessel assigned to the expedition, noted that there was considerable opposition to this use of government property. A rather strange defense of the project came from the New York correspondent for the *Alta* who argued that the government's action could be justified as a national defense measure. According to this argument, the west coast was too sparsely populated to defend itself, and the expedition would bring young women capable of bearing children, as future soldiers.[22]

Mercer soon learned that the advance publicity he had stirred up was premature. Back in New York for a second conversation with Van Vliet, Mercer now learned that the government was not going to send the *de Molay*, or any other government transport, to the Pacific, after all. Mercer said that Quartermaster General Montgomery Cunningham Meigs had refused to honor Grant's "order," contending that it was not in accordance with the law. Actually, as we noted above, Grant had in fact not given any order at all.[23]

The next events were reported in a Mercer interview in the *Times*, and in Mercer's later account to Clarence Bagley. The two versions

[21]Dr. Kellogg of Whidby Island said that he could take thirty women. Clarence B. Bagley, "The Mercer Immigration," 12, Deutsch *Mercer's Belles*, 13, and *Seattle Weekly Gazette*, September 23, October 7, 1865.

[22]The *Alta* also noted that the "Copperhead" press, particularly the New York Express, were opposed, setting up a "steady howl" for several weeks. *Daily Alta California*, September 8, 1865.

[23]Bvt. Major General Rufus Ingalls to Brigadier General Stewart Van Vliet, July 18, 1865, and E. D. Townsend to Gardiner Tufts, August 22, 1865.

diverge considerably, as can be seen in the table on the next page. Mercer told the *Times* that he and Governor Andrews went to Washington and once more met with Colonel Bowers, only to learn that Grant himself was absent in Canada, so there was no opportunity to lay the problem before him.[24]

Mercer went all the way back to New York before he decided to write to General Meigs, apparently after another meeting with Van Vliet, who may well have suggested that Asa should write to the Quartermaster General. In any case, the letter to the Quartermaster General was written from Mercer's room at the Merchant's Hotel, and in this letter, Mercer reminded Meigs that 300 of his party were "daughters of slain Union soldiers," perhaps hoping thus to soften the old general's heart. Mercer told Meigs that he had gone to General Van Vliet with Grant's "order," in order to obtain the two steamers he required, but that the Van Vliet had received no comparable orders from Meigs to dispatch them.[25]

The day after Mercer wrote, Van Vliet also wrote to Meigs, suggesting that if the latter were to send ships to the west coast, they should be the *S. R. Spaulding* and the *Continental*, because both had good machinery and boilers. He noted that he had received Grant's letter, and advised the only practicable way to transport the women to the Pacific Coast was to send government ships, because it was impossible to make the alternative arrangements Grant had suggested with any private shipping line.[26]

The correspondence from New York brought a response from

---

[24]It is entirely possible that Governor Andrews went to Washington with Mercer, as the *Lowell Courier* expected the Governor to go to New York for the departure of the expedition. *The Lowell Daily Courier*, September 18, 1865.

[25]Mercer's "daughters of slain soldiers" assertion would likely have been as difficult to prove then as it is now. In this tangled affair, this is the only mention of a requirement for two vessels, and it must have arisen from knowledge of the letter Van Vliet was writing to Meigs, offering the latter a choice of vessels for the journey. A. S. Mercer to Colonel George D. Wise, Chief Quartermaster, August 1, 1865.

[26]Stewart Van Vliet to the Quartermaster General, August 2, 1865, and George D. Wise, Third Division of the Quartermaster General's office to A. S. Mercer, August 4, 1865. The next day, the Quartermaster General sent a copy of Mercer's letter to Van Vliet, at the same time asking whether Van Vliet had received any such "order" as Mercer had mentioned. J. D. Bingham (for Colonel G. D. Wise) to Brigadier General S. Van Vliet, August 5, 1865.

Mercer in 1865 *Times* Interview[27]	Mercer in 1901 letter to C. B. Bagley[28]
Mercer arrived in the east on April 14, 1865, the day Lincoln was assassinated, so was unable to see the President.	Mercer remembered Lincoln's "funny stories" as a five-year-old, but when he reached his hotel in New York, he heard the news of Lincoln's assassination (i.e., on April 15).
He then went to Kansas to explore a possible overland journey, and when this failed, he went to Massachusetts to see Gov. John Andrew, who gave him a letter of introduction to Secretary of War Stanton.	[The Kansas journey is not mentioned in the 1901 letter.]
In Washington, Mercer saw Gen. Grant, who said he would tell the President; the next day, Grant said the President approved of the project, and Grant had spoken to Stanton, who also approved. Mercer was then sent to see Maj. Gen. Howard, who also recommended the project, and Grant then issued an order to Gen. Van Vliet to assign a steamer to Mercer.	Mercer saw "everybody, from President Johnson down the line. . . ." He called on Grant, who told him to read the morning paper, while Grant went to a meeting with the President and the Cabinet. Half an hour later, Grant returned, directed that an order be prepared, and signed it. [The meeting with Gen. Howard is not mentioned in the 1901 letter, or elsewhere.]
Back in New England, Mercer visited 100 towns, signing contracts with 400 girls with free passage.	In New England, Mercer signed up "nearly 500" women.
In New York, Gen. Van Vliet said Gen. Meigs refused to release the vessel.	[This meeting is not mentioned in the 1901 letter.]
In Washington with Gov. Andrews, Meigs said Mercer could use the vessel if he paid cost of manning, coal and provisions. Mercer agreed to this, although he said the cost to him would be $70-80,000, of which he would recover not more than $10,000 from the girls. He added that there would be no fewer than 700 young women sailing the 1st week of October.	Mercer went back to Washington to get the vessel, taking Oregon Senator George H. Williams with him. They met with Gen. Meigs, who refused to honor Grant's order. Weeks later, Mercer received a letter from Gen. Meigs saying he would sell the *Continental* to Mercer for $80,000 cash.

[27] *The New-York Times*, September 18, 1865.
[28] Quoted in Clarence B. Bagley, "The Mercer Immigration," 12-18.

General Montgomery Cunningham Meigs, Quartermaster General of the U. S. Army at the time Asa Mercer was trying to obtain a ship to transport his passengers to the West Coast.
From the collections of the Library of Congress.

the Quartermaster General, who wrote to tell Mercer that the government was not sending a vessel to the Pacific, thus confirming in writing what Mercer already knew. In a desperate effort to salvage the situation, Mercer said that he went to see George Henry Williams, Republican senator from Oregon, who took him to see Secretary of War Edwin M. Stanton. Mercer said that Stanton was in a "belligerent" mood, and would not overrule Meigs, although Asa said the secretary "favored" the project.[29]

The State of Massachusetts also maintained an office in Washington, and Mercer was able to get Gardiner Tufts, who was the State's agent in that office, to try to intervene with Stanton. Tuft's letter, dated August 10, asked why there had been a delay in carrying out Grant's order, thus leaving the Secretary flexibility to inter-

[29]Williams was later Attorney General under Grant. *San Francisco Examiner*, June 25, 1893.

pret the Grant letter as an order. Tufts' letter was referred back to the Adjutant General, and a few days later, General Townsend responded to Tufts, repeating the substance of Grant's letter.

Clearly, Tufts' inquiry through Stanton's office was given more thought than Mercer's earlier efforts, for someone had now gone to the trouble to find out what alternative arrangements could be made with a private shipping line. Townsend said that cabin accommodations could be booked for $127.50 each, and deck accommodations could be had for $77.50, the deck passengers "finding themselves," that is, bringing their own sleeping accommodations.[30]

Upon receiving his copy of Townsend's letter, Stanton asked the Quartermaster General for a report, and at the end of August, Meigs himself wrote to the Secretary. Whether this referral shows that Mercer had been correct in asserting that Stanton favored his project, we cannot say, but in any case, Meigs was taking the matter seriously, although he had not changed his conclusion. All communications from the Secretary were treated with respect, and it was now time for Meigs to set forth the Army's position at some length. After summarizing Grant's letter to Van Vliet, Meigs noted that he presumed that Grant had intended to propose a loan of a vessel to send the emigrants, but when he learned the cost of doing so, he considered it "not advisable."[31]

It then became clear that Mercer had been expansive in his conversation with Meigs, for the Quartermaster General noted that Mercer himself had proposed to pay the entire cost of sending the ship. Meigs had no objection to such a proposition, since he saw "certain advantages" of having one or two "good propellers" on the Pacific Coast, but he reminded the Secretary that there was no appropriation available for such purpose. He added rather archly, "it is not supposed that the Lieut Genl intended to order any such expedition." So much for Grant's "order."[32]

Learning of Mercer's unwise offer, Stanton at once approved the

[30]Edward David Townsend to Gardiner Tufts, August 22, 1865.

[31]M. C. Meigs to E. M. Stanton, August 30, 1865.

[32]Clearly, Meigs was construing the Mercer "offer" as covering the cost of fuel and provisions, but the use of government employees on the voyage would still have required appropriated funds.

Secretary of War Edwin M. Stanton, who finally made the decision to sell the ship *Continental* for use to transport Asa Mercer's passengers.
From the collections of the Library of Congress.

loan of the vessels at Mercer's expense, and Meigs directed that the necessary papers be prepared. The *Continental* cost over $430 per day for victualing, manning, and running, and the *Spaulding* nearly $320 per day, and Mercer estimated that it would cost $70-80,000 to man, coal, and provision the vessel the voyage, of which $30,000 was for coal.

One would suppose these numbers would have stunned Mercer, but incredibly, he now said he would pay all of these costs, although he said he would not collect more than $10,000 from the passengers. There was not even a hint of where he would find such an sum of money. The government's draft contract called for Mercer and other—presumably adequate—sureties to guarantee the safe delivery of the vessel back to the government in San Francisco.

Faced with the need to provide a bond, Asa wrote to Governor Andrew from New York, asking if the governor could arrange the bond. The governor's private secretary responded the following day, saying that Andrew did not think it would be possible for the state to help, and blandly advising Mercer to strike an agreement with the War Department, or with the commander of the vessel. When Mercer got this response, he did not sign the contract he had been offered by the government.[33]

Meanwhile, the passengers who had signed on for the voyage were getting restless. On September 7, the Boston *Herald*, once again using the "Anxious and Aimless" headline, responded to inquiries from "fair correspondents," who were concerned about the timetable for the Mercer project. The *Herald* relayed the information undoubtedly provided by Mercer himself, to the effect that he was to be at the United States Hotel in Boston on that very day, and he would furnish "all desired information."[34]

Early in September, Mercer issued a circular signed by Edward Everett Hale, advertising for emigrants "who will improve the religious morals and tone of society" in Washington Territory. This circular abandoned all talk of free passage, except for children under three, and promised "comfortable" accommodations for $150, while other ladies would be accommodated for $125. These fares appear to have been designed to recoup the $80,000 it would cost to run the ship, based upon perhaps 700 passengers, as we shall see.[35]

In spite of the incredible financial hurdle he faced, Mercer began acting as if success were within his grasp. He began listing all his passengers and notifying them of the sailing, and he gave an optimistic interview to the New York *Times,* in which he said the

[33]H. Ware to Asa S. Mercer, September 12, 1865. Massachusetts State Archives.

[34]*The Boston Herald*, September 7, 1865.

[35]Children over six years were carried at half price, 3-6 years at quarter price, and under three, free.

Continental would sail the first week of October, with 700 young women, 30 or 40 families and 20 young men. The group from New England would be the largest, chiefly daughters of soldiers, 16-25 years of age, "some few" older. At the beginning of October, Mercer told the *Times* that "nearly a thousand" women were to go West, and the newspaper responded to this news by saying the mission was "full of heroic poetry." Two weeks later, the Rev. Bagley told the Seattle *Gazette* that he had a wire from Mercer stating that he had sailed on the 22nd of September, with 700 aboard.[36]

The *Times* story of September 18 contained a curious reference that was never again repeated by Mercer. The *Times* said that after Grant talked with Mercer, he sent the matter to the President and to Stanton, and both of those men approved the project, but suggested that it be placed under Major General Oliver Otis Howard, who was then in charge of the Freedmen's Bureau. This, of course, harks back to the fuss in Washington Territory, when Mercer was accused of planning to bring freed slaves to the Territory. The *Times* story said that it was General Howard who recommended that Grant write his so-called "order" regarding shipping for the emigrants, and it would be odd for Howard to involve himself, unless freedmen were intended to be included in the expedition.

There were numerous other press comments, the Seattle papers noting that the "solid men" of Boston were opposing the emigration, as they were finding it difficult to hire women for the textile mills. The west coast editors assured the Bostonians that the women whom Mercer was recruiting were not likely to be "useful members of society," but instead would be "school marms" and other "ornamental" types, a description that could not have endeared the editors to the prospective passengers. In the East, opposition came only from editors who disputed the claim that there was a surplus female population, and the Boston *Gazette* now declared that there was actually a scarcity of females. Early in September, the Springfield *Republican* said that if the expedi-

[36] *Seattle Weekly Gazette*, October 14, 1865, and *The New-York Times*, September 18, October 2, 1865.

tion didn't sail soon, there would be no need for the women to leave, as demand for female help was so high.[37]

In Boston, the *Herald*, which for the first time dropped its "Anxious and Aimless" headline, speculated that Governor Andrew would probably be in New York to make a speech when the *Continental* sailed on September 30. The passenger list was said to consist of 700 Massachusetts women, 300 of whom were said to be orphan daughters of dead soldiers. Mercer was once again on the "free passage" bandwagon, and the *Herald* assured its readers that "Mr. Mercer pays all the bills, and looks to the future for his reimbursement, if he gets it at all."

Unfortunately, a week later, the *Herald* moved the sailing date to October 7, and on October 6, the date was again moved, to October 14; two days later, the *Herald* resurrected its "Anxious and Aimless" headline to report a new delay, with sailing in "a few days." The following week, reporting on a letter Mercer had written to the New York papers, the editor's sarcasm was poorly concealed, as he noted that Mercer's letter was "full of hope," and that Asa expected to improve the society of Washington Territory by introducing his female passengers there. Finally, the *Herald* noted that Mercer "still has an office open" in New York, and that the sailing was to be "about the 1st of November." All of these sailing dates, which must have come from Mercer, were published at a time when he still lacked the right to use any ship.[38]

Soon, Asa would make a deal that would give him the use of a ship, but to make that deal, he had to place the fate of the expedition in the hands of a man whose only interest in it was to make money for himself.

---

[37] *The Pacific Tribune*, September 23, 1865, and *The Lowell Daily Courier*, August 7, September 8, 1865.
[38] *The Boston Herald*, September 25, October 2, 6, 16, 24, 1865.

Chapter V

Enter Ben Holladay

If the press reports were only substantially correct, Asa Mercer had succeeded in attracting a large number of people to accompany him to the Pacific Northwest, although it is unlikely that even most of them had the resources to pay the fares he was asking. The government had offered him a vessel for the voyage, but at a high cost, which had to be paid with cash that he did not have. If he were to salvage the expedition, Mercer would have to look elsewhere for help.

Although Mercer had actually made little progress in arranging for a ship in the period from the beginning of September to early October, press reports in early October continued to be optimistic. The *New York Daily Tribune* reported that Mercer had been offered the *Continental*, which was then at Pier 13 in the North River, on condition he pay to man and coal the ship. The paper said that 700-900 had already agreed to go, and estimated that ultimately there would be nearly 1,000 passengers. The *Tribune* said the fare for regular passengers was now $175, but that orphans and the wives and daughters of slain servicemen were to pay only $25, if they furnished their own bedding, and agreed to repay the $150 balance in the future.

The *Tribune* said the women, who were guaranteed employment at four dollars in gold per week, plus board, were mostly sixteen to twenty years of age, although there was a small number of elderly women. Some "fallen women" had applied, but Mercer firmly rejected them. On the passenger list were a number of men, including machinists and other mechanics, and there were special incentives for particular skills. Mercer was paying ten boot and shoemakers of custom boots $2.50 in gold per pair of boots,

Benjamin Holladay, who saw Mercer's troubles as an opportunity to purchase the *Continental* for use in his operations on the West Coast. Courtesy of Oregon Historical Society, Negative No. OHI 49501.

and advancing half their fare to the West, provided they agreed to work thirteen months for him in Seattle.[1]

Although the *Tribune* story contained errors, Mercer's persistence was beginning to pay off. Someone had been able to reach Stanton's ear, for on October 14 the Quartermaster General once again wrote to the Secretary, his tone weary, if not actually testy. "I cannot recommend that the United States supply any more than has already been granted," he said, and noted that sending the vessel to the west coast would cost at least $50,000. To do this would require spending that sum from the appropriation for transportation of the Army, on a project of "civil emigration."[2]

[1]*New York Daily Tribune*, October 6, 1865.

[2]M. C. Meigs to E. M. Stanton, October 14, 1865. Stanton directed that a copy of this letter be given to Mercer, and this was done on the same day.

Stanton referred Meigs' letter back down to Grant, who supported the position of the Quartermaster General, but suggested that the government's position be softened to the extent of permitting Mercer to give his own personal bond for the safe delivery of the vessel. To protect the government's interest in the vessel, an agent of the Quartermaster's Department could be sent on the voyage. Stanton approved this recommendation, which eliminated the guarantee problem in the draft contract, but obviously nothing was solved thereby, for Mercer simply did not have the money for fuel and provisioning.[3]

In his 1901 letter to Clarence Bagley, which has formed the basis for most subsequent accounts, Mercer said that he was in New York some weeks after receiving Van Vliet's negative response to his request for a ship, when he received a letter from Meigs. Meigs said that the *Continental*, a 1,600-ton ship, could be sold at its appraised value of $80,000, cash.

Leaving aside the fact that the story is wrong in detail, including the price, this was a dramatic turning point in Mercer's troubles. Up to this point, the government had been offering to let Mercer use the ship for the single voyage, after which the ship would still belong to the government, and there was no indication that Mercer had ever offered to buy a ship. Moreover, the tone of the correspondence does not suggest that anyone was considering selling him one, either. Nevertheless, this strange and sudden shift in government policy occurred at the time that a formidable person entered the scene.[4]

Ben Holladay, who was born in Kentucky in 1819, was then the stagecoach king, but he was also a significant factor in the shipping business on the west coast. When Holladay learned of Meigs' offer to Mercer, he would clearly have perceived it as a cheap way to replace one of his old side-wheelers. We have no way to judge the price Mercer had been quoted for the *Continental*, but if it was a

[3]U. S. Grant to the Secretary of War, October 16, 1865.

[4]The *Continental*, built in Philadelphia in 1862, was 235 feet long, and had a beam of 36 feet. The figure of $80,000 is by coincidence the same amount Mercer had given the *Times* for the cost of manning, provisions, and coal, but the details Mercer gives are far from the facts.

bargain price, Holladay would have seen that Mercer could be used as a front to acquire the ship for the Holladay company.

Mercer's publicity efforts would have made it easy for Holladay to learn of his efforts, and Holladay owned houses in Washington as well as in New York, so that he was often in the same neighborhoods Mercer was scouring for help. But we need not look so far afield for clues, since in all likelihood, the key source of information for Holladay was none other than his good friend, Major General Rufus Ingalls, in the U. S. Army's Quartermaster's department.[5]

Mercer said that Ben Holladay called on him at his room in the Merchants Hotel, and if Holladay did so, the act was certainly consistent with the personality of this flamboyant man. According to Mercer's recollection of their conversation, Holladay offered to buy the *Continental* and carry the women to the West Coast for "a nominal figure." Mercer quickly accepted the offer, and he gave two different stories as to the contract involved; in one story, Holladay brought in two lawyers to draft a contract, and in a later account, the deal with Holladay was a "plain verbal agreement."

Actually, neither statement was strictly correct. The agreement with Holladay was contained in a brief statement signed by Ben Holladay himself under date of October 17, saying that in the event the Holladay company was able to purchase the *Continental*, Mercer could send 500 passengers "as proposed" from New York to Seattle for $50,000. This worked out to a fare of only $100 per passenger, which was obviously a bargain, but the total of $50,000 was anything but nominal to Asa Mercer.[6]

Even if Holladay did not need a lawyer to write the letter to Mer-

---

[5]The Oregon and California Steam-Ship Company, in which Benjamin Holladay was a principal, had been organized in 1861 to purchase six steamers from the Pacific Mail Steam-Ship Company. F. N. Otis, *Illustrated History of the Panama Railroad*, (New York, 1862), 150, John Haskell Kemble, *The Panama Route, 1848–1869* (Columbia, S. C., 1990), 98 and Roger Conant, in Deutsch, *Mercer's Belles, passim*. General Ingalls was the executor under Holladay's will.

[6]Years later, Mercer claimed that he was outwitted by lawyers' drafting, but in his speech in Yesler Hall on his return from the East, he said that the first agreement with Holladay was verbal. *Puget Sound Weekly*, May 28, 1866. The Holladay letter, written on the stationary of the California, Oregon and Mexico Steamship Line, 84 Broadway, is in the Weintz collection.

cer, he was not lacking for lawyers, and influential ones, at that. For the next step of this transaction, the really heavy work, Holladay called on Judge Edwards Pierrepont, one of the most famous lawyers of the time, and extremely well connected politically. Pierrepont, who was born in 1817, was a War Democrat, who had worked for the reelection of Lincoln in 1864; Grant was also his friend, and he helped to raise $100,000 to lift the mortgage on the general's Washington home.[7]

Pierrepont also knew Secretary of War Stanton, for he had served on a special commission, reporting directly to the Secretary of War. We do not know when Pierrepont first approached Stanton on the Mercer scheme, but he produced results. On October 25, Stanton wired Pierrepont, offering to sell the *Continental* to Mercer for the appraised value (which was $130,000), and the next day, the lawyer wired acceptance. Obviously, Pierrepont was representing Holladay as well as Mercer, but that nuance is not revealed on the official record.[8]

Having made the deal with Pierrepont, on November 4, Stanton wearily wrote to General Meigs, saying that to avoid "all further trouble" with the Mercer scheme, he had offered the *Continental* to Judge Pierrepont at its appraised value, and the Judge had accepted. Stanton directed Meigs to issue the necessary orders to effect the sale. Of course, Mercer did not have any sum approaching $130,000, but he did not need to raise it, either, for the steamer *Continental* now passed under the ownership of Holladay's company, The Oregon, California and Mexican Steam-Ship Company.[9]

[7]When Grant later ran for President, Pierrepont is said to have contributed $20,000 to his campaign, and he later served as Attorney General in the Grant administration. Kenneth D. Ackerman, *The Gold Ring: Jim Fish, Jay Gould and Black Friday, 1869* (New York, 1988), 68, 73. Pierrepont was born in North Haven, Connecticut, on March 4, 1817, and died in New York, March 6, 1892.

[8]J. G. Randall and David Donald, *The Civil War and Reconstruction* (Lexington, Massachusetts, 1969), 301 and Edwin M. Stanton to Hon. Edwards Pierrepont, October 25, 1865, and Edwards Pierrepont to Hon. Edwin M. Stanton, October 26, 1865.

[9]Although the ship was sold privately, for some unknown reason, the Army reported to the Congress that it had been auctioned, even supplying the name of J. H. Draper as the auctioneer. Edwin M. Stanton to Brevet Major General Meigs, October 26, 1865, and *House of Representatives Executive Document 337 (40th Congress, Second Session) Vessels Bought, Sold and Chartered by the United States, July 16, 1868.*

Mercer at once wrote to the *New-York Times* to give yet another sailing date. He said that after the many delays, "success has awarded the effort," adding that "friends" had advanced the means so that the *Continental* could be purchased from the government. The ship would sail at noon on November 25, and there was still room for "about forty" additional passengers.[10]

As a footnote to this frenetic season, it was at this time that Mercer wired Acting Governor Evans to resign his seat in the Washington territorial Council. He gave no explanation for this action, which gave rise to the need for a special election to fill the seat. Asa could not have foreseen that the man who was elected to the seat was not friendly to Mercer's project, and would sabotage his later plea for financial help from the territorial government.[11]

Mercer always spoke bitterly of his dealings with Holladay, but in fairness, Holladay was the man who made it possible for the expedition to go forward, with 500 passengers, rather than 700 or 1,000. Indeed, if no other large obstructions had loomed before him after he made the deal with Holladay, he could have reflected that all his tribulations of the past months had at last borne fruit, and his troubles were over. Unfortunately, it was not to be so.

[10] *The New-York Times*, November 6, 1865.

[11] *Seattle Weekly Gazette*, October 21, 1865.

Chapter VI

The Forgotten War with Anna Dickinson

It must have seemed to Asa that once his enormous problems in making a deal for the *Continental* were conquered, nothing worse could happen to his project. But that proved not to be true, for the opponent he now faced threatened his greatest accomplishment: his contracts with the long list of women who had signed on to be his passengers. Oddly enough, in the reports of Mercer's many references to his expedition, there is no evidence that he ever mentioned the name of the person who brought him so close to total defeat.

The publicity attending Mercer's recruiting efforts in the East had brought him to the attention of the feminist movement, with grave consequences. Although Mercer was careful not to respond to feminist criticism, the New York *Tribune* noted that a prime source of opposition in the East was none other than Anna Elizabeth Dickinson, the famous female lecturer.[1]

A Quaker woman, anything but gentle, and not yet twenty-three, Anna Dickinson had begun her lecture career when she was only seventeen, and in 1863, before she was twenty-one, she had been enlisted to stump for the Republicans. After Dickinson's surprising success in the New Hampshire gubernatorial election in the spring of 1863, Republicans everywhere in the East were clamoring for her as a speaker, and she was even sent to campaign in the coal mining regions, where no man dared go. Although she was fired upon, she stood her ground, and the rugged miners heard her out. With cre-

[1]While we do not know which of the several *Heralds* ran the item in the East, it is clear that the editor of the *Alta California* in San Francisco was particularly vocal in opposition to the Mercer expedition.

dentials of this sort, Anna was able to attract a capacity crowd of 5,000 at New York's Cooper Union, and soon she could book lectures at $100 per night, the same fee Henry Ward Beecher was then getting.[2]

In September 1865, Miss Dickinson announced that she had written three new lectures to be delivered that season, and one of those new lectures, entitled "Home Thrusts, or Marriage and Its Relations," devoted a great deal of time to Mercer's emigration scheme. She delivered all three of these lectures in a series at New Haven, Connecticut, and then she toured New England, coming to Boston on November 1, and to Lowell on December 7, where she delivered the "Home Thrusts" lecture. The crowd who came to hear Anna Dickinson at Lowell packed the hall, and was said to be the largest ever known for this sort of presentation. Her voice was in good form, and in the crowded hall she could "definitely" be heard at the farthest point of the auditorium.

Miss Dickinson began her lecture by pointing out that young girls were being taught that their highest aim was to become wives, rather than a goal of womanhood, and usefulness in the world. On the other hand, boys *were* trained for manhood, and usefulness in the world. As a consequence, every girl was taught to view every single man as a possible future husband, and if she reached age thirty with the word "Miss" attached to her name, all assumed she could not attract a mate. Anna even suggested that newspapers should publish a list of "Offers and Rejections," so that a woman might have a means of disproving this assumption. As a consequence of these societal assumptions, it was only after marriage that a woman could awaken to the uncongenial temper and tastes of her spouse, and the result that there was a long life of misery for her.

All of this was by way of preface to Anna's treatment of the Mercer scheme, on which she spoke at length. She said she had asked Governor Andrew how the women who were emigrating would support themselves in the West, and he replied that they could become teachers. She reminded her audience that the 10,000 or so single

[2]Giraud Chester, *Embattled Maiden: The Life of Anna Dickinson* (New York, 1951), *passim.*

Anna Elizabeth Dickinson, the young woman whose critical lectures effectively decimated Asa Mercer's passenger list for the 1866 expedition. From the collections of the Library of Congress.

men these women would meet in that remote region, were "wandering about in a half savage state." She asked rhetorically, "And we are told they are going to teach children?" Instead, she said, the fathers of these women should tell them that they already have a home in the East, no matter whether they are fifteen or fifty years of age. Anna called attention to the fact that women had fewer occupations to choose from in the West than on the east coast, and she poured scorn on the stereotype of "women's" occupations, referred to in Governor Andrew's message.[3]

If Asa refused to mention Anna Dickinson's name when he recalled his expedition, she apparently returned the favor. While newspaper accounts of the Dickinson lectures make it clear that she was talking about the Mercer expedition, she may not even have

[3] *The Lowell Daily Courier*, December 8, 1865.

mentioned Mercer by name, for her chief target was Governor Andrew, whom she regarded as Mercer's sponsor. After all, she had spoken on the floor of Congress at the invitation of that body, and she would be unlikely to expend energy on a mere immigration commissioner from a "half savage" territory; certainly a sitting governor was a more worthy target.[4]

Early in the new year, while Mercer was making the final arrangements for the expedition to sail from New York, Anna Dickinson came to town to deliver her "Home Thrusts" lecture at the Cooper Institute on the evening of January 9. It was her last lecture of the season in New York, and was apparently well attended. The New York *Times* said the lecture was brilliant, and was greeted by "frequent" plaudits, and it may well be that this lecture was the key factor that so thoroughly decimated the numbers Mercer had hoped to enlist.[5]

Others now took up the case against the Mercer expedition. Early in January, 1866, the *Alta California* declared that the fate of the women who were to come west with Mercer was "one to shudder at," and condemned the project as a Utopian scheme "which could only be conceived in the brain of a subject for a lunatic asylum. . . ." The following week, a long letter to the editor of the *Alta*, signed "Hagar," asked Governor Andrews to halt the expedition.[6]

Mercer was no match for such a performance. The New York *Tribune* later said that the "full force" of Anna's "earnest invective" had been directed at the Mercer project, and undoubtedly caused many of the women to withdraw from the expedition. Mercer's own account said that two-thirds of the passengers he had signed up now declined to go with him.[7]

---

[4]To Anna Dickinson, the Mercer expedition was not merely a topic for the 1865 lecture season, for she was still fuming about the subject as late as the summer of 1869, when she was delivering her lecture, "A Struggle for Life," on the West Coast. *The Daily Herald* (San Francisco), July 15, 1869.

[5]The admission for the Dickinson lecture in New York was 50¢ for those in the reserved circle, while others paid 25¢. *The New-York Times*, January 9, 10, 1866.

[6]*Daily Alta California* (San Francisco), January 11, 19, 1866.

[7]*New York Daily Tribune*, January 18, 1866.

If Anna Dickinson provided Mercer's chief opposition, there were also other new impediments to his recruiting efforts. The mills in New England were reopening, drawing women back from their jobs as servant girls and housekeepers, so that there was a scarcity of workers in those areas. Finally, Mercer's plans had been delayed so many times, and changed so frequently, that some of the women who originally agreed to go with him simply ran out of money, or patience, or both.[8]

For whatever reason, Mercer now did not have enough passengers to meet the minimum in his contract, and he had to go back to Holladay. Mercer told the tycoon that the 500 passengers he had hoped to find would now be only "perhaps" 200, and asked that the minimum rate be extended to this smaller group. Holladay replied that their earlier contract was at an end, and that he would only take the smaller group at "regular" rates. Mercer later said that he had no choice but to agree. Actually, Holladay did not raise the fare much above the level Mercer had previously regarded as "nominal," for the contract he signed with Holladay's company early in January called for Mercer to pay $8,000 to transport 75 passengers to San Francisco, or an average of $106.67 per person.[9]

It is not possible to put together any estimate of Mercer's finances during the 1865-66 period, but he had clearly been spending money for some months, and he now had signed a contract calling for the payment of $8,000. Most of his passengers had vanished, including the craftsmen, who would likely have been the ones most likely to afford the passage. Where was the money to come from? It is futile to speculate, but it is possible that Holladay paid Mercer a consideration to acquire the right to buy the *Continental* from the government. Mercer never said that was so, and there the matter rests.

In any case, Mercer needed to raise the money, if only to pay the expenses occasioned by the long delay, during which a number of

[8]Deutsch, *Mercer's Belles*, 16.

[9]The new fare was not strictly comparable to the $100 in the original deal, which involved passage all the way to Seattle.

his passengers had gathered in the New York area. To get people to sign up for the voyage, Mercer agreed to pay their expenses in New York. With all these expenses mounting by the day, in December 1865, Mercer asked Governor Pickering to arrange for a loan of $3,000, and in the same communication, he set another sailing date. Asa apparently neglected to mention the shrinkage in the passenger list after the Anna Dickinson affair, for the governor told the newspapers that 500 widows and orphans would sail on December 22.[10]

Mercer did not sail in 1865, but then the governor did not make the "loan," either. Instead, he took Mercer's request to the legislature, which was then in session, and a bill was introduced in the Council to secure the funds. The bill presumably was drafted by those who were friendliest to the Mercer expedition, but even so, it fell considerably short of a ringing endorsement of the project. The long preamble to C. B. 14 noted that "one A. S. Mercer," who "claimed" to represent Washington Territory, had induced 500 widows and orphans to assemble in New York, on the promise that "pleasant homes and profitable employment" awaited them in Washington Territory.[11]

The legislature was not asked to advance the money on the merits of the Mercer scheme, but for humanitarian reasons, since the newspapers had failed to deny Mercer's representations, and women had been induced to leave their homes, and go to New York, where they spent their meager resources while waiting for the expedition to get underway. Finally, the $3,000 requested was not to be a grant, but a loan.[12]

When the bill reached the Council floor on December 22, debate on the Mercer request was spirited. Leading the opposition was John E. Denny, the Seattle man who had been elected to replace Mercer in the territorial Council. "Uncle John" Denny, who was born

---

[10] *Seattle Weekly Gazette*, December 29, 1865.

[11] Council Bill 14, which was introduced by Mr. Clark, was printed in full in the *Daily Alta California*, January 11, 1866.

[12] In an apparent effort to reassure those who expected additional requests would follow, the lawmakers were informed that the governors of Oregon and California had agreed to take those women who did not settle in Washington Territory.

in 1793, was tall, white-haired, witty and wise, and he was "immensely popular." His opposition must have been a bitter pill for Asa, since Uncle John was the father of Mercer's friend, A. A. Denny.[13]

Denny, an orator "who never came off vanquished," had disliked the immigration scheme from the beginning, and his opposition apparently doomed the bill in the Council, where it failed to receive second reading by a vote of 4-2. A similar bill in the House failed in the house ways and means committee, where it was defeated 8-18.[14]

Notwithstanding the opinion of the Washington Territory lawmakers, there were Mercer supporters on the west coast, and in January, a woman writing to the Vancouver *Register* took the solons to task for their failure to support the project. She said the legislators, all of whom were men, had acted out of spite because the governor and Mercer had carried off the scheme without their consent, and they were afraid that "refined" women would "discover and reject" their lifestyle in the frontier West. She ended by upbraiding the men who had native wives, noting their "tender regard" for "the dusky daughters of the soil."[15]

At the end of 1865, Mercer once again set a sailing date of "about" January 1, and this time he attributed the delay to the extensive repairs and alterations to the *Continental*, to accommodate so many passengers. If there were extensive repairs, they were not occasioned by the large number of passengers, as we shall see, and a more likely reason for repairs was to make the roughly-used cargo and military transport ship once again fit for civilian passenger service.

Whatever the reason for this last delay—and it was the last—the *Continental* was finally ready to set sail from New York under the command of Captain Charles Winsor, an ex-Navy officer, on

[13]Denny, who was born in Kentucky, and had served with Lincoln in the Illinois legislature. Denny had acted as peacemaker during the controversy over Daniel Bagley's handling of the University lands, and he went to Washington with Bagley to straighten the matter out. Roberta Frye Watt, *Four Wagons West: The Story of Seattle* (Portland, Oregon, 1931), 264, 296-97.

[14]*The Pacific Tribune*, December 23, 1865.

[15]The letter is quoted from the Vancouver *Register* by the *Morning Oregonian* (Portland), January 26, 1866.

January 16, 1866. There were 100 passengers, plus two babies, bound for Seattle, and four passengers for Rio. Mercer's passengers assembled at his office at 91 West Street, and were told the ship would sail at 11:00 A.M., although the ship did not actually leave its berth in the North River until 3:00 P.M.[16]

Although his contract only called for 75 passengers, Mercer no longer had enough orphans to fill even that reduced number, and the final passenger list were a diverse group. Among them were only thirty-six unmarried women and ten widows, seven of whom had children with them. There were fourteen single men, and the rest were couples, some with children. One of the single men was Roger Conant, a reporter with the New York *Times*, who kept a journal of the voyage, and sent periodic progress reports back to the *Times*.[17]

Mrs. Boardman, a blind woman, sang and played the piano to entertain the passengers on the voyage, and later gave birth to a child. Mercer's 1864 voyage actually contributed three of the passengers, for Mrs. Sarah Pearson, with two children, were on their way to join her husband and their other two daughters, who had gone west with Mercer the year before. Finally, on the passenger list were Mr. and Mrs. W. Lewis Mercer, cousins of Asa.

The delays had taken a fearful toll on the passengers' resources, for Mercer's promise to pay the New York expenses proved to be mostly empty, and the son of one of the passengers recalled that the hotel owner attached their luggage until payment could be made. One of the women who made the trip recalled rumors that Mercer was about to slip away, leaving his bills unpaid, but this did not happen, although Roger Conant said that it was "well known" that Mercer's bank account was empty.

The *Continental* cleared New York harbor on January 15, only to steam to Staten Island, where it again stopped. All passengers were sent below, and then they were called up, one by one, so that the captain and the representative of the owners could check their tickets. Mercer's contract with Holladay was a bulk purchase for seventy-

[16] *The New-York Times*, April 22, 1866.

[17] A bachelor, Roger Conant was born in Maine in 1833, and he had served in the Union Army during the Civil War, where he also was a reporter for the *Times*.

five passengers, and Mercer issued his own individual tickets to each passenger. When the tickets were examined, it was apparent that there were more passengers on board than Mercer's contract permitted, and two families and sixteen single women without valid tickets were taken back to New York. While the tickets were being checked, Mercer was apparently in hiding, perhaps even in the coal bin, for Conant recounted that when he reappeared after the ticket-checking incident, there was coal dust in Mercer's red hair. [18]

Two of those without tickets were orphan girls, and their plight was noticed by Miss Mary Bermingham, sister of Captain Bermingham, the San Francisco agent of the shipping company. Through her intervention the two girls were permitted to remain on board. Conant said that some of the people removed from the ship had received what he called "a half promise" from Mercer that they "might" go, and he said it was their own fault that they had to be put off at Staten Island. This comment, written in April, displays more patience with Mercer's business methods than Conant would afterward exhibit.[19]

Even though Mercer and the *Continental* had left New York, he had left plenty of trouble behind, including at least three lawsuits. Elizabeth Thorne and her children were among those left behind, and she brought suit against Mercer, the shipping company, and Hale's New England Emigrant Aid Society. She said that on January 3 she had booked passage with Mercer for herself and her children, giving him $400 in cash and turning over to him $200 worth of bedding and furniture. She claimed that the ship set sail without notice, leaving her behind. Mrs. Sarah A. Balch also filed suit, and she accused Mercer of selling more tickets than his contract permitted.[20]

When the cases were heard in New York, Mercer was safely at

[18]Mercer's tickets did not even show the name of the shipping company. Flora A. P. Engle, "The Story of the Mercer Expeditions," 229, and Deutsch, *Mercer's Belles*, 32.

[19]The incident with the two orphans apparently soured Mercer's relationship with Miss Bermingham. The shipping company later claimed that five of those without tickets were permitted to stay on board as charity cases. Conant, in Deutsch, *Mercer's Belles*, 34, 34n, and *New York Herald*, January 28, 1866.

[20]*The New-York Times*, January 26, 1866.

sea, and the only defendant to appear in court was the ship line itself, represented by its vice president, William L. Dall. Dall produced the contract with Mercer, and noted that the ship sailed with many more than the seventy-five provided for in the contract. At Staten Island, all who had not paid were put off, except for what Dall called "a few charity cases," which undoubtedly included the two girls for whom Miss Bermingham interceded. Dall noted that the tickets Mercer had issued to his passengers did not even bear the company's name, and he denied any responsibility for them.[21]

A third complaint was that of William Carleton, who had booked passage for himself, his wife, and two children. He had sold his farm in New England and brought his family to New York, only to learn that the ship had already sailed. When a boat took him to the ship at Staten Island, Carleton shouted wildly, "Where is Mercer?" but Mercer could not be found. When he refused to accept the assignment of three single berths for the entire family, the ship sailed without them, and Carleton, by then penniless, was forced to return to New York.[22]

At the trial, Judge McCunn called Mercer "a most consummate villain," and in his formal opinion the judge concluded that Mercer had collected fares from "a much greater number" than seventy-five, and then did not notify the excess passengers of the sailing date, hoping to avoid trouble with them. Unfortunately, the ship had already departed, so that the judge could not seize anything of value, and he suggested that the cases be filed in San Francisco, which, as we shall see, the plaintiffs proceeded to do.[23]

Writing from Lota, in Chile, Mercer tried to defend what he had done. He admitted that he had given Elizabeth Thorne four and a half tickets, but said that she did not pay for them, and he had to pay more than $500 on her account from his own resources, which was now a clear loss. As to those who had paid their fare, but did not make the voyage, he claimed he had sent letters with

[21] *The New-York Times*, January 26, 1866.

[22] *The New-York Times*, January 31, 1866

[23] *New York Herald*, January 28, 1866.

the pilot from Sandy Hook, advising them they could receive a refund.[24]

The New York *Times* had been relatively kind to Mercer, during the months when he struggled to achieve his emigration objectives, but after the *Continental* sailed, the *Times* lost patience with him, and recounted the large number of his broken promises. The *Times* suggested that the thousands of Irish and German girls then arriving from Europe could be diverted to the West Coast with less difficulty than the Mercer expedition had occasioned.

Although Asa Mercer did not retreat from the battlefield with Anna Dickinson, he was no match for her polemical style of oratory and she effectively destroyed his appeal to single women. When large numbers of them cancelled their bookings with him, there was neither time nor money to secure replacements. The long delays and the expense of the complex negotiations left Asa with no funds to meet his legitimate obligations, and he fled New York, leaving many debts behind. Although he was later able to refurbish the memory of the expedition, in January 1866, he must honestly have felt that he had failed.

[24] *The New-York Times*, May 6, 1866. Four and a half tickets would have cost Mercer $480, which may be most of the sum he claimed to have spent from his own resources. The Collins Mercer mentions was not otherwise identified, and he may have meant Carleton.

Chapter VII

At Sea, At Last

Although Mercer knew he had left many unsettled obligations behind, he must have been considerably relieved to be at sea, albeit with a much shorter passenger list than he had hoped for. He was twenty-six years old, and although he was no Alexander the Great, he was in charge of an expedition, sailing in its own vessel, on a mission that he still believed in, despite all the attacks. Indeed, he would spend the rest of his life burnishing its memory.

The *Continental* was built in Philadelphia in 1862, and she had seen two years of government service. She displaced 1,626 tons, was 285 feet long, with a 36-foot beam, and could accommodate 100 passengers. Mercer's circular claimed that the *Continental* was the "finest" passenger vessel in the service of the government. That comparison aside, it is clear that the *Continental* had seen rough treatment while carrying troops and stores between New York and New Orleans, and cargoes of sixty tons of oats and 4,000 bales of hay did not enhance the appearance of the appointments. Captain Charles F. Winsor commanded the vessel, and he brought along his wife and Minnie, his daughter of seventeen, plus the Bermingham sisters, Mary and Bessie, whose brother, Captain Bermingham, was the company's agent in San Francisco.[1]

Mercer's contract with the shipping company provided that the company would provide food and cook it, but otherwise the passengers were to be responsible for cleaning and keeping the ship in good order. Unfortunately, there were no standards specified for the

[1]There are numerous references to the *Continental* in *The War of the Rebellion: A Compilation of the Official Records of the Union and Confederate Armies* (Washington, D. C., 1884). During much of the war, the ship was actually chartered by the government; it was not purchased until August 1, 1864. *Morning Oregonian* (Portland), February 28, 1867.

performance of these duties by either the company or the passengers. One of the women who kept a diary of the voyage complained that although they boarded the *Continental* in the morning on the first day, no meals were served until evening. She said that during the voyage, the quantity of food was adequate, but "it was the quality that jarred," and for seventeen days, the principal dish was beans, "only slightly parboiled."[2]

At first, Mercer ate at the captain's table, but his passengers criticized him so severely for this sign of elitism that he began eating with them. While many of the passengers regarded him with something approaching awe, Conant identified two who were not so favorably inclined. One of these was Mrs. A. D. Chase, a widow, who was a "clairvoyant physician," whatever that may have been, and Conant said she was a "regular thorn" in Mercer's side.

On their first Sunday at sea, Mercer determined to hold services. Conant asked Mary Bermingham whether she would go to hear him, she replied, "No, Mr. Conant, I think that Mr. Mercer is a hypocrite and my conscience would smite me if I should encourage him in such a course." Undaunted, Mercer led his congregation in a hymn, offered a prayer, read the fifth chapter of Matthew, and then read one of Henry Ward Beecher's sermons. The following week, his efforts were distracted by some passengers who made faces at him, and one left in the middle of his sermon, knocking over the stand holding his papers.

Soon, Mercer was asserting his own ideas of discipline. He established a rule forbidding passengers to fraternize with the officers or the crew, and his enforcement efforts extended to the point of breaking up a game because officers were participating. When the "Old Man," as the girls now called Mercer, invited one of the girls to his stateroom to reprimand her for flirting with the officers, she replied that he was no better than they were, and rejected his assertion that she had agreed to place herself in his charge. Mercer related this to Conant, with the judgment that the girl was "ruined."

---

[2]The contract also provided that no more than three passengers were to be assigned to each stateroom.

Asa also had a rule against card playing, and he tried to set a 10 P.M. curfew for the ladies. The Captain agreed the curfew would be a good idea, but advised that it could not be enforced. One cultural resource for the journey was a library, which Peter Cooper had contributed for the use of the passengers, but Mercer refused to let them use the fine editions included in the collection, for fear that the books would be injured.[3]

For a time, the captain privately ridiculed Mercer's efforts to prevent the officers from fraternizing with the women, and was even heard to remark after Mercer had made yet another of his demands, "I wish that confounded old Jackass would jump over board and drown some dark night." Later, these affairs among the younger officers got out of hand, and the captain found they were involved with the passengers, to the neglect of their duties. He then ordered the officers not to speak to the ladies, and he had more success enforcing his rules than Mercer had.

If Mercer's rules forbade some amusements, he did try to introduce alternatives, and he invented games to amuse the ladies. In one, which he called the *Continental* Game, he would write a subject on a card taken from the deck, and distribute cards, face down. The one receiving the card must speak for five minutes on the subject he had written. Unfortunately, this activity did not noticeably diminish the ladies' flirtations with the officers.

The *Continental* crossed the equator on the way south on February 2, and then stopped at Rio de Janeiro, where it remained for eight days. The captain and Mercer went ashore, and left orders that no one else should leave the ship until they returned. On his return from the city, Mercer told the passengers that there was cholera and small pox, making it unsafe for them to go ashore, unless they went in his company. At first this news was accepted calmly, but when Mercer asked whether the passengers accepted the restriction, only one lady rose. Mercer then partially relented and permitted two girls to go ashore with two of the officers, but to his

[3]Mercer said Peter Cooper came to his office in New York, and offered the books. *San Francisco Examiner*, June 25, 1893.

dismay, this party did not return to the ship until 1 A.M. The next day he relaxed his strictures altogether.[4]

At the Straits of Magellan, the ship stopped again, and received the governor of the Chilean military post in that region. Some of the passengers went ashore to the governor's residence, and then a number of soldiers came aboard, bringing with them skins and feathers to exchange for whiskey or other items the passengers might offer.

At Port Gallant, a cove in the Straits, Mercer even indulged himself in a bit of impromptu, and highly irregular, foreign relations. Accompanied by three other men, Mercer climbed the highest mountain they could see in the area, reaching the summit, above timberline, by late afternoon. There they planted a pine tree they had brought from below, and to this makeshift flagpole they attached three ten-foot strips of bunting, in red, white and blue. Then, Mercer delivered to his audience of three a short oration he had written for the occasion, in which he expansively declared that one day, the American flag would float over the land from this point to the Bering Straits, if not from Cape Horn to the North Pole. When the little group returned to the *Continental*, those in the lower saloon agreed to call the eminence Mt. Mercer.

South America was then troubled by a confrontation between Spain and its former colonies, but fortunately no one in authority took notice of Mercer's nonsense at the tip of the continent. However, when the *Continental* continued up the west coast of the continent, it unwittingly sailed into a more serious situation, for the captain missed the harbor for Lota, and instead ran into Coronel, which was then blockaded by the Spanish fleet.[5]

When the captain realized he was in the wrong port, he steamed back toward the entrance to the port, but was met by a Spanish warship, which fired a shot across the bow. Two of the ladies fainted,

[4]Before the ship departed from Rio, Mercer invited six of the ladies to go with him to call on the American Consul in the town of Sebastian, across the bay from Rio.

[5]The speech Mercer delivered is preserved in the Weintz collection. Lewis A. Treen, a shoemaker, later married another passenger, Nina Manning. John Wilson and his wife were from Massachusetts. Conant, in Deutsch, *Mercer's Belles*, 148, 156-57. The Spanish blockade of this Chilean port was in retaliation for Chile's support of Peru's dispute with Spain. The Spanish fleet had also bombarded Valparaiso.

while others screamed and wept, but in the end there was no great cause for concern. The gallant young Spanish officer who came aboard was most "gentlemanly," and only insisted upon an extended examination of the ship's papers.

At Lota, the ship paused again for twelve days, and it was here that Mercer first had an opportunity to see a copy of the *Times*, which included reference to the lawsuits then pending against him in New York. He at once sat down to respond, saying, "I deny any fraud or deception in the entire transaction. The enterprise is a success, and God sparing my life, it will be repeated next summer." Fortunately, the last prediction did not come to pass.

The ship was virtually overrun by Chilean officers at Lota, who offered various inducements to the ladies to remain in Chile, and this time, Mercer did not try to enforce any rules of conduct, although he still watched their card games in "grim silence." Only when the Chileans sent a boat to carry away some of the ladies and their luggage, did Mercer take action. The captain was ashore, and Mercer stood in the gangway with a pistol, saying, "No one takes one of these girls from this ship except they pass over my dead body." When the captain came aboard and ordered the ladder drawn up, the crisis passed, and the ship weighed anchor, and made its way up the coast to its last port of call before San Francisco, the Chilean port of Talcahuano.[6]

Asa obviously had been considering his heavy financial obligations, for when the ship was only ten days out from New York, he distributed skeins of yarn, so that the ladies could knit stockings for sale in Seattle, as a means of defraying the cost of the expedition. Some of those who had paid full passage declined to join in this activity, and this enterprise cannot have contributed much to Asa's depleted treasury. On the day after the departure from Talcahuano, he began a series of interviews with some of his passengers, designed to yield more substantial results.

He called one of the widows, Mrs. Eugene Chase, to his stateroom, and told her that he had been put to great expense in organ-

[6]The paper Mercer saw was the issue of February 3; his reply was printed May 6, 1866.

izing the expedition, and asked that she give him her note for $250. She responded that he had promised her passage for herself and two children for $60, and as she had paid that amount, she would pay no more. Mercer continued to argue with her, saying that she would probably find a husband in Seattle, who would undoubtedly pay the note.

Mrs. Chase replied, "Yes, Mr. Mercer, if I can find a man with white hairs, his pockets well lined with gold, one foot in the grave and the other just ready to go in, I might get married, but mind, none of his money shall ever find its way into your pocket." The interview then became testy, and Mercer threatened to leave her without a cent in San Francisco, to which she responded, "Do it if you dare, Sir," and swept from the room.

With Miss Barry, who was nicknamed "Aunt Berry" by the passengers, he was more successful, when he repeated the assurance that the husband she found would pay the note. The poor woman said, "Oh! Mr. Mercer, do you think that there is any body up there who would be willing to marry me?"

Mercer said, "Certainly. There is one nice old farmer who lives near me, who wants a wife, and he promised to take whoever I brought." He did not mention whether the old farmer had already paid him $300 for the errand of matrimony.

Aunt Berry replied, "If that is the case, I will give you my note for any amount, if you will promise to recommend me to him." Thereupon, she signed the note, and according to Conant's account, she did not even notice that it was for $550.

Some of the others also signed notes for Mercer, while some indignantly refused. Conant took upon himself the role of advisor to the ladies, telling them that Mercer was not a "responsible" person, and assuring them that the notes, given in this fashion for no consideration, were not worth the paper they were written on. Actually, Conant's assurance that there had been no consideration may have been an overstatement. It will be recalled that Mercer had said that those women traveling at reduced fares would have to repay the amount of the discount. It may be that Mercer's notes were an effort to commit this agreement to an enforceable writing.

Annie E. Stephens Mercer, Asa Mercer's long-suffering wife. Courtesy of Chester Mercer, Hyattville, WY.

Notwithstanding his non-fraternization rule, Mercer, himself was not immune to all of the amorous intrigues around him, and before the end of January, he was already in love. He sent a note to the lady of his choice, and wisely asked her to return the missive if her answer should be negative. The target of his affections chose to make the return at a time when he was talking with some other ladies, saying, "Here is your note, old Pap." Conant said that Mercer, who was then only twenty-six, was so depressed by this turn of events that he took to his bed for a few days.

By early April, Asa had recovered from his first disastrous courting effort, and he then fastened his attentions on an Irish girl, Annie Stephens, then twenty-six, who was the daughter of John Stephens, owner of a Philadelphia hat factory. Conant gives us the added information that Annie was "a most bigoted Catholic," who was apparently "a willing victim" of Mercer's blandishments.[7]

The ship crossed the equator for the second time on April 8, and passed through the Golden Gate on April 24, reaching the end of the first part of the journey to Seattle. The only serious mishap during the voyage was the loss of a deck hand, who fell overboard. Although Mercer threw him a life preserver, and a lifeboat was lowered to look for him, the man was not recovered. A less serious incident was that of the poor woman who was bent over the rail while seasick, and lost her false teeth in the ocean, causing her fellow shipmates to call her "toothless" for the remainder of the voyage. Two babies were born during the voyage, Mrs. Stevenson's daughter, fittingly named Continenttalla, and another baby born to Mrs. Boardman, the blind woman.[8]

At San Francisco, the pier was lined with men, all eager to catch sight of the women, and a "strong" force of police was necessary to keep them off the ship. The passengers were lodged at the Fremont House and International Hotel, while they awaited passage north. In Olympia, the *Tribune*, which had loyally backed the venture, urged a pleasant reception for the women, but said that any further schemes of the sort "should and will be promptly frowned down."[9]

There were thirty-six defections from Mercer's expedition at San Francisco, some of whom were influenced by stories they heard of the dismal conditions in Washington Territory. Those left behind included five married men, their wives and children; two widows and the sons of one; eleven unmarried women and five single men. Roger Conant also stayed on the west coast, and after a later trip to Seattle, he returned to spend the rest of his life in California.

Once again, rumors flew among the passengers that Mercer was about to take passage for Seattle and desert his charges, but this

[7]Annie's sister, Mamie, who was nine years younger, was also on board. Annie E. Stephens was born in Philadelphia, January 4, 1840. Mamie later married John F. Atkinson and moved to New York. Clarence B. Bagley to Julia H. Emery, January 3, 1908. Weintz collection.

[8]Flora P. Engle, "The Story of the Mercer Expeditions," 231 and Deutsch, *Mercer's Belles*, 38n.

[9]*Daily Alta California*, April 26, 1866, and *The Pacific Tribune* (Olympia), April 28, 1866.

did not happen. Nevertheless, Asa was in extreme need of money, and he later said that he arrived in San Francisco with only three dollars in his pocket, and with the obligation to pay for his passengers' fare to Seattle.

According to his story of that crisis, Mercer spent $2.50 of his remaining funds to wire Governor Pickering for more money. Surely this was an act of faith, considering the response to his earlier request for help from the territorial government, but nevertheless, he anxiously waited for the reply. When the telegraph office notified him that there was a wire waiting for him, Mercer hurried down to pick it up, only to learn that the answer had been sent collect, with charges of $7.50 against it. Since his resources only amounted to fifty cents, Mercer asked the superintendent of the office to read the message and see if it contained an order for money. To his horror, the wire consisted of more than 100 words of congratulations, with not a word about money.[10]

Here the story becomes hard to follow, for somehow, Mercer was able to find money for another telegram, this time to ask his old friend and sponsor, the Rev. Daniel Bagley, to arrange bond, so that he could borrow $2,000. Bagley did not arrange bond, and instead authorized him to use the $2,000 which Bagley and others had given him to buy wagons and some other farm machinery in the East, for shipment back to Seattle.

The sources differ as to what happened next. Clarence B. Bagley claimed that Mercer had already spent the Bagley money months before, thus implying that the machinery was never purchased. Bagley is silent as to how Asa raised the money for the journey north to Seattle. Asa, on the other hand, said that when he arrived in San Francisco, he found that the machinery, which he earlier had shipped to Seattle, was still in a San Francisco warehouse. According to his account, he was able to sell the machinery in San Francisco, to pay transportation for the women.[11]

We do know that Mercer raised a total of $2,100 from two passengers, and he used this money to pay the most pressing claims

[10]Clarence B. Bagley, "'The Mercer Immigration,'" 17-18.

in San Francisco. John Wilson, from Massachusetts, loaned Mercer $2,000, and Mercer repaid this obligation by transferring his farm on the White River, just south of Seattle, in Washington Territory. Although the farm was not of great value at the time, the land subsequently became quite valuable. A month after the transfer to Wilson, Asa also sold his half interest in 150 acres north of Seattle to another passenger for $100. By some means, Mercer was able to pay for the transportation of the women from San Francisco to Seattle. The accommodations he secured for them were not deluxe, for they had to make their way north in lumber ships.[12]

Mercer's own departure for Seattle was delayed by legal actions in San Francisco, some of which had followed him from New York. The sheriff attached what appeared to be Mercer's assets on board the *Continental*, and the items levied on included the merchandise Mercer had bought for William F. Watkins, in another typically impulsive Mercer transaction.

The Watkins affair began in New York, at the end of 1865, when Mercer was distributing his circulars there. Watkins, a California miner and legislator, later said that at the time he met Mercer he had $8-9,000, and that Mercer induced him to buy a quantity of merchandise to be shipped to Seattle for resale. The initial conversations resulted in a written contract, whereby Mercer was to buy the merchandise and arrange for its shipment. For this service, he was to receive a 10 percent commission.[13]

---

[11]The investors were Thomas Mercer, Rev. Daniel Bagley, and Dexter Horton. Delphine Henderson quotes Archie Binns to the effect that Mercer sold the machinery in San Francisco; in any event, the investors lost their money. Delphine Henderson, "Asa Shinn Mercer, Northwest Publicity Agent," *Reed College Bulletin*, XXIII (January, 1945), 23. Roger Conant died at Sawtelle, California, October 19, 1915. Also, telegram Asa S. Mercer to Daniel Bagley (from San Francisco), April 30, 1866, and Asa S. Mercer to Julia Emery, October 26, 1915, Weintz collection.

[12]The transfer of land to John Wilson was dated May 3, 1866, and that to Hout O. Hills was dated June 1, 1866. Book 1 Deeds, 437, 454, King County Recorder. Conant said that after the last of the passengers boarded the *Huntsville* for Seattle, Mercer took a piano belonging to one of the ladies, and gave it to the hotel for the unpaid bill.

[13]Roger Conant said that the shipment consisted of wedding suits to be used in the large number of weddings that were expected to result from the voyage, but Watkins did not add this detail in his later testimony.

Mercer said that the merchandise actually cost about $13,000. Whatever the correct amount was, money did change hands; a check for $6,000 was handed over on the sidewalk on Broadway, and a further $2,000 was also paid, hopefully in some less public place. According to Mercer's inexplicable calculation, these transactions left a balance of $3,000 due to him, plus $400 for shipping, all of which was to be paid by Watkins before delivery in San Francisco.[14]

As we have noted, the Sheriff's attachment in San Francisco included the dry goods Mercer had bought for Watkins, and the latter was forced to file suit to recover his property. These legal difficulties completely soured the relationship between Mercer and Watkins, and Asa later declared that Watkins was a cold-blooded murderer, who had killed several men. Watkins was finally able to salvage some of his personal fortune from the sale of the recovered goods, and he took up journalism again in California, writing under the pseudonym Sniktaw.[15]

When the Balch and Thorne lawsuits came to trial in San Francisco, Mercer was on hand to answer the charges, in contrast to the situation in New York. He said that Mrs. Thorne only had one trunk and two packages on board ship and that they were in the shipping company warehouse. He denied that she had paid him the money she claimed, saying he had paid over $400 on her account. He acknowledged that she had spent money to live in New York while waiting for the ship to depart, but quoted her as saying she could live as cheaply there as in Philadelphia. In support of Mercer's account, the captain obligingly testified that he waited two hours in New York for Mrs. Thorne, and she did not appear.[16]

As to Balch, Mercer admitted that Balch had paid for his tickets, but said that Balch had not appeared to claim passage. Mer-

[14]Conant, who by this time was less than charitable about Mercer's financial dealings, said that Mercer diverted Watkins' money to pay the passage money, but this was clearly untrue, as we shall see. Roger Conant, in Deutsch, *Mercer's Belles*, 33.

[15]*Daily Alta California*, May 4, 1866, and Asa S. Mercer to Julia Emery (from Omaha), October 26, 1915, Weintz collection.

[16]*Daily Alta California*, May 4, 1866.

cer's defense in both these cases was aided by the absence of any such testimony as Dall had given in New York, regarding Mercer's sale of more tickets than were permitted under his contract.

The first group to go north left on the bark *George Washington* on April 30, others left the following month, and the last did not reach Seattle until June. Mercer did not travel from San Francisco to Seattle by ship, but instead chose to go overland, so as to be able to meet the first group to arrive there. It was a rigorous journey, on the train from San Francisco to Red Bluff, then by stage to Portland, on a boat down the Columbia to Monticello, and finally ninety miles on horseback to meet the steamer.[17]

At Seattle, Mercer addressed a meeting chaired by Rev. Daniel Bagley, to give his account of the expedition, and the audience was kind to him, "frequently" interrupting him with applause. He was already rewriting the history of the transaction to buy the *Continental*, saying that Holladay had bought the ship for $100,000 (he would later lower this to $80,000). He claimed to have paid bills of $10,000 during the period the expedition was delayed in New York, and a further $3,000 "in gold" in San Francisco. The source of all this money was then, as now, a mystery. The *Gazette* said the meeting resulted in a vindication of Mercer, and that it adjourned, "apparently with the best good will" toward him.[18]

At Olympia in the middle of June, another meeting was held at the Methodist Church, and by this time, Mercer had hit his stride in the elaboration of the story. He said that when the government asked him for bonds of $300,000 for the safe delivery of the ship in San Francisco, he got fifteen governors and ex-governors, plus a number of gentlemen of wealth, to petition the government to

[17]The bark *Scotland* sailed for Puget Sound with some of the Mercer passengers, including Watkins and his merchandise, on May 4, and was in Seattle by May 27. Others sailed on the brig *Sheet Anchor*, which also sailed on May 4, for Victoria; this group arrived in Seattle on June 3. Finally, the last of Mercer's passengers may have taken the bark *Huntsville*, which sailed for Puget Sound a week behind the *Sheet Anchor*. Deutsch, *Mercer's Belles*, 127n, *Puget Sound Weekly* (Seattle), May 28, June 4, 1866, *San Francisco Examiner*, June 25, 1893, and Asa Mercer to Julia Emery, October 26, 1915, Weintz collection.

[18]The Seattle meeting was held in Yesler Hall on May 23, 1866. The *Gazette* was quoted in the *Morning Oregonian*, June 8, 1866. Also, *Puget Sound Weekly* (Olympia), May 28, 1866.

waive the bonds. Grant, who had actually been the one to recommend waiving the bond, was now relegated to giving Asa warm assurances, saying, "Mercer, give yourself no uneasiness, the thing can be arranged." Notwithstanding such influential support, when Asa went to see Stanton, the secretary insulted him. The reader is once more assured that the audience frequently applauded this stirring speech.[19]

In Seattle, Asa had a day of reckoning with those who had contracted with him to bring them brides. On their arrival in Seattle, some of the girls would not even speak to those who had paid Mercer $300. One man came to Seattle, and asked Mercer to give him two or three of the girls to take out to his farm, in the hopes that one would find the place attractive, and remain. There were no takers on this offer. Miss Barry's old farmer did not show up, and that lady told Mercer that she would not pay her note until he produced a good husband for her. If there were additional scenes in this little drama, record of them has vanished.[20]

Conant recounted an incident where a man from Washington Territory had asked Mercer to contact a young lady from Ohio and bring her back to Washington Territory. Mercer made no attempt to contact the Ohio lady, but when the Washington man saw the passenger list from the *Continental* in the newspaper, he found a name that he took to be that of his lady, and went at once to see her. She was annoyed, telling him she had paid her own passage, and he realized he was mistaken when he learned she was from New York, not Ohio.

Nevertheless, these were the worst examples, and there were also a number of others who were happy with the opportunities they found in Washington Territory, including at least one couple, who were married by the Rev. Daniel Bagley. Despite all of the difficulties in getting the expedition underway, those who did make the journey were generally positive about it. For example, Harriet F.

[19]The Olympia meeting was held June 16, 1866. *The Pacific Tribune*, June 23, 1866.

[20]Flora Engle, who carefully researched the subsequent lives of the passengers, said that Miss Barry had married a man from Seattle named Melson. Flora A. P. Engle, "The Story of the Mercer Expeditions," 237.

Stevens wrote that the voyage was the happiest three months of her life, and she was extremely laudatory of Mercer.

For Asa, certainly the most important of the marriages which resulted from the *Continental* voyage was that of Asa Shinn Mercer to Annie E. Stephens, on July 15, 1866. Bagley conducted the ceremony at the Methodist Protestant Church in Seattle, so clearly, Annie's "bigotry" did not extend to the Methodists. It was to prove a durable union, for Annie would make her home with Asa for better or worse—and it was often the latter—until she died, in northern Wyoming, after the turn of the century.[21]

Some supposed that Mercer was making a profit from the project, but it actually seriously impaired his finances, as well as those of some members of his family, including his brother Thomas. Another brother, Joshua Dickerson Mercer, had hoped to go west with the party, and had sold a good deal of property in preparation to leave Princeton, only to change his mind when conditions proved unfavorable. He then had to buy again, at a higher price, causing a "sore tax" on his cash. J. Dickerson added, "If Asa would only keep out of speculation," he could get along financially.[22]

Although few seriously contended that Mercer spent the money for his personal benefit, still he had signed contracts with men who had been promised a "suitable" wife, and those contracts seemed to promise financial gain to Mercer. Moreover, there was the matter of Mercer's unrealistic optimism: Clarence Bagley sourly commented, "He was ever prone to take whatever he urgently hoped for as certain of accomplishment." As a consequence, those who had given him the funds were at best financially crippled, and at worst bankrupted, leaving them with the feeling that Mercer had robbed them, even though he did not thereby benefit personally.[23]

The *Continental*, which had brought this motley group to San Francisco, was soon placed in service for Holladay, replacing the

[21]Weintz collection.

[22]Thomas had apparently been forced to bail Asa out, for he asked J. Dickerson for a loan, and the latter could not comply, suggesting that Asa should at least pay his "security" debts. J. Dickerson Mercer to Thomas Mercer, February 3, 1867. Weintz collection.

[23]Clarence B. Bagley, "The Mercer Immigration," 23-24.

John L. Stephens, and she was to sail for Mazatlan and other ports on May 1. After a few months in the Mexican service, she was placed on the run to Portland, replacing the *Oriflamme*. Her colorful life ended when she was caught in a gale in the Gulf of California in the fall of 1870 and foundered.[24]

Washington Territory could count fewer than 4,000 souls (excluding Indians) when it was created in 1853, but it was already growing rapidly in 1860, before Mercer began his efforts to import females to counterbalance the large single male population. By 1870, there were nearly 24,000 living in the territory, and only a few of that number owed their presence to Mercer's activities, although the second expedition had generated a good deal of publicity—both good and bad—for Asa Mercer, himself. In time, the bad feelings that surrounded the expedition evaporated, and were replaced by praise for the concept of the venture. In 1888, when Mercer returned to Seattle, he was welcomed enthusiastically.[25]

As Asa repeated the story of this unusual enterprise in the years afterward, the tale changed in curious and sometimes fanciful ways. An extreme example was the account Mercer gave to the Cheyenne *Leader* at the end of 1910. He began by asserting that when he arrived on the Puget Sound in 1861, there was not an unmarried woman there. After his first experiment with importation of an "even dozen" young women, he determined to go back to Washington, D. C., and ask President Lincoln for a fully-provisioned ship to carry 500 widows to the West Coast.

In this version, Lincoln was assassinated the night after Asa arrived in New York, and Mercer obtained the assistance of Massachusetts governor John Andrew to secure the necessary order for a ship from Grant, whom Mercer now promoted to Secretary of War. He then found 500 women and provided them with tickets to New York. But then the governor refused to honor Grant's order for the ship. Mercer was then forced to negotiate the purchase of

[24]*Morning Oregonian* (Portland), April 26, August 4, 1866.

[25]Flora A. P. Engle, "The Story of the Mercer Expeditions," 232, 236, and Angie Burt Bowden, *Early Schools*, 192.

the *Continental* from the government at private sale, and he permitted "one Ben Holliday [*sic*]" to buy the ship for $130,000, although it was worth $250,000. Holladay then agreed to transport the 500 women free. Holladay did not honor this agreement, however, and Mercer paid $100 to transport 300 women, an expense he bore personally. And so ends this version of the tale.[26]

A more credible assessment of the 1866 expedition was given after Mercer's death by Clarence Bagley, who knew Asa well, and had intimate knowledge of the voyage. Bagley flatly declared that the venture was "largely a failure," because Mercer's optimism was not tempered by judgment.[27]

There were many people who were called upon to help Mercer with the expedition, giving of their time and their money. The failure of his overblown expectations would make it impossible for him to find the means to repay any money, but perhaps the most serious of his personal failings in this affair was his failure to express his gratitude to those who had helped him. Edward Everett Hale, who had done so much to help him to kick off his great campaign, complained that although he saw Asa "almost every day" when he was helping Mercer organize the emigration project, after Asa left on the *Continental*, Hale did not even hear "a syllable" from him.[28]

Asa can be forgiven for failing to deliver on one promise he had made, namely, to repeat the 1866 expedition the following year. There was unanimity that this experience should not be repeated, and Asa soon left Washington Territory without a backward glance. His new endeavors would be of an entirely different nature, but the university teacher had already become an immigration commissioner. Who could say that he might not succeed as a customs officer?

[26] *The Big Horn County Rustler*, December 23, 1910.

[27] Clarence B. Bagley, *History of King County Washington* I, (Chicago, 1929), 231.

[28] Edward Everett Hale to Frank B. Cooper, November 16, 1903.

Chapter VIII

The Smuggling Charges

On his return to Washington Territory in 1866, Mercer did not try to organize another female immigration expedition, as he had publicly promised to do, but instead he left Seattle for Oregon. His years in Oregon would be filled with entirely new adventures, and there he would win the best job he was ever to hold, and also be charged with a serious federal crime for the only time in his life. It was an interval he seldom mentioned in later years, and obviously the bad memories heavily outweighed the good ones.

For a time after he came to Oregon, Mercer had to clear up some of the many remnants of the personal financial debacle that the *Continental* voyage had been. One such case involved the excessively tangled story of a loan of $100 Asa had made in New York, which he hoped Clarence Bagley would collect for him. The debtor did not like Asa, but did like Captain Winsor. Unfortunately Winsor was not friendly with Asa, and therefore, Asa hoped Bagley could approach Winsor, and ask him to collect the debt.

Since Winsor also owed Asa a sum that exceeded $100, Asa hoped that the captain could be induced to pay over the money, if Bagley asked him to. The reason why Winsor would pay the $100 to Bagley for Mercer, when he would not pay Mercer directly, was not explained. Nor do we know what was to become of the additional sum Winsor owed Asa. We do not know what success Bagley had in this collection effort, but the sheer complexity of the explanations would seem to give the project a low probability of success.[1]

By the middle of March 1867, Asa had secured a very good gov-

[1]Asa S. Mercer to C. B. Bagley, January 15, 1867. Weintz collection.

ernment position at Astoria, where he was appointed special deputy collector for the custom house. The customs service was the oldest branch of the federal government, and in 1867 it was a far more important source of revenue than it is now; in 1867, customs receipts still accounted for $179 million of the $490 million the U. S. government received from all sources. Positions in the customs service were much sought after (the New York customhouse was the most lucrative post in the United States government), but the service has also been called the "most dramatically flawed agency in government."[2]

Asa's position in Astoria paid $3,000, a handsome sum in those days, and there was the chance to earn a great deal more than the salary, for the collector also shared in forfeitures. If goods were imported without declaring and paying the proper duty, the entire shipment was subject to forfeiture, not just the amount of the unpaid duty. Half of the forfeiture, after deduction for the duties and other costs of the case, was then distributed one-quarter to any informant in the case, and the balance was spread equally among the collector, the naval officer involved (if any), and the surveyor in the customs house. While the law on forfeitures made the collector's position a lucrative one, it also gave a powerful incentive to informers who could hope to gain a share by turning others in to the prosecutors.[3]

This compensation feature made the New York collector's office the prime source of political patronage in the country, and while Astoria did not enjoy the traffic New York had, there was still considerable opportunity to enhance the collector's salary. It was a truly golden opportunity for Asa, and he promptly nominated the cousin who had come West on the *Continental*, W. Lewis Mercer, to serve

[2]In the early days of the Republic, nearly all of the government revenues were from customs receipts, and until 1849, the customs service paid its expenses out of the revenues it collected. Carl E. Prince and Mollie Keller, *The U. S. Custom Service: A Bicentennial History* (Washington, D. C., 1989), 140, 147, and Michael N. Ingrisano, *A History of Enforcement in the United States Customs Service* (Washington, D.C., 1988), 1, 57.

[3]The 1799 law had given the entire forfeiture to the informant and the collector, but the amendment of July 1866 paid half into the Treasury. 1 *Statutes at Large* 627, March 2, 1799, and 14 *Statutes at Large* 546, July 18, 1866.

under him, in a position at Portland that paid $1,300 per year. This was probably the best job Asa ever held, but unfortunately, he did not enjoy its benefits for long.[4]

The first sign of trouble came in May 1867, when the *Oregonian* ran a small item reporting the arrest of several men, whom the paper declined to name, for smuggling liquor from Victoria, British Columbia. According to the news article, the arrest was based on information obtained from a confederate of the defendants, and from subsequent developments, we can assume that this confederate was Frederick A. Sargent. Sargent, who was 28, was a distant relative of the Commissioner of Customs in Washington, but whether he owed his job as customs inspector to the family relationship, we do not know. Sargent was arrested on May 15, 1867, for smuggling four barrels of sherry wine and two barrels of Scotch whiskey at the end of March. It soon became clear that Mercer was involved in these matters, although he was not immediately arrested.[5]

The grand jury charged that Asa Mercer and four other men brought four casks of brandy into the United States from Victoria in the middle of December 1866, the first of two shipments investigated by the grand jury. The more serious incident, which became the focus of the government case, involved the second shipment, made at the end of January 1867, when the same men brought four casks of wine and four casks of Irish whiskey to Portland from Victoria on the steamer *Fideliter*. The required duties were not paid on either shipment. Three men were arrested and charged in the middle of May, but at this time, the government did not move against Mercer, who was then in charge of the custom house.[6]

---

[4]Asa S. Mercer to Secretary of the Treasury, May 8, 1867.

[5]Further confirmation of Sargent's identity as the informant comes from the fact that he was not brought to trial on the March 30, 1867, incident, for which he was arrested in May. Sargent was on the federal payroll at four dollars per day, to inspect in the area east of Olympia to the Chehalis River. Nathan Sargent, the U. S. Commissioner of Customs, was born in Putney, VT, May 5, 1794, while Frederick's father, who was Nathan's fourth cousin, was born not far away, in Chester, Vermont, in 1817.

[6]The warrant for Frederick Sargent's arrest was issued May 3, and he was taken into custody May 15. U. S. vs. A. S. Mercer, *et. al.*, Case No. 614, Federal District Court for the District of Oregon. Details of the case are taken from these files, without further citation herein.

Judge Matthew Paul Deady, who presided at Asa Mercer's three trials for smuggling.
Courtesy of Oregon Historical Society, Negative No. OHI 4138.

The prosecutors believed the leader of the smuggling ring was Samuel Ball Parrish, born in 1838, who had become one of Portland's "high-toned" entrepreneurs, and was a member of the Stock and Exchange Board in Portland. One of Parrish's employees, H. W. Rappeleye, prepared the fraudulent documents, in the name of a fictitious person, and Mercer approved these documents. A third participant, George A. Ladd, was a drayman, who arranged for the delivery of the smuggled goods to a house which Parrish owned in Portland. Bail was set at $3,000 for Parrish, and $1,000 each for Rappeleye and Ladd, although bail for the last two was subsequently raised to $2,000. All of these men posted bond and were released from custody.[7]

Mercer was soon swept into the criminal case, and when the fed-

[7]Parrish left Portland in 1874 to become Indian Agent at the Malheur Agency, and he would later become chief of police in Portland. The U. S. attorney, in an affidavit dated November 3, 1868, asserted that the signature of one "H. L. Gorven" was in fact made by Rappeleye, and that Mercer knew that the goods on the documents were in fact smuggled. Samuel B. Parrish came to Oregon with his father in 1830. He was Indian agent from April 18, 1874, through April 25, 1876; he died July 12, 1897.

eral grand jury brought in an indictment of five men for smuggling, he was one of those indicted. On the day the indictment was filed, Addison C. Gibbs, the former governor of Oregon, who was now acting U. S. attorney, brought an action against Asa Mercer and three others. This, of course, meant the end to Mercer's job with the Customs Service.

The defendants were represented by David Logan, age forty-two, who has been called "the greatest jury lawyer of his time," and was noted for his powers of oratory, which were apparently not diminished by his considerable thirst for liquor. Logan was joined by William Strong, who had been a judge, both in Washington Territory and in Oregon. Despite a family connection between Strong and the trial judge, Matthew Paul Deady, the latter disliked him. The defendants pleaded not guilty to the charges.[8]

Judge Deady, then 42, was a formidable figure in the Oregon judicial system, and had a colorful history of his own. A large, awkward redhead, Deady had made his living teaching before working his way to Oregon as a teamster and part-time smith. He was appointed to the territorial bench in 1853, was president of the constitutional convention, and was elected as a state judge after statehood, but decided to accept appointment to the federal bench instead. Deady was also a correspondent for the *San Francisco Bulletin*, an unusual role for a federal judge, and Bancroft called him a "graceful" writer.[9]

Frederick Sargent was not charged in this case, but he was sub-

[8]Addison C. Gibbs, second governor of Oregon, was born in New York, July 9, 1825; he had been a collector of customs back in 1853. Gibbs died in London in January 1887. Logan had lost an election contest against Matthew Paul Deady, the judge who would hear the smuggling case, and after Deady accused Logan of having raped an Indian woman on the public street of Jacksonville, Logan began carrying a pistol and threatening the judge's life. At the time of the smuggling case, Strong was almost exclusively occupied in representing the Oregon Steam Navigation Company. Malcolm Clark, Jr., ed., *The Diary of Judge Matthew P. Deady 1871-1892*, 2 vol., (Portland, Oregon, 1975), 44n, and Malcolm Clark, Jr., *Eden Seekers: The Settlement of Oregon, 1818-1862* (Boston, 1981), 250, 270-71.

[9]In 1867, Deady was assigned to hold the U. S. Circuit Court in San Francisco, in addition to his duties in Portland. Matthew Paul Deady was born in Easton, Maryland, May 12, 1824; he died March 24, 1893. *History of the Bench and Bar of Oregon*, (Portland, Oregon, 1910), 264. Also, Hubert Howe Bancroft, *History of Oregon* (San Francisco, 1888), 151, and Malcolm Clark, *Eden Seekers*, 233, 266

poenaed as a material witness. When the first case came to trial, Sargent failed to appear, and three other government witnesses were also missing; the government was forced to ask for a continuance. The problem of missing witnesses was not uncommon in the Oregon courts of this period, and although the case was set for trial in the next term of court, these early difficulties suggested that the government's case might not be easy to win.[10]

The smuggling case came to trial in November, and since Frederick Sargent was still missing, the government decided to put on its case without his testimony. Whether for lack of Sargent's testimony, or some other reason, when the case went to the jury, they could not agree. The *Oregonian* said that on the first ballot, the jurors were 7-4 for conviction, with one not voting, and at the final ballot they were 7-5 for conviction, except that there were nine or ten votes for acquittal for one defendant, whom the paper did not identify. The case was then set to be retried at the next term of court.[11]

The second trial took place in May 1868, against the original four defendants, plus Frederick Sargent, the reluctant witness. When this case was called, Asa Mercer was absent in the East, and the case was defaulted against him, causing forfeiture of his recognizance. At the trial, the jury was again unable to agree, this time standing 9-3 for conviction. At the end of the trial, John C. Cartwright, the U. S. attorney, moved to dismiss the charges against Parrish, Rappeleye, and Ladd, leaving only Mercer and Sargent to stand trial for yet a third time.[12]

After the Portland court issued a default judgment against him, Mercer hurried back from New York, and filed an affidavit with

[10]The grand jury indicted A. S. Mercer, Samuel B. Parrish, George A. Ladd, and H. W. Rappeley. William Strong was born in St. Albans, Vermont, July 15, 1817; he died in April, 1887. David Logan was born in Springfield, Illinois, in 1824. Hubert Howe Bancroft, *History of Oregon*, II (San Francisco, 1888), 102, 158, and *Morning Oregonian* (Portland), May 17, July 4, 8, 1867. Also, *History of the Bench and Bar of Oregon*, (Portland, Oregon, 1910), 269-70, 276-77.

[11]*Morning Oregonian* (Portland), November 6, 9, 11, 1867. Since the government subsequently dismissed the cases against all of the original defendants except Mercer, it was unlikely that he was the defendant favored by the jury in the first case.

[12] In a separate action, the government also proceeded directly against the steamship *Fideliter*, the ship involved in the smuggling incident; trial in that case was set for the next term of court.

the court, in which he claimed he had planned to be present for the trial, but could not make the journey because of illness. He attached the sworn testimony of a New York doctor, who said that Asa had, indeed, been suffering a severe attack of the lung fever, which incapacitated him from April 21 to May 23.

Mercer's pleas did not mollify the U. S. attorney, who plainly wanted to make a statement about smuggling by customs collectors. Early in July 1868, the U. S. attorney filed the government's third case, against A. S. Mercer and Frederick Sargent; the government immediately asked for a continuance to the November term, and this was granted. Unfortunately, the case continued to unravel for the government, for when the summons was issued to bring Sargent to trial, he apparently could not be found. Moreover, Parrish, whose testimony would have been of considerable value, could not be found, either, now that the charges against him were dismissed, although he still resided in Portland. Accordingly, when the third case was called in November, the U. S. attorney was forced to ask for yet another continuance, until the December term of court.

The final case in this long process was styled merely *United States vs. A. S. Mercer*, the Sargent case having been separated. When summons were issued for Ladd and Rappeleye to testify, neither could be found, although Ladd was arrested while the case was still being heard. Ladd was too ill to testify in court, but his deposition was taken.

The legal representation of the defense changed with the dismissal of charges against Parrish and the other two defendants, undoubtedly because Parrish had advanced the legal fees. At the trial on December 7, 1868, Mercer was represented by E. D. Shattuck, a former legislator and a director of the Oregon Central Railroad. On the third day of the trial, the U. S. attorney asked Judge Deady to place Mercer under bail, and the judge ordered Asa to be held on $3,000 bail, or committed to the custody of the marshal. It appears that Asa was then taken into custody, for the only time in his life. Nevertheless, his salvation was close at hand.

Later in the same day, the jury again deadlocked, and was discharged. On December 10, the long-running drama ended when John C. Cartwright, acting for the U. S. attorney's office, moved *nolle prosequi* (literally, "I will not further prosecute") in the case, and Judge Deady allowed the plea, discharging the defendant. The deputy U. S. marshal released Mercer before the day ended.[13]

As one of the footnotes to the Mercer smuggling case, the government continued its action against the ship *Fideliter*, even though the cases against the individuals had been dismissed. Not only had the ship carried smuggled goods, which was ground for forfeiture, but there was an additional blot on its record. The *Fideliter* was British-built, and had originally sailed to Victoria in March 1864, where she was refitted and placed in service between Victoria and Portland.[14]

Later, the *Fideliter* was purchased and resold to a Russian resident of Alaska, before the effective date of the treaty by which the United States acquired that territory. The new owner hoped that the sale to a Russian would enable him to register the ship under U. S. flag, so that she could trade in domestic service. In the fall of 1869, the U. S. district court in Portland declared the ship forfeited, and gave judgment against the sureties for $30,000.[15]

The forfeiture case against the *Fideliter* was reversed on appeal, and Frederick Sargent's case dragged on until the spring of 1870, when it was also dismissed. Thus, all of the prosecution efforts in the Mercer smuggling case proved futile, except for one exaction from Asa Mercer. After he was released from custody, Mercer asked the judge to remit the penalty levied against him for failure to appear, and the judge refused, which must have caused a considerable drain on Asa's finances.

---

[13]In 1911, Asa wrote a long letter to B. H. Tillotson, in which he reviewed the history of the Mercer family, summing up by saying, "no member has ever been in jail for a crime or been suspected." His memory must have faded by this time. A. S. Mercer to B. H. Tillotson, April 15, 1911, Wyoming State Archives, Cheyenne.

[14]E. W. Wright, *Lewis & Dryden's Marine History of the Pacific Northwest*, (Seattle, 1967), 127.

[15]The *Fideliter* was wrecked near Victoria, and was then purchased by Kohl; he resold the ship to Joseph Lugebil, a Russian inhabitant of Alaska. *Morning Oregonian*, September 21, 1869. The forfeiture judgment was later reversed on appeal to the U. S. Circuit Court.

A mildly amusing footnote to the Sargent case is found in an inquiry from Alanson Hinman, who replaced Mercer at the Astoria customs house. Hinman wrote to his superiors to ask, hypothetically, if an informant who was released on bond and then fled from the jurisdiction was still entitled to a share in the proceeds of the forfeitures from the case. This description must have applied to Frederick Sargent, who hoped to receive his one-quarter of the value of the forfeited liquor for turning his colleagues over to the authorities. Unfortunately for Sargent, the assistant secretary of the Treasury predictably assured Hinman that the hypothetical informant would not be entitled to a share of the forfeiture.[16]

We have found no reference to the smuggling affair, either in Mercer's own writing, or in that of his friends. The case against the alleged smugglers seemed doomed at the outset by the influence of Parrish, and even the newspapers were reluctant to make any substantive comment on the matter. The prosecution failed because the government could not bring witnesses to court, and there is the additional question as to how diligent the search for them really was. Finally, while the jury did not agree, it appears that a considerable majority believed the defendants were guilty, and a verdict was prevented because of a recalcitrant minority.

For Asa, one of the few pleasant memories of his customhouse tenure was the birth of his daughter Janet in 1867. Moreover, in spite of all the trouble of that period, Asa once more demonstrated his ability to survive, even if his opponent was the United States attorney. Now, with his legal problems behind him, he was ready to devote full time to a new venture, and if it succeeded, he could revolutionize the shipping industry on the west coast.

[16]*Morning Oregonian*, March 8, 1870, and J. F. Hartley, assistant secretary of the Treasury to A. Hinman, August 31, 1868.

Chapter IX

Salvage, Shipping and More

Mercer's ventures were so varied, that it is often difficult to imagine what information may have piqued his interest in the next enterprise he chose. Nevertheless, it is clear that he never doubted that he could do what had to be done, even if others before him had tried, and failed.

Asa was involved in at least two salvage schemes involving wrecks in the Columbia River. The first was a large packet ship, the *Silvia de Grasse*. The ship was heavily laden with lumber for gold-rush San Francisco, and the owner had been able to offload much of the cargo. She struck a large rock and sunk in the river, just off Astoria, late in 1849. Mercer now wanted to raise the ship, move it on shore and salvage the timber and iron from it. Examination of the hulk confirmed that the timbers of locust and oak were still sound, but after this initial work, there is no further mention of the salvage project. The old ship remained on the river bottom, where she attracted scavengers from time to time.[1]

Another salvage project seemed at first to have a bit more substance. The French bark, *Duc de Lorges*, had sunk at the mouth of the Willamette River in 1849. The ship was loaded with a speculative cargo of goods then in demand in that region, and it had been partially unloaded when a storm sunk her where she was moored. Soon after, various items were salvaged from the hulk, and a flag from the ship was used in a Masonic ceremony in 1850, but rumors

[1]The *Silvia de Grasse* brought the first news of the storming of the Bastille to the United States in 1789. Don B. Marshall, *Oregon Shipwrecks* (Portland, 1984), 160-161.

circulated over the years that the remaining cargo still in the river included twenty-five to fifty barrels of whiskey and cognac.[2]

The claimants of the sunken hulk sent a diver down to examine the ship, an operation which drew a crowd of several hundred people, and a few days later, a diver went down again for nearly an hour, and brought up the ship's compass. The ship was found to be in forty feet of water at the bow end, but only fourteen feet at the stern; she was lying on her side against a sand bar, and the underwater inspection resulted in the conclusion that her wood was sound. It was expected that the copper in the hull could be salvaged and sold for enough to pay the entire cost of raising the ship.[3]

A few days after this examination, Mercer announced that he had arranged to attempt to raise the vessel, using a concept originated by John Pike, the inventor of a submarine hydraulic dredging machine. At the beginning of April, Mercer's first test of the Pike invention was made on location, with the inventor's son in attendance. Mercer borrowed a hose and nozzle from one of Portland's fire engines, and a diver was sent down to the sunken vessel, where for over an hour he cleared sand from 35-40 feet of the deck. Although this initial test was encouraging, the next attempt on April 8 was not, because the engine was not powerful enough to perform the task, and by the next week the project was suspended. Although Mercer claimed to be "confident," he did not resume the attempt, and the old ship continued to interfere with shipping in the river for years afterward.[4]

After he was fired from the Customs Service, there was added urgency for Mercer find a new source of livelihood, and even though there was no lack of wrecks in the river, salvage operations did not appear to offer promise. His new idea also involved shipping, but this time, ships that were still afloat.

Mercer's new project, if he succeeded, would bring him into com-

[2] *The Oregon Sunday Journal*, August 5, 1928.

[3] *Morning Oregonian* (Portland), March 21, 22, 26, 1867, October 7, 1870.

[4] At least three attempts were made to blow up the old ship, and in 1928, divers for the Pacific Bridge Company still found the remains of it. *Morning Oregonian*, April 4, 8, 13, 1867, July 24, 25, 1874, and Don Marshall, *Oregon Shipwrecks*, 205.

petition with his nemesis, Ben Holladay, and that factor may even have influenced his thinking. Asa wanted to establish a ship line that would ply between Portland and New York, thus eliminating the need to route all Portland shipping through San Francisco. After the Civil War, wheat production in California and Oregon, particularly in the former state, had increased sharply, producing an exportable surplus. Most of this surplus was shipped from San Francisco to Liverpool, and soon the business of shipping fell into the hands of the California commission merchants. This control over their shipping, and ultimately, their markets, created discontent among businesses and farmers in Oregon, who blamed low prices on this factor.

Mercer's idea was not new, and he was undoubtedly inspired by the example of the Opposition ship lines which sprang up from time to time, in an effort to take trade away from the established lines, by offering lower rates. None of these lines had been successful, but, as usual, Mercer was confident that he could avoid their fate.

Mercer once again turned to the U. S. government for help, and apparently he saw no irony in asking for help from one branch of the government, while another was still trying to put him behind bars for smuggling. Of course, his efforts in Washington and New York in 1864-66 had given him plenty of possible names to call upon; we also assume that he welcomed a trip to the East, far from Judge Deady's court in Portland. His first trip to promote the new ship line, which extended from the middle of 1867 until late fall of that year, apparently did not accomplish much.

After the mistrial at the end of 1867, the government still expected to try Mercer for smuggling. Nevertheless, he set out again for the East, taking with him Judge Cyrus Olney of Astoria, and this time he received substantive support for his shipping idea. In New York, Mercer met with General Rufus Ingalls, who was the New York assistant quartermaster, and Ingalls gave him a letter promising that he would use his "influence and patronage" to assist the shipping scheme. Down in Washington, both

Oregon senators wrote letters to the Secretary of War, endorsing the shipping project.[5]

These efforts bore fruit, for in March 1868, General Daniel H. Rucker wrote from the quartermaster general's office in Washington to the Secretary of War, reporting that Mercer's shipping line had been established, and noting that the various Army departments had been instructed to use it. The new line was assured of the Army's business as well as that of the Indian service, so long as it was "beneficial to the service."[6]

Mercer was not planning to make use of the latest technology in shipping, but instead he was going to place sailing ships in service on the long run from New York to Portland. He made this choice because there were plenty of sailing ships available for charter at low rates—for a good reason.

Steamships had been operating in regular service since the 1840s, and by 1858-60, steamers of 2,000-2,500 tons offered formidable competition to sailing ships. Indeed, the important competition was between propeller-driven vessels and the older paddle wheel steamers. The new propeller vessels were slower than the paddle wheelers, but much cheaper to operate, and they soon claimed most of the premium passenger and freight traffic. Ship lines using sailing ships had to try to survive on the business the steamer traffic left for them, and for a time, they continued in business cutting back on their fleets, and carrying bulk cargo and the low-fare steerage passengers. When 400-foot steamers began to come off the ways, even those lines of business became vulnerable to competition from the steamers.

The idea of still another shipping line was at first greeted with derision in Oregon, but this criticism became more muted after Mer-

[5]Olney had been a justice of the Oregon Supreme Court in 1853-57, before moving to Astoria, where he invested in a subdivision, a venture which would also involve Asa. At the beginning of July 1868, Mercer, who had just returned from the East, told the *Oregonian* that he had been in New York nearly a year, but, of course, he had been in Portland for the trial the previous November. *Morning Oregonian* (Portland), July 1, 1868.

[6]Rufus Ingalls to A. S. Mercer, February 10, 1868 and D. H. Rucker to the Secretary of War, March 27, 1868, quoted in Charles W. Smith, "Asa Shinn Mercer," 358-59. Senators George Henry Williams and Henry Winslow Corbett endorsed Mercer's project.

cer wired that he had chartered the brig *Sallie Brown*, a new vessel, only six months old, and she was being loaded with a cargo destined for Portland. The Pioneer Line, as he called the enterprise, was in business.

The business did not involve heavy capital investments, and in fact, there may have been almost no money invested, as the vessels were all chartered, and Mercer's offices on both coasts were apparently shared with those of his agents, who were shipping brokers. Nor was there the need for him to hire his own employees, for the agents at both ends of the line bore the responsibility for soliciting cargoes.[7]

The San Francisco *Commercial Herald* now applauded the idea of the Pioneer Line, and complimented the promoters offering this alternative to the neglect of the region by Holladay's shipping line. It took Mercer more than a month to assemble the first cargo for Portland, but the ship finally sailed on May 11, carrying a cargo of 800 tons. Mercer immediately announced that the second ship on the run would be the bark *Osmyn*.[8]

The *Sallie Brown* finally arrived in Portland on November 2, in tow of the steamer *Julia*, as was the practice for most sailing vessels coming up the Columbia. She had been 120 days in passage, including a number of calm days. Nevertheless, when she arrived in Portland, all her rigging was in good order, and she at once prepared to take on freight for a return voyage to New York.

Only ten days after her arrival in Portland, the *Sallie Brown* was able to go down the river to take on a cargo of grain for her return voyage. This time, she was bound on a truly pioneer voyage, all the way across the Atlantic, to Liverpool. The man who arranged for this cargo was Joseph Watt, a pioneer entrepreneur in the area, and although he obviously worked in association with Mercer, the accounts are silent on that subject. Watt conceived the idea that the abundant Oregon wheat harvest, now being sold only in the

[7]The New York agent for the Pioneer Line was Brockway and Baker, and in Portland the agent was McCraken, Merril & Co.; by the end of 1869, Bently, Miller & Thomas had replaced Brockway and Baker in New York.

[8]*Morning Oregonian* (Portland), March 23, July 1, 1868.

California market, could be shipped all the way to Liverpool, where it could enter the British market. He traveled through the valley, soliciting wheat from farmers, to make up the cargo for the *Sallie Brown* to take on her incredible return voyage.[9]

By early December, the *Sallie Brown* was back at sea, carrying that first cargo of Oregon wheat, bound for Liverpool, according to the account given by James R. Robertson. The *Sallie Brown* was in New York by the end of April, 1869, when the cargo was consigned to Francis & Hathaway, and the vessel was returned to the master, which presumably meant that the charter was completed. She did not leave New York until August 18, when she cleared New York for Falmouth, under charter to another house.

Clearly, this voyage did not end profitably, for Robertson says that when the wheat was finally delivered in Liverpool, the inspectors looked at the large kernels and condemned them, as obviously water-soaked, and therefore unfit for consumption. If the cargo lay in New York harbor from the end of April until the middle of August, it would have been in poor condition, in any case, and the details of the logistics do not survive. We simply do not know if the wheat actually was shipped to Liverpool on the *Sallie Brown*, as the Robertson account says, whether it was sold in New York, or whether it was offloaded in New York, and shipped to Liverpool on another vessel.[10]

Whatever the details may be, the idea—if not the feasibility—of shipping wheat to the British Isles had been established. Thereafter, a number of cargoes of Oregon wheat made their way to that market, and the *Adeline Elwood*, another of the sailing ships Mercer chartered for the Portland run, was the second vessel to carry Oregon wheat in the Liverpool trade. The shippers learned that the wheat should be sacked, not carried loose in the holds, to guard against excess humidity during the two equatorial passages necessary on the trip, and these direct shipments of grain to England

[9]Watt had also organized a project to build a woolen mill in the Willamette valley. *Morning Oregonian* (Portland), November 3, 16, 23, December 8, 1868, May 14, 1869.

[10]James R. Robertson, "A Pioneer Captain of Industry," *The Oregon Historical Quarterly*, IV (June, 1903), 166. In order to partially offset the light weight of the cargo, the wheat sacks were cut so they could bleed some wheat down among the sacks on the bottom of the hold. Also, *The New-York Times*, August 19, 1869.

eventually became a significant trade. Soon British ships were also being sent to Portland direct from Liverpool, and there was even talk of a new direct shipline between Liverpool and Portland.[11]

Obviously, the Pioneer Line was a business where delivery was measured in months, rather than weeks or days. The second ship dispatched from New York was the bark *Osmyn*, and the *Oregonian* said her cabin was finished in a style "almost as fine" as that of the saloons of the steamships. This attention to luxury did not benefit the economics of the vessel, however, for the *Osmyn* was a relatively slow sailer, and took 160 days' passage from New York. She then ran aground for a day or two in the Columbia below St. Helens, before she was towed to Portland by the steamer *Okanogan*. Her cargo included 100 tons of railroad iron, for use in the building of railroads on the west coast. After unloading, the *Osmyn* left for San Francisco the middle of March, but at the Columbia bar she had to suffer through another delay of eleven days before the pilot came to take her across the bar.[12]

Meanwhile, Asa was busy chartering more vessels, finding cargoes for them, and dispatching them around the Cape to Portland. The bark *Hattie C. Besse* followed the *Osmyn* from New York, and she was followed in turn by the bark *Meldon*, the bark *Adeline Elwood*, and the barkentine *A. Heaton*.[13]

Mercer left for New York again at the beginning of 1869 to promote the new ship line. In a letter to the *Oregonian*, Mercer said that he was loading a vessel in New York for the Oregon trade every forty-five days, with a cargo of 800 to 1,000 tons. He repeated the objective to increase the market for local produce, by shipping wheat direct from Portland to overseas markets, and he promised that if the farmers would support him, he would "whiten every sea with the sails of noble ships bearing Oregon produce.[14]

---

[11]The British bark *Alpha* sailed January 10, 1870, from Liverpool, on a direct voyage to Victoria and Portland. The *Adeline Elwood* cargo to Liverpool included 100 cases of salmon, in the hope of introducing this product to the British, and a pair of elk horns were sent to the Royal Botanical Gardens in London.

[12]*The Daily Oregonian* (Portland), February 23, 24, 25, March 13, 25, April 5, 1869.

[13]*Oregonian* (Portland), February 9, August 13, 1869.

[14]*Oregonian* (Portland), August 13, 1869.

The third vessel in the line, the *Hattie C. Besse*, under Captain William H. Besse (who was also a part owner of the ship), was a 1,300-ton four-masted bark, 220 feet long with a 35 foot beam. She was the first fourmaster to enter the Columbia River, and among the largest vessels in terms of carrying capacity to visit the river. The passage from New York took 127 days, and on the way, storms washed two men overboard and carried away her main topgallant mast. Her cargo included 297 tons of coal from the east and 13,000 oak planks.[15]

Mercer reported from New York in July that the *Adeline Elwood* was then 100 days at sea on the way to Portland, and the bark *Edward James* was loading in New York and would sail in ten days. He advised that he would set up a special reading room in the New York headquarters of the shipping line, where he would make available all the Oregon publications that were sent out to him; he also expected to display Oregon products in this place.[16]

Mercer was receiving a good deal of favorable press coverage, but a transportation system based on obsolete sailing vessels was not an idea with a future, and the Pioneer Line was certainly no threat to the big shipping lines. It took one of Mercer's sailing ships nearly a year to make a round trip to New York, and the big steamers passed his ships as they plied the routes to the Isthmus and back, bringing freight shipped to Aspinwall from the East Coast.

Moreover, the Cape route was beset by unpredictable weather, and more than one of Mercer's ships suffered damage from storms. Finally, the completion of the transcontinental railroad in 1869 brought a new and powerful competitor into the transportation business, although at first it was not a direct benefit to Portland. Mercer himself recognized the advantage of the railroad, for he now traveled overland to New York in only seventeen days by stage and railroad, rather than the four months required by one of his own vessels.[17]

The use of ships that were slow and undependable made it difficult for the Pioneer Line to secure return cargoes to New York, and

[15] *The Daily Oregonian* (Portland), April 16, 1869.

[16] *The Morning Oregonian* (Portland), July 20, 31, 1869.

[17] Soon it was possible to make the overland journey in only ten and a half days.

consequently most of the ships Mercer chartered went into other service once they reached the west coast. The *Hattie C. Besse* was sent to Hong Kong, the *A. Heaton* took a cargo of lumber to Montevideo, and the *Edward James* took a load of lumber to San Francisco.[18]

Ever the promoter, Asa hatched a new scheme in the spring of 1870. Perhaps prompted by the voyage of the *A. Heaton* to Montevideo with a load of lumber, Mercer conceived the idea of chartering a vessel to take a load of lumber to the treeless pampas along the La Plata, near Buenos Aires. He expected to sell the cargo to pay for the charter and the fare for fifteen to twenty men from Oregon, who would then settle in a small colony in Uruguay, to raise cattle and sheep. The cost of the charter was to be raised from eight investors in a corporation, who would put up $500 each.[19]

One might think it ironic that Asa, who had been prominently associated with the idea of bringing settlers to the sparsely settled Pacific northwest, and was at least nominally charged with promoting immigration to Oregon, should now be promoting the emigration of men *from* Oregon. Perhaps he saw this as another way to reduce the excess male population on the Pacific coast.

The Oregon press was not friendly to the Argentine venture, and the editor of the *Oregonian* opined that there was no good reason to leave Oregon, which was a better country than the one Mercer was promoting. Although Asa said six men had agreed to go, and asserted that he could sail in early May if only two more willing to pay the passage of $150 came forward, there is no indication that any action followed these statements.[20]

Apparently a total of nine vessels ultimately saw service for the Pioneer line, including the barks *Ida F. Taylor* and the *C. L. Taylor*, both added in 1870, but after that the line disappears from public notice. The railroads building on the west coast continued to ship railroad iron from New York direct to Portland in sailing vessels,

[18]The *Hattie C. Besse* was wrecked in November, 1871, near Cape Flattery. *Morning Oregonian*, November 30, 1871.

[19]*Morning Oregonian*, March 10, 23, 1870.

[20]It is interesting that Mercer at first promised free passage to Argentina, but later was charging $150 per man, a pattern reminiscent of his efforts in 1865-66, with the female immigrants.

even after the Pioneer Line disappeared, but their best transit time was 115 days, and this traffic disappeared altogether once the railroads were built. Thereafter, most of Portland's trade with the East Coast was once again conducted via San Francisco.[21]

Mercer seemed to be more successful with projects where he merely handled the promotion, while others financed and operated the enterprise. When the Astoria Chamber of Commerce was incorporated in the spring of 1873, Asa Mercer became secretary, and he immediately plunged into a scheme to build a wharf and grain warehouse at Astoria. The three-member committee on which he served reported that if Astoria could be established as a major shipping point, vessels using that port could avoid pilotage costs and delays which averaged nearly $800 for a vessel 600 tons capacity. They also held out the hope that a better understanding of conditions at the mouth of the Columbia would eventually bring insurance rates down.[22]

After consideration of this report, a corporation was organized to build the necessary wharf and warehouse at Astoria, and Asa was one of the first subscribers, pledging $250. Construction got underway by October 1873, and the offices of the Astoria Farmers' Company moved into the new quarters at the beginning of 1874.[23]

The idea of a direct shipline from Portland was a good one, but Mercer lacked the financial resources to offer a line of efficient, fast, and competitive ships in this service. While the publicity he attracted clearly pointed the way for others who did have the necessary resources, his own efforts ended in failure. Nevertheless, he had not limited himself to the shipping business, for he was also involved in other ways to make money.

[21]The *Ida F. Taylor* was the eighth vessel, and the Oregonian noted that the *C. L. Taylor* was in the same shipline; the latter vessel was at Astoria on its way from New York in July, 1870. The *A. M. Small* made the trip from New York to the bar outside Astoria in 115 days, a record for a sailing ship. *Morning Oregonian*, February 22, July 19, October 5, 1869, February 14, 1870. Also, E. W. Wright, *Marine History*, 178.

[22]The report was dated May 31, 1873. *Tri-Weekly Astorian*, July 1, 1873.

[23]Apparently control of the new docks passed into the hands of Col. Joseph Teal, of the Wallamet Transportation Company by the spring of 1874, and the facilities were then substantially expanded. *Tri-Weekly Astorian*, July 3, 5, October 4, 16, 1873, January 20, May 7, August 13, 1874.

Chapter X

Real Estate Speculation

During his sojourn in Oregon, Mercer also got involved in a sizeable real estate speculation. We have already noted that he had purchased real estate before, but in Oregon, for the first time, he was making larger commitments.

The Mercers had owned Washington Territory property before, and while he was in Oregon, Asa bought two pieces of property in that territory for more than $2,000; Annie bought two more parcels for $840, apparently investing her own money. This land was well located, north and south of Seattle, near Admiralty Inlet. But it was in Astoria that Asa and Annie made their largest real estate investments.

In the spring of 1867, before his smuggling case had come to trial, Asa and Annie purchased 300 lots in Astoria from Cyrus Olney, who had been so helpful in the promotion of the Pioneer Line. The Mercers gave four promissory notes in payment, each for $2,625, payable one, two, three, and four years in the future, respectively. Because the paper money of the United States was not received on a par with gold, Olney required the notes to be payable in gold coin.[1]

In 1868, Asa decided to build houses on two of the lots they had purchased from Olney, and for this purpose he purchased $544 worth of lumber and other building materials for one house, and $368.50 for the other. When the Mercers failed to pay for the materials, the

[1]The details of the Mercer purchases are given in J. W. Robb, as administrator of *Estate of Cyrus Olney, deceased, plaintiff, vs. A. S. Mercer*, Annie Mercer, D. K. Warren and Hiram Brown, Administrators of the Estate of George W. Warren, deceased, Frances E. Warren, widow, and William E. Warren and Marcus S. Warren, minor heirs of George W. Warren, deceased, defendants, filed in the Circuit Court of Clatsop County, Oregon, November 18, 1876.

lumber dealer filed a lien on the incomplete buildings for the unpaid balance. In another case, the sheriff sold one of the lots the Mercers had purchased from Olney to pay a judgment of $115. Obviously, the speculation in city lots was not a paying proposition for Mercer.[2]

Ten of the Astoria lots were sold in 1867, but only one in each of the following years, and of course the notes to Olney were coming due each year. In June and December, the Mercers gave Olney a mortgage on seven other lots they owned in Astoria, as further security for their indebtedness to him. Finally, at the beginning of 1871, the Mercers conveyed all of the lots purchased from Olney to George W. Warren, subject to the Olney mortgage.

Olney had been considerate of the Mercers' financial straits, and had not demanded prompt payment on his mortgages, but after Olney died in December 1870, his executors sued the Mercers to foreclose on the mortgages. At that time the amount due on the original notes, plus interest and taxes paid by Olney, had grown to nearly $17,000, in gold coin, but when the property was sold at auction in 1875 by the sheriff, he only recovered a little over $8,000. Costs and interest had continued to accumulate in the meantime, so that the balance due was still more than $16,000.[3]

On a positive note, the Mercer family continued to grow. The first boy, Thomas Cecil Mercer, was born in Seattle in the summer of 1868, but we do not know if that fact implies that Asa had temporarily moved to Seattle, or whether Annie went there to have the baby. At intervals during their married life, Annie would depart for her "health," and there is no comment in the Mercer papers on this subject. A second girl, Anita Loretta, was born in Portland, Oregon, in July, 1870, but when the next boy was born, the event occurred in California.

---

[2]The John West case is *John West & Co. vs. A. S. Mercer*, filed November 13, 1869, Clatsop County Circuit Court, Astoria, Oregon, and the other case was *John Warrenstaff vs. A. S. Mercer*, in Justice Court, Astoria Oregon, March 23, 1870.

[3]The foreclosure decree erroneously omitted six lots, and more litigation was necessary in order to have them sold, which finally occurred in the spring of 1877, the sheriff realizing an additional $1,250.

At this time, Asa clearly moved to San Francisco to engage in the real estate business, but he could not have been there very long, for he was back in Astoria in the spring of 1873. In any case, Ralph Dickerson Mercer was born in San Franciso, near the end of 1872, and we have no further information on this brief business venture.[4]

The list of ventures in this chapter does not complete the catalogue of Mercer activities during this period, for Asa got himself appointed as marine insurance agent for a group of eastern underwriters, and he even tried his hand at prospecting. He joined a party who spent ten days prospecting in the mountains near Tillamook, west of Portland near the coast, without success.[5]

Legal difficulties continued to dog Asa during these years, although we do not know the details of the legal controversies. In the Portland courts, Mercer was sued by one A. R. Elder, and also by Joseph Gaston, a newspaper editor. The Elder case was handled by Addison Gibbs, Asa's old nemesis from the smuggling case days, and Elder finally won a verdict for $452.56. The records do not even make it clear whether Mercer hired a lawyer for these actions.[6]

We lack many of the details on the profitability of the Mercers' Oregon real estate speculation, but the signs clearly point to an unhappy result. At the end of 1876, the administrator of the Olney estate tried to collect on Mercer's notes to Olney, a sum of $8,500, plus interest and costs, but the sheriff could find no further property belonging to the Mercers, and the court was informed that the Mercers were "insolvent."

It is worth noting that the census taker who interviewed the Mer-

[4]Thomas Cecil Mercer was born July 9, 1868. The San Francisco city directories for 1872-73 and 1873-74 list Mercer as a real estate agent in that city. In the first of those directories, his residence is shown as Portland, but the following year, a dwelling in San Francisco is listed.

[5]Rumors of gold discoveries in the Tillamook area continued into the following year. *Morning Oregonian*, April 29, 1870, February 17, 18, 1871. Mercer was reappointed as marine insurance agent early in 1870.

[6]The notation "To be dismissed" appears on the docket for the Gaston case, and "No service" is the comment on the Elder case. Counsel are listed for the plaintiffs in these cases, but there is none listed for Mercer. C. F. Russell, Terry and Woodward also sued Mercer in 1873, and this case was stricken from the docket in the spring of 1875. Multnomah County circuit court files, and *Morning Oregonian*, March 23, 1875.

cers for the 1870 census gained a very different view of the financial condition of the household. The census states that Asa owned real estate worth $5,000 and personal property worth $3,000. Unfortunately from the historian's perspective, the census did not inquire into liabilities, and it was the liabilities that always troubled Asa. Nevertheless, he did have funds to employ Matilda Cary as a domestic to help Annie, and Annie's sister Mamie, who had come west on the *Continental*, also lived with them.[7]

At the end of October 1873, the *Astorian* noted that Asa would "soon" leave Astoria for Albany, Oregon. Although Asa had suffered a number of setbacks since he made his home in Oregon, he was in no way discouraged, for he was about to start a new career, one that would hold his interest, with only a brief interruption, for the rest of his life.[8]

---

[7]Asa Mercer received land from Ansel Hulbert on January 13, 1871, and 603 acres from George Warren on August 2, 1871; on May 8, 1871, Annie Mercer paid Jefferson L. Perry $840 for a total of 150 acres in King County. Book 4 Deeds, 324, 695, 696, King County Recorder, Seattle, and Charles W. Smith, "Asa Shinn Mercer," 351.

[8]*Tri-Weekly Astorian*, October 30, 1873.

Chapter XI

Newspaperman and Tobacco Farmer

Most people remember Mercer for his female expeditions, or for his later work as a journalist. The latter career would occupy him for nearly twenty years, and its beginnings were in western Oregon, where he established the first of the string of papers he once owned. He had displayed a flare for writing in the promotional book he authored for the second Mercer expedition, but he would now take up the pen as a newspaper journalist.

The newspaper business in the West was growing more rapidly than the population, and the number of Oregon newspapers doubled in the decade between 1860 to 1870, from fourteen in the earlier year to thirty in 1870. By 1880 there were seventy-four newspapers in the state, and twenty of the twenty-three counties had at least one. Most of these papers were weeklies, and they were modest enterprises: average gross revenues were just about $5,000 per year, equally divided between advertising and circulation, and even that low figure was inflated by the seven dailies included in the averages.

The prospectus Mercer prepared for his Albany newspaper called for publication to begin at the end of November 1873 and continue weekly thereafter, appearing on Thursday mornings under the masthead *Oregon Granger*. Asa loftily declared, "The Paper will be neutral in politics and religion, reserving only the right to criticise flagrant acts of injustice in State or Church." He pointed out to his potential readers that the name was intended to signify an intention to promote social values, support development of the material resources of the State, and recognize the tiller of the soil as "the man of capabilities, and the peer of the greatest." The paper could be had for a year for $2.50, cash in advance.[1]

The newspaper Asa had in mind was to be a "niche" newspaper, with the granger movement as its special constituency. The seventies were years when there were many "movements" afoot in Oregon, including a woman suffrage movement and a strong temperance movement, complete with Carrie Nation-type saloon raids, but the granger movement was particularly active.

The National Grange of the Patrons of Industry, a secret organization formed at the end of 1867, was conceived by Oliver Hudson Kelley, a clerk in the agricultural bureau, who had traveled through the South in 1866, and observed the devastated condition of agriculture in that region. He conceived of a secret national organization that would be dedicated to reconstructing southern agriculture, and advancing the agricultural class throughout the country. The resulting organization was the first national farm organization, and the only rural fraternity.

While the impetus for the organization came from conditions in the South, the reasons for its rapid growth can be traced to problems in other regions. After the Civil War, agricultural production was stimulated by a five-fold increase in immigration by 1873, much of which was directed to the farming regions, and a doubling in railroad mileage in the seventies provided much better transportation to the new farming regions opened up by the Homestead Act. As a consequence, there were agricultural surpluses that forced prices down, and the farmers focused their discontent with these low prices on the perceived monopolies of the railroads and other large corporations.[2]

The National Grange responded to this discontent, and granges were organized at the local, state, and national level. Officially, granges were prohibited from taking a position on political matters, but local granges immediately began working on issues that were hot political subjects. The granges were opposed to high rail-

[1] *Tri-Weekly Astorian*, October 30, 1873.

[2] War-restricted immigration was under 90,000 in 1862, and rose to 459,000 in 1873.

road tariffs and to trusts, and they were in the forefront of the "greenback" campaign against hard money.[3]

Nebraska and Kansas were the center of Grange organizational activity, but the granger movement was also strong on the West Coast, especially in Oregon. The first nine Oregon granges were organized in the spring of 1873, and by 1875, Oregon ranked third behind Nebraska and Kansas in the relative density of the movement. Oregon granges formed a number of cooperative buying organizations for farmers, and they erected warehouses to sell farm products cooperatively.[4]

But the Grange also had important social and educational objectives. In particular, all of the leaders of the Grange insisted that members be encouraged to read. The larger granges established libraries, and they subscribed to the leading agricultural newspapers, which were soon supplemented by newspapers that functioned as organs of the farmers' movement. It was this newspaper movement which Mercer joined when he began his new publication.[5]

The site he chose for his first newspaper was Albany, a town on the east bank of the Willamette River some eighty miles southwest of Portland. The seat of Linn County, Albany was established in 1848, and its population in the seventies was perhaps 2,000. When the Mercers came to Albany in the fall of 1873, the town was in the midst of a boom, and there was not a dwelling house for rent. A visitor two years later noted that twenty to twenty-five new houses were then under construction.[6]

The area around Albany was wheat farm country, and there was over a million bushels of wheat storage in the town, but the town was also in the midst of a $54,000 public works project to build an extensive canal system from the Santiam River to the town. This system was designed to provide waterpower for manufacturing, including a gristmill the grangers were planning to build. The grangers had

[3]O. H. Kelley and six others formed the National Grange in December 1867. The National Grange consisted of seven degrees, and was open to farmers and their wives.

[4]By 1875, 177 granges had been organized in Oregon. Solon Justus Buck, *The Granger Movement* (Cambridge, 1913), table after p. 58.

[5]Solon Justus Buck, *The Granger Movement* (Cambridge, 1913), 289–90.

[6]*Morning Oregonian*, February 22, 1873, May 17, 1875.

a farm warehouse in Albany, and they were also involved in a shipping company, organized in the spring of 1873, to build and operate steamboats and barges between Albany and Astoria.[7]

With over 8,700 people, Linn County was comfortably larger than the 2,500 or so that represented a minimum to support a weekly western newspaper. Nevertheless, Albany was not lacking in newspaper coverage; Mercer's new paper would be the third in the town, where the *Democrat* and the *Register* already were being published. Nor was the competition easy, for the *Democrat* was edited by a wit who had a flair for introducing humor in his news columns, and this paper later grew to become a daily. Nevertheless, Asa could expect that a newspaper pitched to the granger population would enjoy a competitive advantage his competitors did not have.[8]

The first issue of the *Granger* was published on December 4, 1873; it was eight pages, published weekly, with an annual subscription price of $2.50. The *Granger* seems to have enjoyed a measure of success, and at the beginning of 1874, the *Oregonian* noted that new type had been purchased for it. There were granger promotional functions, and of course, the *Granger* editor was in the midst of them.

In the summer of 1874 the grangers organized an excursion of some 200 farmers on the *Willamette Chief* from Corvallis to Astoria, and Mercer was on board; at Astoria, where the ship received salutes from the ships in the harbor, Asa addressed the welcoming party. In the spring of 1875, the *Granger* reported on the results of the plowing contest. When the farmers produced exceptional crops, the editor duly reported that fact, as when the *Granger* called attention to a wheat head weighing one ounce, and containing 123 kernels.[9]

Nevertheless, the *Granger* did not command much respect among

---

[7]The canal system was completed by the beginning of 1874. *Morning Oregonian*, March 8, 1873, December 10, 1875.

[8]The *Democrat* converted its printing operation to water power in the fall of 1875. In the spring of 1874, there were forty-four newspapers in Oregon, led by Portland with ten and Salem with four, which placed Albany third in that ranking. By the spring of 1876, a fourth newspaper, the *Call*, was publishing in Albany. *Morning Oregonian*, August 21, 1875, February 23, 1876. Also, Barbara Cloud, *The Business of Newspapers on the Western Frontier*, (Reno, 1992), 11.

[9]*Morning Oregonian*, February 21, June 2, 1874, May 21, August 6, 1875.

its peers, and the prestigious *Oregonian* continued to favor the *Democrat* in its exchanges, giving scant attention to the *Granger*. Nor did the enterprise seem to be a satisfactory business venture, and in the fall of 1874, Mercer sold the newspaper to the Granger Publishing Company, expecting to continue to serve as editor. After only nineteen weeks, this arrangement apparently collapsed and in October 1875, Mercer sued the new owner for the purchase price, and for his salary as editor. At the end of the year the *Oregonian* noted that Mercer's connection with the paper had "ceased."[10]

Mercer now appears to have reverted to his former specialty as promoter of immigration to the Pacific coast, although this time he concentrated on promotional activity, and he did not try to organize immigration expeditions. Oregon Governor George L. Woods appointed him as special immigration commissioner for the State of Oregon for a period of one year, and in 1876 Governor La Fayette Grover named him as honorary commissioner of emigration to Oregon.

Asa was obviously working on promotional material the year before the latter designation, as he published two promotional booklets patterned after his earlier work on Washington Territory. In 1875, he published *The Material Resources of Linn County, Oregon, Embracing Detailed Descriptions and Business Directory*, and followed this the next year with *The Material Resources of Marion County, Oregon, With A Complete Business Directory*.

While this promotional work may have been spiritually satisfying to Asa, it could not have yielded much in financial terms, and soon the Mercer family was once again preparing to move. Before they left Albany, Oregon, a second son was born there in the spring of 1876; he was christened Asa, Jr. The family's next move was a

[10]Mercer asked for $430 for editorial services, $728.50 for office furniture and fixtures, and $1,225 for the subscription list, plus interest; the defendant admitted that Mercer was entitled to $380 for editorial services and $1,228 for the subscription list, but stated that he had settled with Mercer, and nothing further was due. *A. S. Mercer vs. The Granger Publishing Company*, Case No. 2179, Linn County Circuit Court, and *Oregon Granger*, December 11, 1873, November 11, 1875. Also, *Morning Oregonian*, December 11, 1875. Mercer was replaced as editor by H. W. Garretson, "a writer of reputed ability," according to the *Oregonian*.

long one, away from the west coast, and at the beginning of June the *Astorian* bade farewell to Asa, calling him "an enterprising advocate of immigration."[11]

The next Mercer family home would be across the continent in Maryland, on a 200-acre farm with the pleasant name of Calvert's Hope, which Annie bought in Charles County in August 1876. It was not a expensive property, for the purchase price was only $2,000, and Asa and Annie immediately mortgaged the property for $977.50, perhaps to provide working capital for the farm. The following spring, it was again necessary to borrow, this time $275. The loan was secured by a mortgage which may have covered virtually all their assets in Maryland, a fourteen-year-old gray mare, a mule of the same age, harnesses, a plow, two harrows, and Asa's interest in the growing crops.[12]

Asa's new livelihood was yet another clean break with his past experiences, and we have very little information to suggest why he chose to go into tobacco farming. Since Annie purchased the property they acquired in Maryland, it is possible that some family connection or inheritance attracted them to this unlikely occupation. While Maryland ranked perhaps eighth among tobacco-growing states, it was by no means the most productive, and its average yield per acre lagged considerably behind the largest tobacco states. Dorothy Weintz gives us only the terse comment that Asa operated a tobacco "plantation" for a season, with "poor success," and from the meager details we have her description seems apt.[13]

Tobacco farming clearly did not capture Asa's imagination, and the family's sojourn on the East Coast was a brief one, but before they left Annie gave birth to her third son at the beginning of 1877.

---

[11] *Tri-Weekly Astorian*, June 9, 1876.

[12] Mercer's interest in crops included a one-third interest in a crop of wheat, together with an interest in a crop of tobacco, corn and oats.

[13] Maryland ranked eighth in tobacco production in 1899, and its yield was less than 600 pounds per acre, 100-200 pounds below the yields of Kentucky, North Carolina, and Virginia, the three largest tobacco producers. Dorothy Weintz also said the Mercers moved to Philadelphia, where Asa may have commuted to New York to work on the New York *Sun*, but she gave no further evidence of this assertion, and it cannot be confirmed.

This boy was christened Francis Bowman Mercer and the Maryland adventure found mention in his obituary seventy-eight years later when his birthplace was described as a "plantation."[14]

Although the first Mercer newspaper had not been a financial success, that experience obviously had whetted his appetite for journalism. Leaving the Maryland tobacco fields behind, he now turned his face back in a westerly direction, to a region where new settlements and new potential readers were appearing daily.[15]

---

[14]Newspaper clipping dated November 30, 1954, courtesy of Asa's grandson, Chester Mercer, Hyattville, Wyoming.

[15]Weintz collection.

Chapter XII

Texas Newspaperman

Asa already had experience setting up a new paper, so the fact he did not immediately establish his own newspaper in Texas suggests that the Maryland interlude may have seriously strained Mercer finances, to the extent that he lacked the several hundred dollars necessary to set up his own enterprise. Instead, his first journalistic venture in Texas was to be city editor for another publisher.

Mercer never explained why he chose Texas as the place to start a string of small-town newspapers. It is tempting to assume that he was drawn by dreams of opportunities in the frontier setting of a state still in turmoil after the Civil War. While the turmoil in Texas was real enough, the signs of opportunity were not so evident in the post-Civil War economy of the state. Following the defeat of the South, the bitterly-resented northern carpetbaggers took over the state government until 1874, when Texas Democrats resumed control of the state under Governor Oran Milo Roberts. In these circumstances, why would Asa expect Texans to welcome him to their midst, rather than treat him as a symbol of their northern oppressors?[1]

By choosing the market in northern and western Texas, Asa was looking for rapid growth, although the sparse population meant that the initial market could not be large; even if his writing was first rate, the initial rewards would be limited. Indeed, north Texas then had many of the characteristics of a frontier, and Texas newspapers

[1]Texans' grievances were sometimes well founded, for federal appropriations favored the victorious North over the defeated South. The Fort Worth *Democrat* printed a long, state-by-state list of appropriations for public works on rivers and harbors, saying, "The South pays its share of the taxes, but the North very kindly receives the benefits for the entire country." *Fort Worth Daily Democrat*, March 4, 1879.

used that word to describe the region. Although the cattleman was well established, there were still reminders of an even earlier time, for bison still roamed the plains in some numbers, and Fort Griffin was the headquarters of the buffalo hunters, who slaughtered the great beasts for their hides.[2]

Although the Texas legislature had drawn counties on paper for the entire region, including the Panhandle, many of these counties were not organized, for the cattle industry dominated northwest Texas, and county government, with its appetite for tax money, was unwanted and unneeded. The coming of the railroads changed all that, at least in the counties outside the XIT grant, as new settlers arrived to take up the school lands and the farmers' towns became the seats of the newly organized counties.[3]

The coming of the railroads transformed the economy of this area, although the big ranchers, who recognized the threat that settlers represented for the cattle industry, were at first not enthusiastic about the coming of the rails. Later their attitude gradually changed when the railroads became a reality in the area, and ranchers began using the new rail lines to ship their cattle from Texas points, thus avoiding the long trail drive to Dodge City, Kansas.[4]

Sherman, Texas, where Mercer first came to work for the *Sherman Courier*, was a town of more than 10,000, located sixty-four miles north of Dallas, on the Missouri, Kansas & Texas. Grayson County, of which Sherman was the seat, lay just south of the Red River, partly in the Blackland Prairies and partly in the Post Oak Belt. The county had been created and organized in 1846, and by 1880 was such an important agricultural area that it had become the most populous county in Texas. Sherman had also been established in 1846, and by the time Mercer arrived it was already some-

[2]One or two hunters, using needle guns equipped with telescopes, could kill thirty or forty buffalo in an area of one or two acres, and the remainder of the herd would gather around the scene of carnage, pawing and bellowing, oblivious of the hunters firing on them from concealment. The hides, worth $1 to $1.60 each, could be stripped from a carcass in five minutes. *Denison Daily News*, December 29, 1877.

[3]The huge land grant managed by the XIT sprawled across ten counties, and there was no school land within its boundaries, which could be taken up by settlers.

[4]Dodge City had been the railhead for cattle shipments after the Santa Fe reached that point in 1872.

times called the "Athens of Texas," a reference to its drama club and three colleges.[5]

Sherman was an important business center in North Texas, and it may have been an "Athens" in a relative sense, but it was far from a polished city, and complaints about the mud, which created actual hog wallows in the streets, was a favorite topic in the papers. The rich, black soil made particularly ugly mudholes, and even the *Courier* admitted that at times the courthouse was an island, surrounded by a sea of mud. Fire was another scourge that affected Sherman, as it did most western communities, particularly those with inadequate water systems. For a time, the natural causes of fire in Sherman were also abetted by arsonists, who fired a number of buildings.[6]

The water shortage in Sherman was forcefully brought to public attention when the ice factory, which produced ice from well water, shut down, causing the stoppage of three mills and the cotton gin, all of which depended on waste water from the factory. Eventually artesian wells were drilled to alleviate the water shortage.[7]

There was a newspaper boom in Texas, and the Dallas *Herald* estimated that in 1880 there were more than 200 papers in the state, including at least one in nearly every organized county. Innovative names were common, and although some owners called their organs *Journals* and *Heralds*, there was also a *Hesperian*, a *Cresset*, a *Hawkeye*, a *Jimplecute*, and a *Link*, to cite only a few on a long list. For the most part—and especially in North Texas—these were tiny enterprises, so that a circulation of even four or five hundred would confer bragging rights. Indeed, the *Herald* boasted that it paid more postage to send out papers than all of the other papers in north Texas combined.[8]

Editors scrambled for the limited readership available in the sparsely populated region, and the financial condition of the papers was often desperate. Public printing was an important source of

[5]In 1880, 30,000 bales of cotton were shipped from Sherman. After Mercer left Sherman, the Texas and Pacific also built into the town, in 1880. *Denison Daily News*, February 20, 1878.

[6]*Denison Daily News*, November 2, 1877, January 12, May 3, July 16, 1878, January 11, 1880.

[7]*Fort Worth Daily Democrat*, October 4, 1879.

[8]Although the *Herald* was the largest newspaper in North Texas, the Galveston *News* dwarfed the Dallas paper. *Denison Daily News*, December 30, 1877, February 26, 1880.

revenues for the small papers, so that the county seat was a preferred location for a new paper. Indeed, when the Texas legislature in the spring of 1880 eliminated the requirement that delinquent taxes be advertised in the newspapers, the Dallas *Herald* headlined the move as a "War on the Press."[9]

The small papers were hampered by the many shortcomings of small businesses, and the rising cost of paper threatened their profitability. So many of these organizations opened, closed, suspended and moved from one marketplace to another, that it would be a daunting task to keep track of them. When the establishment of the Belton *Courier* burned down, it purchased the plant of the defunct Brenham *Reporter*, and it was said the equipment still was comparatively new, although it had been used to print three papers in succession, under six different proprietors, all of whom had failed financially.[10]

The Associated Press and Western Union Associated Press were available in the West, but only the larger papers, such as the Dallas *Herald*, could afford the monthly charge of $150 or so for telegraph coverage. Even the Fort Worth *Democrat* canceled its AP coverage in the spring of 1879, because the telegraph lines insisted on exclusive patronage by a participating newspaper, so that when an editor obtained signed up with one service, he was cut off from competing services.[11]

Even though they printed only a few pages, editors were often hard-pressed to find enough local news to fill the space, and the Denison *News*, scouring the town for news items, complained that people on the streets were "silent as the Egyptian Sphinx." Those smaller papers without wire service were forced to fill their pages with "exchanges" from their competitors, plus letters from unpaid correspondents, serialized novels, and excerpts from almanacs and encyclopedias.

---

[9]The *Herald* was a forty-eight-column broadsheet, and the Dallas postmaster obligingly certified the comparative comment on postage paid by the paper; the letter was then run by the *Herald* as a promotional statement. *The Dallas Daily Herald*, May 27, 30, 1880, January 6, 1881.

[10]The *Denison Daily News* of February 11, 1880, reported that the Chicago dailies were forced to add one cent to their nickel price because of paper cost increases, and the following month the same source said paper costs were up 50 percent in a month or two. *Daily Democrat* (Fort Worth) November 27, 1881.

[11]*Fort Worth Daily Democrat*, February 26, March 1, 1879.

The subscriber, starved for reading material, seemed not to object to the varied fare, for as the Dallas *Herald* said, "There is no class or variety of news that will not be read by almost everybody, and with avidity by some." Thus, the reader might be puzzled to open his paper to find a long letter recounting gossip from some remote area, perhaps even in another state, while late breaking news from the next town was ignored for lack of a source for the information.[12]

Although the content of these papers depended heavily on the offerings in the stack of other newspapers on the editor's desk, the unwritten protocol governing the use of exchange material required that the editor acknowledge the source, and competitors were quick to note when this courtesy was omitted. Thus, the Denison *Herald* accused the *News* of copying all of its local news, and the *News* called the charge a lie, saying the *News* "will never do that."[13]

Those small-town editors who had a particular flair for writing could expect to be picked up in printed exchanges by other papers, and they enjoyed more frequent mention than their competitors of the more prosaic sort. This factor encouraged colorful writing, and commentary on the competitor's efforts. During what must have been a slow news season, the Sherman *Courier* said, "If a scurvy yaller dog comes loafing around your premises, shoot him on the spot," and the Denison *News* promptly rejoined, "The *Courier* should be more explicit and point out the particular spot to be aimed at."[14]

The "Personal" columns of the papers were a collection of brief references to the activities of people in the area. The editor's reason for making favorable mention of these people in the column was often little more than a visit at the newspaper office to pay an advertising bill, or for a year's subscription. Consequently, while those who were mentioned might be leaders of the community, they often were only ordinary folks whom the editor had seen, and much otherwise unavailable information was packed into these notes. The Denison *News* needled the Sherman *Courier* over the frequent listing of the travels of a local lawyer, and it is clear that in some cases,

[12]*Denison Daily News*, June 19, 1880.
[13]*The Dallas Daily Herald*, May 27, 1881, and *Denison Daily News*, September 5, 1877, July 25, 1879.
[14]*Denison Daily News*, July 20, 1878.

the paper may well have been compensated by other favors received from the person mentioned.[15]

There was little restraint on the language used in arguments between editors, and the more colorful conflicts were good for business. When the Denison *Herald* said the Denison *News* was "as filthy as it is cowardly," the exchange doubtless sold newspapers on both sides, and was printed for that reason. Even the harshest comments directed at competitors tended to be composed more with an eye to increased circulation than from any deep-seated enmity, so that when an editor's daughter performed in a school play, the competitor's effusion could be positively saccharine.[16]

The Sherman *Courier*, established by Kit Owsley and Charles Miller, was the first newspaper in Grayson county when it began publishing as a weekly in 1867, but its beginnings were rocky for it changed ownership three times in its first year. Apparently, the paper was a daily for a time, but by the fall of 1877 it was a weekly again, although the twenty-four-column daily appeared in September 1877. At this time there was plenty of competition, for there were now two other newspapers in Sherman, and two in Denison, only a few miles away. None of these papers enjoyed much circulation, and in Sherman, the *Courier* only sold 170 copies at the beginning of 1879, and its local competitors were smaller; the two papers in Denison only sold 600 papers in their town.[17]

The editor of the *Courier* was Thomas J. Crooks, a short, somewhat rotund, red-haired, and otherwise colorful Confederate veteran, who thrived on controversy. After the *Courier* criticized a letter printed in another paper, the author of the letter, who did not disclose his name, challenged Crooks to a duel, saying, "Either publicly apologize or fight me in Louisiana, opposite Orange, with six-shooters, till one falls. Retract, fight, or take the name of a coward."[18]

This gave Crooks a welcome opening, and he eagerly seized on

---

[15] *Denison Daily News*, October 26, 1878.

[16] *Fort Worth Daily Democrat*, May 29, 1879.

[17] *Denison Daily News*, June 19, August 23, September 21, 1877, January 8, 1879. Also, Mattie Davis Lucas and Mita Holsapple Hall, *A History of Grayson County, Texas* (Sherman, Texas, 1936), 162.

[18] Thomas J. Crooks served in the 27th Texas Cavalry during the Civil War.

the opportunity to build circulation. First, he argued that the duel would confer little credit on his challenger, because of the smallness of the target, "both in size and reputation." Then, he called attention to the fact that under the dueling code, the challenger did not have the right to select the place for the duel. Next, Crooks pointed out that the proposed duel would be competing for public attention with a similar challenge to one McDade, printed in the Galveston paper. Crooks suggested that they should not divide public attention between the two duels, but since "we are full of other business just now," the McDade duel should go forward first. After McDade was laid away "in his little box," the Crooks duel could then be taken up when it would command a full audience. Finally, returning to the original cause of the challenge, the unrepentant Crooks said to the challenger, "In the meantime, we would admonish him to write the truth to his paper, and not indulge in slander."

The Denison *News* joined in the fun over the dueling challenge by needling Crooks, who apparently had a well-deserved reputation as a good shot. The *News* editor said, "We are glad to note that the meeting, if it ever occurs, is to take place at a distant point. Owing to Crooks' bad sight, no one in the vicinity will be safe while the shooting is going on."[19]

Crooks obviously took pleasure in his work, and he was able to survive in this rough and tumble era of journalism, apparently enjoying the friendship, or at least respect, of many of his colleagues in the press. In this period, Texas politics was very much a matter of Democratic party politics, and Crooks was very active in the Grayson County Democratic organization. The greenback party, which was an outgrowth of the Grange, had by 1878 displaced the discredited Republicans as the second party in Texas, and Crooks tried to keep the greenbackers in the Democratic organization. He even offered the *Courier* office for a greenbacker meeting in the fall of 1877, but he soon learned that his guests were bent on offering their own candidates, and he quickly severed relations with them.[20]

[19]*Denison Daily News*, January 14, 1879.
[20]*Denison Daily News*, August 17, 1877.

The local editor of the *Courier* was J. N. Bartholow, who had come to Sherman from the Dallas *Herald* in September 1877. Bartholow held this position until the end of 1878, when the job was given to Asa Mercer; no other reason for the change was given to the public. Because we have no precise date for Mercer's arrival in Texas, we do not know whether he started working for the *Courier* in some more junior position before he took the local desk, or whether he only came to Sherman at the end of 1878.[21]

Soon after Asa became local editor, the *Courier* ran a long, scolding editorial in which it chided the Sherman merchants for their lack of advertising support for the daily edition, which was not "prospering." It was particularly galling to the editor to note that a dry goods store in Denison was taking more advertising space in the *Courier* in a week than all the dry goods stores in Sherman took in a month.[22]

Mercer brought with him from Oregon an intimate knowledge of the grangers, who were a potent political force in Texas at this time; in 1877 the grangers counted 46,000 men and women in their membership in an electorate of fewer than 200,000. When the grangers met in Sherman at the beginning of 1879, Crooks and Mercer both spoke to the gathering, and the latter undoubtedly capitalized on his granger experience from the days of the *Oregon Granger*. Mercer's speech on this occasion was on the topic, "Texas, the Coming Empire," and we have no further information on his remarks, which were likely of the sort he had perfected in his previous promotional writing in Washington Territory and in Oregon.[23]

In common with a many other western editors, Asa had a tendency to moralize, and the *Courier* of this period has a number of examples which freely sprinkle editorial opinion along with news reporting. One story told of a young man, an employee in

[21]*Denison Daily News*, December 5, 1878. Dorothy Weintz's notes in the Bagley collection indicate that Asa worked three years for the *Courier*, but she also said that he worked two years for the New York *Sun*, and that he spent one season on a tobacco plantation; taken together, there is not enough time between his departure from Oregon in the summer of 1876, until his departure from Sherman at the beginning of 1880.

[22]*Denison Daily News*, September 21, 1877, December 12, 1878, May 31, 1879.

[23]Billy M. Jones, *The Saga of Texas, 1875–1900: The Search for Maturity* (Austin, 1965), 37.

a Sherman store, who approached a young lady on the street, asking her some "impertinent questions," the nature of which the editor failed to state. When the lady declined to speak to the man, he blocked her passage, and after she finally got away from him she reported the incident to a friend, who thereupon located the young man and thrashed him with a cane. Mercer weighed in with his righteous judgment: "He should have been taken out into the public square and stripped, and then had thirty lashes upon the bare back."[24]

A few days later, Mercer called attention to the habit of "one or two" young men, who made "remarks" about "respectable women:

> [T]he first they know some one will split their heads open with a bois d'arc cane that will not break. If there is any one thing for which a young man should be hung and quartered, it is for standing on the streets corners and making insinuating remarks about respectable women.[25]

When a man in Denton County was tried for murder, the *Courier* rushed to judgment on the matter:

> It is a killing—a cowardly and unprovoked killing—such a killing as calls for the most speedy punishment possible for the law to give. And in fact, in such a case, the law is too tardy, it matters not how swiftly it may be handled, nor how exacting the justice may be.[26]

In the summer of 1879 the town of Dexter, in Cooke County, was shot up by a crowd of men armed with pistols and rifles. The *Courier* turned its passionate prose on the unfortunate town, lecturing the inhabitants: "The reputation of Dexter has grown from bad to worse, until it stinks in the nostrils of all decent people.[27]

At the other end of the moral spectrum, the *Courier* was equally quick to magnify the effects of the good influences it detected, and when a Methodist camp meeting came to Collin County, the *Courier* noted the strong response to the message, saying "The cow boys

[24] *Denison Daily News*, May 13, 1879.

[25] *Fort Worth Daily Democrat*, May 16, 1879.

[26] A few days later, the *Courier* resumed its attack on the accused, whose name was Holt. *Fort Worth Daily Democrat*, March 29, April 2, 1879.

[27] *Fort Worth Daily Democrat*, June 28, 1879.

are deserting their wild ways and flocking to the standard of the cross." Would that it could have been so.[28]

Nevertheless, there were limitations on the moral tone of the *Courier*. The Texas legislature passed a Sunday law, which quickly became very unpopular, and those opposed to the measure sought to gain support for amendment or repeal by calling attention to violations by newspapers, whose staff had to work on Sunday to prepare the Monday editions. Texas newspapers vigorously attacked the law, and the Dallas *Herald* contended that it violated the First Amendment of the U. S. Constitution, and also abrogated legal contracts.

In Grayson County, two newspaper publishers were arrested for Sunday law violations, and one of those was T. J. Crooks of the *Courier*. The *Courier* was thoroughly incensed, and devoted a long editorial to the law:

> We are in favor of morality and good order, but when a fanatical legislature allows a few bigots to impose a law upon the people that works a hardship upon the poor, and only confers blessings upon a few rich men, it is time for the voice of the press to be heard in defense of the people's rights. If your friend dies on Sunday morning, bury him without coffin. . . . The ice man who sells you a piece of ice for your sick child cannot lawfully escape. . . . And last but not least, the minister of God, who for hire goes into his pulpit on Sunday morning and preaches Christ and him crucified, is liable to a fine under this law.

In the end, the *Courier* capitulated, and switched its publication to the afternoon so as to avoid Sunday evening work, a move which immediately called forth derision from the Denison *News*.[29]

In the fall of 1879 the *Courier* was criticized for failing to report the proceedings against a young man accused of counterfeiting; the *Courier* piously declared that it would withhold its coverage until the trial was completed. Apparently, the young man did pass two counterfeit silver dollars, in connection with his handling of large sums of money, but the *Courier* concluded that he did not intend to

[28] *Fort Worth Daily Democrat*, August 5, 1879.

[29] *Fort Worth Daily Democrat*, August 8, 1879, and *Denison Daily News*, August 13, 1879.

commit a crime. Although the trial finally did end in an acquittal, the *News* suggested that the *Courier* thereafter should remove from its masthead the boast that the paper "contains the latest news."[30]

During Mercer's tenure as local editor in Sherman, the *Courier* eagerly promoted the rapidly growing area in north Texas, and it was slow to report incidents that reflected a lawless condition. The *Courier* accused Kansans and others in the North of besmirching Texas, by magnifying "every murder, every killing, and every crime against law and society, possible to imagine," and the editor estimated that such efforts had successfully diverted 10,000 Ohio emigrants to Kansas, rather than Texas, in 1878.

Examples of the agricultural bounty of the land were always welcome, and when a farmer brought a bundle of eleven-foot sugar cane to the *Courier* office, the editor intoned that there were "millions of acres" in Texas that would grow such cane. Asa's interest in growing fruit apparently went beyond his journalistic duties, for when a new Texas Pomological Society was organized in Sherman, in the fall of 1879 he was elected secretary of the organization.[31]

Asa's attendance at the 1879 meeting of the Grayson County Pomological Society in Denison gave the editor of the Denison *News* what may have been his first opportunity to meet the *Courier's* new local editor, and he announced that Mercer had an "open countenance." Perhaps we should not place too much emphasis on this favorable description, as it was used in the context as counterpoint to the *News'* characterization of the editor of the Sherman *Register*, who was described as a man "caught in the act of robbing a hen roost."[32]

Although the area around Sherman was primarily the province of farmers, it was here that Asa Mercer came in contact with the

[30]*Denison Daily News*, September 12, 13, 14, 1879.

[31]*Denison Daily News*, August 31, 1879, and *Fort Worth Daily Democrat*, February 7, July 26, 1879.

[32]*Denison Daily News*, January 17, June 16, 1879. The editor of the Sherman *Register*, J. M. Martin, was caned by his employees, who used a black ebony cane with an ivory handle as their weapon; the cane had been a gift to Martin from employees, perhaps in a happier era. *Fort Worth Daily Democrat*, June 20, 1879.

subject of livestock rustling, a subject that would loom large in his future. The Grayson County farmers found that although their cattle were not numerous, they still suffered from rustling, particularly by thieves who crossed the Red River from Indian Territory. In the spring of 1878 the Grayson County Protective Association was organized, consisting chiefly of farmers, and the *Courier* emphasized that the members would be cooperating with law enforcement officers, and not function as a "Judge Lynch posse." In the fall of 1879, the association recovered three horses belonging to members, and the thieves were brought to justice.[33]

In the fall of 1879 the newspaper business in North Texas was in ferment. The Whitesboro *Democrat* moved to Sherman, where it was renamed the *Sherman Democrat*; soon after, the *Evening Chronicle* appeared in town; and in September the rumor appeared that a greenback paper was to be started, to serve the growing greenback movement in Texas. It was then reported that the vacuum in Whitesboro caused by the departure of the *Democrat* was shortly to be filled by a new weekly, and there was talk of starting a semiweekly in Gainesville, and a greenback paper in Decatur. There were even a rumor that the Dallas *Herald and Commercial* would be purchased by the Galveston *News*, but although that story proved to be without substance, the *News* did decide to open it own paper in Dallas.[34]

All of this newspaper activity must surely have stirred Asa, and we do not know what factors counted most heavily with him, but after his indoctrination as Texas newspaper man for the *Courier* he was now ready to strike out on his own again, to publish newspapers in a different sort of Texas community.

[33]*Denison Daily News*, May 26, 1878, and *Fort Worth Daily Democrat*, September 17, 1879.

[34]Although the number of new newspapers would seem to argue that the business was profitable, it is interesting that at this time the Fort Worth *Democrat* discontinued its daily issue, taking the paper back to a weekly. *Fort Worth Daily Democrat*, August 2, 9, 20, September 20, December 14, 17, 18, 21, 1879, February 8, 1880.

Chapter XIII

Frontier Press Lord

All but one of the newspapers Mercer established in Texas were located in the tier of counties abutting on the Red River border between Texas and Indian Territory; the exception was the paper he located up in the Panhandle, in Wheeler County. In contrast with his newspaper experience in Oregon, Mercer apparently made no effort to identify his Texas papers with the granger movement. Instead, he was pinning his future in Texas journalism on the economic development that followed railroad construction. Again, with the sole exception of the Panhandle location, the counties where he established newspapers were then in the midst of a flurry of railroad building.

When he chose to publish without the support and potential subsidy from a "movement," Mercer was forced to become a small-town newspaper editor, in the usual sense of the word. The content of such newspapers had evolved over the years since the birth of the nation, and only after the Civil War did they pay a great deal of attention to local news, although Horace Greeley had earlier exhorted editors to do so.[1]

We have already noted that much of the content of the small newspaper was derived from "exchanges," or items copied from other papers. Indeed, the Post Office Act of 1793 recognized the importance of exchanges to the small newspapers, and exempted the exchange of newspapers among editors from the payment of postage. In the 1870s newspapers began printing columns gleaned from talking to people on the street, with the objective of printing

[1]David Dary has traced the appearance of "Local" columns to the Santa Fe *Weekly Gazette*, edited by W. W. H. Davis, in the early 1850s. *Red Blood and Black Ink: Journalism in the Old West* (New York, 1998), 158.

the names of as many potential subscribers as possible, in the hopes they would buy the paper to see what had been written about them. Nevertheless, even after he had reported the most trivial items, the editor often still was faced with large areas of potentially blank space.

We should note another innovation that appeared in small newspapers during this period, even though Mercer apparently made little use of it. This was the preprinted page, an idea pioneered by Ansel Nash Kellogg in 1865. The A. N. Kellogg Newspaper Company furnished editors with preprinted sheets, containing serialized fiction, and well-written non-fiction items. One incidental result of Kellogg's efforts was a rapid standardization of the appearance of the local newspapers, because it was desirable that the preprinted items blend with the locally-written portion of the paper, so as not to betray their "imported" origins. We only have a few examples of Mercer's Texas newspapers, but it appears from the evidence that he did not make extensive use of preprinted materials in his newspapers, undoubtedly because he could not afford their cost.[2]

At the beginning of 1880, the Fort Worth *Democrat* noted that Henrietta, the seat of Clay County, and also on the path of construction for the Fort Worth and Denver City railroad, was "beginning to look up in the world," with new building construction, and a general air of "thrift." It was to this place that Asa Mercer came, to open the first of his Texas newspapers.

The Fort Worth & Denver was the most important railroad in the area where Mercer would build his newspaper chain, and it was ready to begin building in earnest. In 1881 the railroad secured the services of General Grenville M. Dodge, who had just completed the Texas & Pacific from Fort Worth to Sierra Blanca. Following the pattern of other railroads, Dodge also organized the Texas Townsite Company, to promote and lay out towns along the line of the railroad.[3]

Clay County, one of the Red River counties, was located in the

[2]David Dary, *Red Blood and Black Ink,* 209. After he moved to Cheyenne, and started the *Northwestern Live Stock Journal,* he published large sections of material from other sources, but it appears this material was set in type in Cheyenne, and not purchased in preprinted form.

[3]F. Stanley, *The Story of the Texas Panhandle Railroads* (Borger, Texas, 1976), 7. The Fort Worth and Denver City Railway was incorporated May 26, 1873; it was to begin at Fort Worth, and then build northwest to Denver.

western Cross Timbers, one of the two wooded strips extending in parallel from north Texas nearly to its southern border; the Cross Timbers were a famous landmark and also somewhat of a barrier for early travelers in the region. Accordingly, when Clay County was organized in 1860, it was still on the western edge of white civilization in northwest Texas, and during the Civil War Indian depredations drove away even the hardy few who had settled there. Also during the war the county became a haven for deserters from the Confederate army, and this situation only ended in 1866, when the cattlemen returned to the area.

This primarily cattle country was a considerable contrast with Grayson County, where Asa first settled in Texas. Although Clay County was reorganized in 1873 and in the years 1875-79 was the judicial center for the entire Panhandle, the county's population in 1880 was only 5,045, half that of the town of Sherman. The Dallas *Herald* quite properly referred to the area as the "frontier," and Clay County had no incorporated towns, although a courthouse had been built in Henrietta, paid for by public subscription. To be sure, the hide hunters had almost completed their destruction of the huge buffalo herds, but only three years before Mercer came to Clay County, Captain E. F. Ikard did find a buffalo among the cattle he rounded up for shipment to market.[4]

From Clay County, Texas cattle were still trailed north through Indian Territory to the railhead in Kansas, where the Santa Fe railroad had built west to Dodge City in order to take the cattle trade away from the Kansas Pacific. The special legal status of Indian Territory was destined to cause considerable trouble for the cattlemen, and in the spring of 1880 the government had issued its first order prohibiting the trailing of Texas cattle through the Territory.[5]

[4]William Charles Taylor, *A History of Clay County* (Austin, 1972), 47-52, 75, and Lorena Katherine Charistian Douthitt, ed., *Romance and Dim Trails: A History of Clay County* (Dallas, 1938), 11. Also, *The Dallas Daily Herald*, May 6, 1880, and *Dennison Daily News*, May 27, 1877, April 5, 1878, February 27, 1880.

[5]Although the anti-trailing order was soon withdrawn, it was only a precursor to the troubles that would eventually end with the expulsion of cattle from Indian Territory five years later. *Denison Daily News*, May 27, 1880. Dodge City's brief, turbulent cattle boom ended with the Kansas quarantine of 1885.

Texans were more than casually interested in the Indian Territory, just across the Red River to the north, for by the time Mercer came to Clay County to live, "boomers" were already using Texas as a base for their move into the Indian Territory. Although the government tried to expel the illegal squatters, the effort eventually proved futile, and the government opened the Territory to settlement, giving rise to the "Sooner" state of Oklahoma in the next decade.

Moreover, close proximity of the Indian Territory undoubtedly contributed to the high incidence of crime in the northern counties of Texas. The lawless element preying on the northern counties of Texas fled with their booty to the relative sanctuary of the Territory, where they were raided only occasionally by Texas Rangers, who crossed the line in pursuit of fugitives from Texas law.

Henrietta was first settled in 1860, but its early existence was turbulent, and the town was abandoned during the Civil War because of Indian problems. Resettled in 1865, it was shortly thereafter evacuated again, and a permanent settlement was established in 1873. When Mercer arrived in Henrietta, the town was not yet incorporated, and although there was talk about opening a bank and a stage line to Gainesville was in the offing, the economic promise of the town was still very much in the future.

One favorable economic factor was the designation of Clay County as the authority to collect taxes in a number of unorganized counties that were attached to it for administration. Unfortunately, collecting these taxes was difficult and expensive, for the payment of taxes to another county was very unpopular. Neighbors of those whose property was sold by the county for delinquent taxes would not bid on the property at the sheriff's sale, and when these outlying counties were finally organized, their taxpayers balked at paying their prior year arrearages to Clay County.[6]

For a time it was not certain that Henrietta would win its fight for the hegemony of Clay County against the town of Cambridge, located only two and a half miles away. The battle turned in Henrietta's favor when it was learned that the extension of M. K. & T.

[6] *Fort Worth Daily Democrat*, July 5, 1879.

railroad would build to Henrietta, and by the middle of April 1880, Cambridge merchants gave up the contest and began to move their businesses to Henrietta. A new flour mill began operating at the end of 1879, and the Baptists showed their confidence in Henrietta by erecting a costly stone church.[7]

Henrietta already had a newspaper, the *Henrietta Journal*, which had begun publishing in 1877, expanded from twenty-four to twenty-eight columns the following year, and had been sold to R. Y. Mangum, a Sherman stationer, in October 1879, who transformed it into a greenback paper. At first, Mercer announced that he would buy the *Journal*, but he later retracted this story and said he had organized a company to bring out a new paper, which he named *The Henrietta Shield*. Mercer reported that "all" parties had subscribed "liberally" to the new enterprise. The new paper apparently began publishing in March 1880, and in the following month, the Dallas *Herald* reported that the *Shield* was enjoying "almost phenomenal" success.[8]

When the town was incorporated in 1882, in anticipation of the coming of the railroad that summer, the Ikard brothers laid out the Henrietta townsite. The arrival of the railroad generated boom conditions for a time, and in the fall of 1883, the Fort Worth & Denver reported that the new towns on its line had more than doubled in population and valuation in just a year. Business seemed so good that another newspaper, the *North Texas News*, commenced publication, dividing further what must have seemed to Mercer to be a crowded newspaper market.[9]

---

[7] *Fort Worth Daily Democrat*, June 7, November 1, 1879.

[8] The Henrietta *Journal* was established by T. G. Williams. The Tuesday, March 9, issue of the *Denison Daily News* reported that the first issue of the *Shield* would be published "next Saturday." Also, *Denison Daily News*, April 12, 1878, April 9, 1879, February 17, 1880, and *Fort Worth Daily Democrat*, October 8, 1879, January 29, 1880. Although Mercer's comments could mean he organized a corporation to publish the *Shield*, a search of the corporation records failed to turn up one; it is probable that a partnership was set up for that purpose. Also, *The Dallas Daily Herald*, April 17, 30, 1880.

[9] John M. Hendrix, "Texas Cowtowns: Henrietta," *The Cattleman*, XXVIII (October, 1941), 17, Richard C. Overton, *Gulf to Rockies: The Heritage of the Fort Worth and Denver-Colorado and Southern Railways, 1861–1898* (Austin, Texas, 1953), 98, 109, and *Fort Worth Daily Democrat*, May 17, 1882. In 1887, after Mercer had gone to Wyoming, the Missouri, Kansas & Texas also built to Henrietta. William Sude Ikard and his brother, Captain E. F. Ikard, were ranchers, and William had brought the first Hereford cattle to the country in 1876.

Soon, Mercer was soliciting advertising and subscriptions in Sherman and nearby Denison, the region he had formerly served for the *Courier*. The *Shield* generated little comment from others in the area, in spite of the eagerness with which news items were "exchanged" in those days, although a Mercer editorial complaining about the absence of polling places in the unorganized counties did get copied in the Dallas *Herald*. Doubtless, the lack of mention of the *Shield* in other newspapers chiefly reflected the fact that there was not a great deal going on in Henrietta.

While editors in Grayson County spent a good deal of time reporting on the cotton market, and the growing of fruits, this type of farming activity was almost totally missing in Clay County. In the frontier of west Texas, the press catered to the livestock interests, detailing cattle shipments and meetings of the annual stock raisers' conventions, which were often held at Henrietta.

Such news as there was in Clay County tended to be of a violent sort, as when a drunk young cowboy rode his horse into one or two stores in Cambridge. The unfortunate man was then shot by one Dawson, another citizen of the area, after the cowboy unleashed a torrent of abuse, "in which Dawson's mother received special notice." The following year another killing was provoked by an argument over a comet that was then making its way across the night sky. It was a wild country.[10]

Asa quickly entered the political scene in Clay County, and in the spring of 1880 he was elected secretary of the Democatic convention, as well as a delegate to the state convention in Dallas. The county platform committed its delegates to oppose the state administration of Governor O. M. Roberts, and to support an efficient system of free public schools.

At Dallas, Mercer followed the instructions he had received, and nominated John Hancock of Travis for governor. Although a Democrat, Hancock had refused to take the oath of allegiance to the Confederacy during the Civil War; he had apparently been forgiven by the Texas electorate, as he would later serve four terms in Con-

[10] *The Dallas Daily Herald*, July 4, 1880, August 10, 1881.

gress. Although Mercer placed Hancock's name in nomination, he did not even vote for his candidate on the first ballot, and Roberts handily carried the convention.

The Texas Press Association held its convention in Dallas at the same time as the Democratic convention, giving the editors the chance to attend both meetings. Unfortunately, Asa was not able to attract much attention in Texas political circles, and despite his early success in Clay county, he never rose to any prominence at the state level in Texas.[11]

Mercer seems not to have been certain whether the farmers or the cattlemen would ultimately dominate Clay County, and he wrote editorials to serve both sides. Noting that the cattlemen were buying up land for grazing, he suggested that the state should not sell the land to them if it could be more beneficially used for farming. However, when it was suggested that rounding up cattle on Sunday violated the new Texas Sunday law, he invoked the Scriptures to claim that this work was necessary, and therefore should be lawful. In response to claims that the cattlemen were driving the farmers' cattle off their range, he piously said, "it is safe to say this is never done with the consent of the owners of the herds," although some cowboys "do it."[12]

Although there were few distinctions that could be identified with the *Shield*, it is interesting that Mercer's staff included one of the few female printers in Texas. Indeed, the Dallas *Herald* could list only five female printers in the state, of whom two were in the two papers in Henrietta, and the other three worked for papers in Sherman, including Mercer's former employer, the *Courier*.

When there was a newsworthy item in the *Shield*, we see the style of journalism that would later mark Mercer's publishing efforts in Wyoming. Writing of the hanging of four horse thieves across the Red River from Henrietta, in the Indian Territory, he commented that there had been a total of eleven such hangings, and said, "It is about time the force of example was having a good effect."[13]

Making Henrietta his headquarters, Mercer now jumped fur-

---

[11]*The Dallas Daily Herald*, April 11, August 3, 12, 1880.

[12]*The Dallas Daily Herald*, February 9, May 26, 1881.

[13]*Denison Daily News*, January 29, February 7, 28, April 18, 1880, *The Dallas Daily Herald*, April 1, 1880, and *Fort Worth Daily Democrat and Advance*, January 25, 1882.

ther into the newspaper craze then sweeping Texas. In an 1885 interview with Ashley Bancroft, Mercer boasted that at one time he had owned all except one of the newspapers between Decatur, Texas, and the New Mexico line. Considering the number of new entrants in the field in these years, this claim is most unlikely to have been true, although it is just possible that during some brief interval so many papers failed that the Mercer papers were left alone in the field. Curiously, in the Bancroft interview Asa did not mention owning the Henrietta *Shield*, but he did assert that he had established the four papers we shall now mention, although the dates Bancroft copied down for them were wrong.[14]

Mercer established *The Texas Panhandle*, a stock journal, in Mobeetie, in the fall of 1881. The town was Old Mobeetie, on Sweetwater Creek, which had been established as a trading post for Fort Elliott in 1875. It was originally a buffalo hunter's camp, called Hide Town, then was called Sweetwater until 1879, when the Post Office Department required a change of name to eliminate confusion, and the Indian word for "sweet water" was chosen. The town was located in the Panhandle, the home of some of the largest cattle outfits in the world. West of Mobeetie was the enormous XIT spread, three million acres in ten counties, and its neighbors in the cattle industry were only smaller when compared with that enormity.[15]

In 1879 Wheeler County was organized, and Mobeetie became the county seat. Although the law required 150 voters for county organization, the promoters of Wheeler County compiled a list that included the names of cowhands from a hundred miles around. Most of Mobeetie's citizens were gamblers, dance hall people, and buffalo hunters, but the wild character of the old town changed dramatically early in 1881, the year Mercer established the *Panhandle*.

[14]Ashley Bancroft met Mercer when he was in Cheyenne in 1885, interviewing people for inclusion in Hubert Howe Bancroft's monumental history of the West; the Mercer interview was February 24, 1885. Mercer gave initial dates of 1879 for the *Panhandle*, 1881 for the *Cross Timbers*, and 1884 for the *Herald*; he did not give a date for the *Guard*. In judging Mercer's assertions in this interview, we should also bear in mind that he also claimed to have brought 300 women to Washington Territory and guaranteed their wages, which was patently untrue. Bancroft interviews, American Heritage Center, University of Wyoming.

[15]The only surviving copy of the *Panhandle* which shows Mercer as owner is apparently that of December 28, 1883, which was Volume 3, No. 17, implying the first issue was September 5, 1881.

In that year a district attorney and a district judge were appointed to administer justice in the twenty-six Panhandle counties, and when J. N. "Honest Jim" Browning arrived in Mobeetie as the new district attorney, the lawless element was finally brought under control. As the first county to be organized in the Panhandle, Wheeler County and its county seat became the administrative center for fourteen other counties attached to Wheeler for judicial purposes, and in the 1880s Mobeetie became a business center for the Texas Panhandle.[16]

Mercer installed Col. William E. Edwards, whom he had hired at the *Shield*, as editor and publisher of the *Panhandle*. The son of a Methodist minister, Edwards was born in Ohio and learned the printing trade in Illinois, where he worked for a time on the Chicago *Tribune*. In the 1870s he came to Texas, to work a cowhand for the Bar X outfit in Archer County before he applied for a newspaper job at Mercer's *Shield* in Henrietta.

Mercer's *Panhandle*, like other small papers, made little effort to write most of its own news stories, but instead relied heavily on "exchanges." There were the usual local advertisements, including those from several banks, but as a livestock paper, the *Panhandle* enjoyed a source of revenue its competitors lacked, for the mainstay of its revenue was brand advertising. The cattle companies paid $10 per year to advertise their brand, and additional brands in the same ad were run for $1.50, making it a lucrative business for the newspaper, because the ad did not have to be reset each week, and payment was for a year, in advance.[17]

Charges for additional brands could be significant for the *Panhandle*, because the big foreign companies who advertised their brands in the paper had plenty to advertise. These companies included the Texas Land & Cattle Company, which advertised its brands on the Canadian River, as well as those for Rancho de Los Laureles, down at Corpus Christi; the Hansford Land & Cattle

[16]J. Evetts Haley, *Charles Goodnight: Cowman & Plainsman* (Norman, Oklahoma, 1936), 358-59. Wheeler County was named for Royal T. Wheeler, former chief justice of Texas. Also, Pauline Durrett Robertson and R. L. Robertson, *Panhandle Pilgrimage* (Amarillo, 1976), 200.

[17]Lorena Douthitt, *Romance and Dim Trails*, 258, 261.

Company; the Rocking Chair Ranche; the Cattle Ranche and Land Company; and the Matador Land and Cattle Company.

Edwards earned mention in the exchanges of the Sherman *Courier-Chronicle*, when he was forced to apologize for printing the *Panhandle* on brown wrapping paper because his newsprint supply was tied up in shipping. The Sherman editor called the *Panhandle* "sprightly," and said the paper was always welcome in his office, so long as it was printed on something that could be read. This exchange was in turn picked up by the Dallas *Herald*, giving Edwards a sort of double bonus for his efforts.[18]

The *Panhandle* was the only one of his Texas newspapers that Mercer retained when he left for Wyoming in the fall of 1883. Mercer had visited Mobeetie in July, before departing for Cheyenne, and Edwards, the editor, noted that Mercer had promised him a new office, but the new setting did not change the personal habits of the newspaper's customers. The following year Edwards sarcastically invited his patrons to spit "on the floor, the table, in the money drawer, or anywhere except toward the stove."[19]

Mercer next opened newspapers at two other towns which the Fort Worth & Denver reached in the summer and fall of 1882. In late September the first train arrived in Wichita Falls, a town that had been organized only a few months before; the townsite company moved the town south of the river to avoid flooding, and opened sale of lots in the new location. The following year Wichita Falls became the seat of Wichita County, and after the railroad arrived in 1882 the town was the terminus of the Fort Worth and Denver for several years. Mercer established the *Wichita Herald* in September 1882, and hired as editor Frank T. Daugherty, who acquired the paper after Mercer left Texas.[20]

Mercer's next newspaper was *The Bowie Cross Timbers*, published at Bowie, a town in Montague County named for James Bowie, of

[18] *The Dallas Daily Herald*, November 5, 1881.

[19] *The Texas Panhandle*, July 6, 1883, November 28, 1884.

[20] The falls referred to in the town's name were created by a dam across the Wichita River, which washed out in 1886, and was not replaced. Jonnie R. Morgan, *The History of Wichita Falls*, (Oklahoma City, 1931), 62. Mercer's paper was not the first in Wichita Falls; the four-page Wichita *Mirror* had begun publication in September, 1882.

the famous knife, after two other names were rejected by the Post Office. Bowie was also laid out on the Fort Worth & Denver in 1882, and it was the only one of Mercer's Texas newspaper towns which was not the seat of its county. The railroad heavily promoted the new towns laid out along its route, and an excursion was organized for Bowie to encourage settlement, and to sell lots in the townsite. A year after the arrival of the first train, the town could boast a population of 1,100, and the most important industry was the brickyard, supplying brick for new buildings.[21]

The name of Mercer's newspaper, which began publishing in November 1882, derived from the local term for the two bands of timber we have already mentioned. Henrietta was on the western belt, while Bowie was located on the east edge of the eastern belt, or Lower Cross Timbers. Mercer's editor of the *Cross Timbers,* O. P. McLean, must have enjoyed a special position in Mercer's favor, or had financial resources of his own, for he was the only one of his editors that Mercer invited to attend the Texas Press Association meeting in Dallas in 1883. After the Dallas meeting, McLean also went with Mercer on an excursion to Monterey, Mexico.[22]

The last Texas newspaper that Mercer established was the *Vernon Weekly Guard* at Vernon, seat of Wilbarger County. When Mercer opened the *Guard,* Vernon was not yet on the railroad, although the Fort Worth & Denver would arrive in the fall of 1886 after Mercer left Texas. Nevertheless, even before the arrival of the railroad, Vernon was an important transportation hub of a different sort, for the town was on the old western cattle trail that led from Texas to the northern ranges in Wyoming and Montana, and over 300,000 head of cattle passed through Vernon in 1884. The town was also an important point on the stage route from Henrietta to the Panhandle, still an important transportation method in the areas not served by rails. Finally, Vernon was the trade center for the impor-

[21]Bowie was end of track from July 1, 1882, until construction reached Wichita Falls later in the year. Harriet V. Morrow, "Coming of the Railroad to County; the Subsequent Founding of Bowie," in Jeff S. Henderson, ed., *100 Years in Montague County, Texas* (Saint Jo, Texas, 1958), n.p.

[22]The *Cross Timbers* was not the first newspaper in Montague County; the *Montague News* began publishing in Montague in 1858. Mrs. W. R. Potter, *History of Montague County, Texas* (Saint Jo, Texas, 1958), 167. Also, *The Dallas Daily Herald,* May 17, 1883.

tant Three D ranch of Daniel Waggoner, which operated on a range that extended more than 30 miles from the town.

Notwithstanding its importance as a hub, the country surrounding Vernon was still sparsely populated, and as late as 1880 the town was said not to contain a single house. However, beginning in 1881 it grew rapidly, soon acquiring three stores, a restaurant, two saloons and half a dozen residences. The next year there were seventy-five inhabitants. The *Guard* began publishing in Vernon at the beginning of 1883, and the first issue estimated that the total population of Wilbarger County at that time was only 500. While we may assume the estimate was inflated, most of the people in the county would have been living in Vernon which would indicate fairly rapid growth in just a year.[23]

The editor of the *Guard* was Benjamin Wilson Edgell, who was born in Missouri in 1852 and had come to Texas to farm. We do not know what Mercer's financial arrangements were for the *Guard*, but indications are that he enjoyed the backing of others; it is possible that Mercer's backers in Wilbarger County were some of the same men who had helped him finance the Henrietta *Shield*.

E. S. "Ramrod" Hendrick, who went to work for the *Guard* in 1888, after Mercer had sold the *Guard*, said that the newspaper was the project of cattlemen from Henrietta and Fort Worth who were interested in having an organ to fight rustlers in Wilbarger County. Hendrick said that because of the paper's editorial stance, Edgell's office was shot "full of holes" by nightriders carrying Winchesters. After Mercer left Texas, Edgell continued to edit the paper, but we do not know if he subsequently became its owner.[24]

Mercer was admitted to membership in the Texas Press Association at its meeting in Dallas in the spring of 1883, and he at once

[23]Vernon was first called Eagle Flats, for the large number of eagles in the area; the name of the town was changed to Vernon, for Mount Vernon, when the post office opened. Dorothy Weintz to Charles W. Smith, October 5, 1931, quoted in Charles W. Smith, "Asa Shinn Mercer," 352n, Douglas C. McMurtrie, "Pioneer Printing in Wyoming," *Annals of Wyoming*, IX, No. 3 (January, 1933), 732, and interview of Asa S. Mercer with Ashley Bancroft, February 24, 1885, Bancroft collection, American Heritage Center, University of Wyoming. Also, *Northwestern Live Stock Journal*, July 4, 1884, and *Daily Democrat* (Fort Worth), April 16, 1881, May 19, 1882.

[24]The first issue of the *Guard* was published January 18, 1883. Charles P. Ross and T. L. Rouse, *Official Early-Day History of Wilbarger County* (Vernon, Texas, 1973), 84, 104.

made his contribution to the business of the meeting by asking the Association to declare all the wives and daughters honorary members. This motion occasioned considerable discussion before the convention agreed to invite the ladies to meetings, without conferring membership on them.[25]

After the conclusion of the serious business of the Association, those who had signed up for an excursion to Monterey, Mexico, departed from Dallas on a special excursion train. Asa Mercer and O. P. McLean, from the Bowie paper, both were on the excursion, which left Dallas in Pullman sleepers on the Texas Pacific. The excursionists first stopped in Austin, where they were dinner guests of Governor John Ireland. From Austin the train crossed the border at Laredo, and the group spent a day in Monterey before returning to Texas.[26]

The cattle-raising dominance of west Texas was threatened by two 1879 land laws which speeded the sale of public lands. The first of these laws priced school lands at one dollar per acre, with a four section limit to each purchaser, and the second placed the remainder of the public domain on the market at 50¢ per acre, with no limit per purchaser. Land dealers thereupon filed on large tracts, signing contracts requiring payment at the end of ninety days; in the time before payment was due they tried to resell the land.[27]

This legislation set off a scramble to acquire the land. Settlers were attracted by the price, while cattlemen wanted to "block up" their holdings. Both groups wanted to control the available sources of water, and they fenced their landholdings with barbed wire, which had been invented in 1873 by J. F. Glidden. Barbed wire fencing appeared in Clay and Montague counties in 1879-80, and by 1883 fencing was also well under way in the Panhandle. While most fencing undoubtedly was located on private land, there were also fences that strayed over on public lands, as well as the private lands of others; some fences even crossed county roads.

[25]The convention did give out a number of honorary memberships to old friends of the profession, and to further identify its constituency the convention approved a constitutional amendment declaring that the Association was open only to managing editors and publishers (except persons of African descent) and not to their backers or landlords. *The Dallas Daily Herald*, May 18, 1883.

[26]The excursion cost twenty to twenty-five dollars per person. *The Dallas Daily Herald*, May 18, 1883.

[27]Billy M. Jones, *The Saga of Texas, 1875-1900: The Search for Maturity* (Austin, 1965), 44-45, 49.

The drought of 1883 brought on the so-called fence-cutting war in Texas. Farmers and cattlemen alike realized that most water was now behind barbed wire fences, and both groups cut fences in order to get water for their livestock. The Red River Land & Cattle Company was the chief corporate ranch in Clay County, and its 110,000 acres behind fences became a prime target for fence cutting by farmers who lived near its pastures. This sort of conflict presented an opportunity to Mercer, and he jumped into the midst of it, taking on the role of mediator. In the fall of 1883 he chaired a meeting of seventy-eight ranchers who met in Henrietta to seek an end to the destruction and violence.[28]

The resolutions adopted by the Henrietta meeting affirmed the right to fence owned or leased land, but condemned other fencing, and particularly that obstructing public roads. They also deplored wire cutting, even when the fences being cut were improper. A special session of the legislature was called to deal with the problem, and the following January a law was enacted making it illegal to fence land that was not leased or owned, and also making it a felony to cut fences.[29]

The small towns where Mercer's newspapers were located did not produce much noteworthy news, and although Mercer could be flamboyant on occasion, he and his other editors never developed a following among their colleagues in the region, so that there are few surviving references to the Mercer publications. In the summer of 1881, Mercer suggested that kerosene could be used as a treatment for snakebite, but although this advice earned him mention in the columns of the Dallas *Herald*, the skepticism of the city editor was evident. The Dallas *Herald* wrote an editorial in the spring of 1880 in which it listed the leading newspapers of the state, but Mercer's efforts did not make that list. It must have been galling for Asa to live in such relative obscurity, with only occasional mention in the exchanges of other Texas papers.[30]

---

[28]The Henrietta meeting was held September 25, 1883. Mercer had just returned from a trip to Cheyenne, where he was surveying the Wyoming area for his new newspaper project.

[29]The later bankruptcy of the Red River company was blamed on the fence-cutting incident. William Charles Taylor, *A History of Clay County*, 90-93, and *Dallas Weekly Herald*, September 27, 1883.

[30]*The Dallas Daily Herald*, May 30, 1880, July 20, 1881.

Indeed, perhaps the most notoriety accorded any of the papers Mercer established in Texas arose after he had departed. In the spring of 1885 the new owner of the Vernon *Guard* became embroiled in a vigilante effort in Wilbarger County to rid the country of "cow thieves, horse thieves and incendiaries, etc." Three men were killed, and the Texas rangers arrested twenty-three for the crimes, including the *Guard's* editor, the county sheriff, and the "best men in Wilbarger County," according to the Dallas *Herald*. The editor of the *Guard* apologized for the slim reportage in the paper during his confinement in jail, noting that it was difficult to write surrounded by "a gang of lawless characters whom he has for the past two years used his best endeavors to rid the country of, and whom he knows would pay a high price for his blood."[31]

While the Mercer family lived in Texas, Annie had two more children, but both died soon after birth. At Henrietta, Joseph Mercer was born in November 1880, but only lived until the following summer. The last of Annie's children, Mathew Philip, was born in 1882, but died in March 1883. Indeed, the Mercer family group was smaller when they left Texas, than when they arrived, for their oldest son, Thomas Cecil, also died in March 1883, and was buried in the same grave as Mathew Philip.[32]

We know few details of Mercer's financial affairs in this period. Asa appeared on the Clay County tax rolls in 1882, when he owned no real estate in the county, and the newspaper property was assessed at only $750. He owned seven head of cattle, and this little herd grew to ten the following year, but even allowing for the usual understatement of assessed valuations, his financial condition was poor.

By the time he departed for Wyoming in 1883, Mercer had sold all of his Texas newspapers except the *Panhandle*, where W. E. Edwards was editor and Mercer was listed as "Manager." Soon the *Panhandle* was printing exchanges from Mercer's new Cheyenne paper, and when the *Panhandle* was also disposed of, Edwards came

[31]The vigilantes included B. Wilson Edgell, editor and owner of the *Guard*, as well as two sheriffs, an ex-sheriff, and a deputy sheriff. *Dallas Daily Herald*, March 14, 18, 19, 23, 1885.

[32]Joseph Mercer was born October 24, 1880, and died of dysentery, July 24, 1881. Mathew Philip was born December 30, 1882, and died March 20, 1883; Thomas Cecil died March 18, 1883. The Mercer graves are in Hope Cemetery, northwest of Henrietta.

to Cheyenne to work for Mercer on the new livestock paper. Although Mercer told Ashley Bancroft he still owned the *Panhandle* in 1885, he must have sold it soon afterward, for a surviving issue dated late in the following year shows the paper under new owners.[33]

Mercer said that while his family was living in Texas there was a disastrous fire which burned a printing office, destroying a $2,500 press outfit and all of the furniture and papers stored nearby. The location and date of this fire continues to be a mystery, but Asa later said that the flames consumed his business papers, some of which were irreplaceable. He said he had come to regret his offhand methods of dealing with important details, for the ashes of the fire included unrecorded deeds to 100 cemetery lots in Brooklyn, New York, which he later lamented could have been sold in 1898 for $300 each. He never stated where the deeds came from, and this detail is as mysterious as the fire itself.[34]

Although Mercer often spoke of his chain of newspapers in Texas, he never gave a reason for quitting the field. It appears obvious that the small towns he chose could not afford to pay much for the privilege of having their own newspapers, but it was also obvious that they were all growing very rapidly. These businesses must surely have still been immature by the time he decided to sell them, and one would suppose that the natural growth of the area would have stimulated them considerably in future years. Nevertheless, by the summer of 1883, Asa had determined to leave Texas and seek out other opportunities.

The Texas experience had given Asa considerable experience serving the range cattle industry, and he now resolved to concentrate on that industry in a new location. This time, he would launch his new venture in Cheyenne, Wyoming, in the region that had been the destination for many of the Texas herds driven past his Texas operations, on their way north.[35]

---

[33]In the 1890s, Edwards returned to Henrietta, where he purchased the *The People's Review*. Lorena Douthitt, *Romance and Dim Trails*, 261.

[34]Asa S. Mercer to Clarence B. Bagley, December 15, 1898. Weintz collection. The Texas fire may also explain why so few issues of Mercer's Texas papers survive.

[35]*Cheyenne Daily Leader*, October 30, 1883.

Chapter XIV

THE *NORTHWESTERN LIVE STOCK JOURNAL*

When Mercer arrived in Cheyenne in August 1883, he was forty-three, and the thick, carrot-red hair which graced his Washington Territory photograph had receded from the top of his head, while that remaining—which a rival Cheyenne editor said was gold—was mostly confined to his face. To his credit, his midsection had "comparatively little" rotundity.[1]

Mercer had a partner in the Cheyenne venture in the person of Samuel A. Marney, a roving ad salesman for the *Texas Live Stock Journal* at Fort Worth, who met Mercer at a livestock meeting in Dodge City in the spring of 1883. Marney was younger than Mercer, and was described as "pushing and energetic," very brown in the face, with a heavy black mustache and a firmly set jaw.

When the Cheyenne newspapers learned of their new competitors, they cast about for information on the new proprietors. In response to this inquiry, the manager of the Fort Worth paper wrote that Marney had come to work there about a year earlier, being "entirely destitute," to solicit ads, wholly on a commission basis. He apparently did well during the first months in this work, but soon Marney was not generating any ad sales, and hence received no money. The Texan volunteered the conclusion that Marney was incapable of success in a newspaper venture.[2]

It was Marney who conceived the idea of publishing a live stock journal, and he apparently approached Mercer with the idea, we

[1] *Cheyenne Daily Leader*, July 22, 1884.

[2] *Cheyenne Daily Leader*, October 30, 1883.

Northwestern Live Stock Journal.

Vol. 4. CHEYENNE, WYOMING, FRIDAY, DECEMBER 3, 1886.

THE STOCK GROWERS' NATIONAL BANK
OF CHEYENNE, WYOMING.
Authorized Capital $1,000,000. Paid in Capital ..... $400,000. Surplus ..... 53,000.
OFFICERS.
H. G. Hay, Cashier,
W. C. Lane, Vice President. E. A. Abbt, Ass't Cashier.
DIRECTORS.
Andrew Gilchrist, I. C. Whipple, W. Sturgis, Jr.
W. C. Lane, H. E. Teschemacher, H. G. Hay.

T. A. Kent, Banker
THE CHEYENNE SAVINGS BANK, CHEYENNE, WYO.
Correspondence Solicited.

NORTHWESTERN
Live Stock Journal
SUBSCRIPTION—INVARIABLY IN ADVANCE:
One Year, - $3 | Three Months, $1
Six Months, - 2 | Single copies, 10c

STOCK NEWS.

Items of Interest Gleaned from All Parts of the Country.

Fort Morgan (Colorado) *Times*: Range cattle came through the recent snow storm in good shape and are in excellent condition to stand actual winter.

Silver City (N. M.) *Sentinel*: Jack Flemming will go to Texas in January and buy from [illegible] to 10,000 head of cattle for his Grant county ranges.

Caldwell (Idaho) *Tribune*: The Oregon Horse & Land company

Mobeetie (Texas) *Panhandle*: The state of Texas vs. W. Groom, theft of cattle; two years in the penitentiary. The state of Texas vs. Jack Rice; theft of horse; five years in the penitentiary. The state of Texas vs. J. J. Joyce; theft of cattle; four years in the penitentiary. The thieves must go!

Las Vegas (N. M.) *Optic*: Fred Garst, the Lincoln county cattle raiser who accidentally shot himself, a week ago, in the right leg, while handling a gun, is slowly mending at the Plaza hotel. After having been wounded, he rode to the city, a distance of nearly a hundred miles, before receiving any medical attention.

Medora (Dak.) *Cowboy*: Monday night's passenger train "made a killing" among some cattle on the section west of here, that looked as though it was running an opposition to the slaughter house. Nine head were killed in less than that

Arizona *Hoof and Horn*: It is with pleasure we note the fact that although nearly all our live stock exchanges are indulging in gloomy anticipations of the losses which may ensue during the present winter, we have yet to hear of a similar croak from any part of Arizona. Throughout the entire territory live stock generally are in good condition, and unless the weather for the next three months is of unparalleled severity the loss experienced by stockmen will be almost nothing.

Winnemucca (Nev.) *Silver State*: Ex-Senator P. N. Marker, of Lovelocks, arrived here yesterday from the north. He made arrangements with cattlemen, whereby 850 head will be driven to his ranch on Big Meadows to be fattened on alfalfa. The Big Meadows, next to the Truckee Meadows, is the most extensive alfalfa producing region in Nevada, and in time it will take

Arizona *Hoof and* [illegible]

Masthead of the *Northwestern Live Stock Journal*,
Mercer's last and most notable newspaper.
Courtesy of Wyoming division of Cultural Resources.

do not know who proposed Cheyenne as the location. In any case, Mercer agreed to pay Marney's expenses for a two-month survey of cattlemen and businessmen in Wyoming, and when this survey proved favorable, the two men agreed on a partnership. They were to share profits, and Marney was to solicit advertising, while Mercer would handle the editorial and publishing functions.[3]

Mercer came to Cheyenne to form his own opinion of the situation, and then returned to Texas, where he somehow secured letters of recommendation from four banks. We do not know how favorable these recommendations were, but they were good enough to permit Asa to go to St. Louis where he purchased, on credit, a Country Campbell press, a safe, and other necessary equipment. By the end of October 1883, Mercer was back in Cheyenne ready to set up the newspaper, which published its first issue on November 25.[4]

The name of the newspaper was the *Northwestern Live Stock Journal*. As the name implies, the new journal hoped to speak to the

[3]The profit split was not equal at first, but after five months, Marney's share was increased to equal Mercer's. *The Cheyenne Daily Sun*, July 22, 1884 and *The Democratic Leader*, July 22, 1884.

[4]*Cheyenne Daily Leader*, October 30, 1883, July 22, 1884 and *The Cheyenne Daily Sun*, July 22, 1884.

entire region, not just Cheyenne, or even Wyoming, and it was intended to serve the livestock industry. Indeed, the *Journal* would be the industry's unabashed mouthpiece. Although the powerful Wyoming Stock Growers Association did not at first lend any direct financial support to the *Journal*, it was clearly a positive force in the background, opening doors for the newspaper, and when financial trouble loomed, more direct help came from that source. These influences paid off for the *Journal*, which sold so much cattle brand advertising to cattlemen that the *Denver Times* sneered that it resembled "a cattle corral."[5]

The Cheyenne *Leader* grudgingly conceded that the initial issue of the newspaper was bright and newsy, well made up and neat. There was the snide comment that Mercer's editorial duties seemed chiefly to involve reprinting items from other papers, but other initial editorial comment was restrained, perhaps in part from an unwillingness to offend the powerful Association. Nevertheless, the polite words did not entirely mask the ill will harbored toward the *Journal* by its competitors in the territorial capital. An obvious reason for their animosity was the degree to which the *Journal* was cutting into their printing business, as well as their advertising and circulation revenues derived from the cattle business.[6]

The first issue of the *Journal* was eight pages, which was expanded to sixteen by the following spring, and the print run was 5,000 copies per week, although the paid circulation was clearly a smaller number. The style of the *Journal* was similar to Mercer's *Panhandle*, and the entire front page was filled with exchanges from other papers, including those he had been connected with in Texas. The back pages of the paper were filled with ads for cattle brands, where many of the large cattle owners were paying the *Journal* to publish their

[5]The *Denver Times* was quoted in *The Democratic Leader* (Cheyenne), July 29, 1884.

[6]One story in the Cheyenne papers claimed that Mercer was the great-grandson of a man who owned 100 acres in Manhattan that was shortly to be reclaimed from a ninety-nine-year lease. This story undoubtedly came from Mercer, who made similar claims regarding his genealogy. Later, the *Sun* printed a variation on the story, now involving a Mercer grant in New York and New Jersey, which in this version consisted of 100 acres in Manhattan, and more land on the Jersey shore. The heirs were supposedly trying to reclaim the property after a ninety-nine-year lease which had been paid in advance, and each expected to receive a million dollars. *The Cheyenne Daily Sun*, April 23, 1886.

brands, at rates the *Leader* said would "paralyze" ordinary businessmen. These ads, which were priced at twelve dollars, rather than the ten dollars Mercer had charged at the *Panhandle*, covered brands from ranches in all of the surrounding states and territories, including California and Oregon. The brand advertisements were in the nature of institutional advertising, since they served little purpose except to keep the owner's name before the public. Peer pressure was strong to show how many brands the outfit owned, and the wide range over which their cattle roamed.

As we have already noted, these brand advertisements were extremely lucrative, since they were paid for a year in advance, and did not have to be reset so that the same copy was run every week without change. While the basic charge was twelve dollars for one brand on a cut of an animal, all of the large outfits listed more then one brand—sometimes as many as forty or more—and there were extra charges for additional brands and for any designs that required special engraving.

When Alexander H. Swan was still managing the Swan Land and Livestock Company, Ltd., that company printed twenty-two cuts of brands for cattle, and nine for horses, a display which cost $200 per year. Both the Arkansas Valley Land & Cattle Company, Ltd., and the great Prairie Cattle Company, Ltd., listed more than forty brands apiece. When the *Journal* was a sixteen-page publication in the fall of 1886, the paper carried more than 250 brand ads, distributed through ten states and territories, of which 135 were from Wyoming.[7]

The *Journal's* patron, the Wyoming Stock Growers Association, was also enjoying substantial growth in membership and revenues in this period, and it could afford to be generous with its new promotional organ. In the spring of 1884 the association paid Mercer to send 150 copies of the *Journal* to members of Congress—certainly as fine an endorsement as he could hope for. At the 1884 annual meeting of the Association in April, George W. Simpson of

[7]Besides Wyoming, the *Journal* carried brand ads from Dakota, Nebraska, New Mexico, Colorado, Oregon, Nevada, Utah, Idaho, and Montana. *Northwestern Live Stock Journal*, December 3, 1886, and A. S. Mercer account book, January 6, 1888, on microfilm, Wyoming State Archives, Cheyenne.

Thomas Sturgis, secretary of the Wyoming Stock Growers Association at the time Asa Mercer established the *Northwestern Live Stock Journal* in Cheyenne.
Courtesy of the American Heritage Center, The University of Wyoming.

Boston, president of the Bay State Cattle Company, took the floor to compliment the newspaper, and to urge members to support it. Mercer responded graciously, as well he might, for he enjoyed far more direct business with the Association than either of the two older papers in Cheyenne, and, of course, his cozy relationship to the individual ranches stemmed from the same source.[8]

The *Journal* reported the proceedings of the Association's annual meetings in full, and the Association's official record of these proceedings in some cases consisted only of a scrapbook, in which the clippings from the *Journal* were pasted, augmented only by such longhand comments as the secretary considered appropriate. The Association convention of 1886 passed a resolution urging its members to support the *Journal*.

[8]At the 1885 meeting, the secretary reported the Association had spent $550 with the *Journal*, as compared with $337.90 with the *Leader* and $435 with the *Sun*. *The Cheyenne Daily Sun*, April 9, 1884, and *The Democratic Leader*, April 8, 1885.

Soon, the partners were effectively functioning as the public relations arm of the Association. At the end of February 1884, Thomas Sturgis, secretary of the Association, wrote to tell Mercer that a cattle meeting at Dallas on March 11 would discuss the pleuro-pneumonia bill then pending before Congress. Sturgis directed Mercer to attend this meeting and oppose the bill, saying he was writing, "at the request of the Ex Com of this Assn." Early in March, Sturgis wrote again, saying that if Mercer could not personally attend the meeting, he should send Marney.[9]

Marney later told the *Leader* that the newspaper earned $8,000 over expenses in the first eight months. The figure was probably exaggerated, but nonetheless, the offices of the paper *were* "finely fitted up," and there was talk of erecting a building for the enterprise. Nor did these pretensions end with the partnership business. Both partners settled into living accommodations furnished with the best they could acquire in Cheyenne, and their taste had already outrun the cash flow of the enterprise, for both partners made their purchases on credit.[10]

At first Asa Mercer rented a house on 17th Street, and Annie Mercer began advertising for piano students. Apparently Annie enrolled the Mercer children in parochial schools in the area, testifying to the fact her Catholic roots had not been erased by her Methodist wedding ceremony in Seattle. Later, the girls were sent away to school at a Catholic academy.[11]

Later Mercer moved the family to a house he rented on the corner of 19th and Evans, from old Margaret G. Henne, a colorful character whose business establishment in another part of town provided

[9]Thomas W. Sturgis to A. S. Mercer, February 29, March 4, 1884, Wyoming Stock Growers Association collection, American Heritage Center, University of Wyoming.

[10]The *Leader* quoted a "well-known" Cheyenne businessman to the effect that the paid circulation of the *Journal* was not half of 5,000, and declining. *Cheyenne Daily Leader*, July 22, 24, 1884.

[11]St. Mary's in Laramie was apparently the first Catholic school in the area, but it was replaced in 1885 by the girls' school conducted at the Convent of the Holy Child Jesus, in Cheyenne; St. John's Catholic Church also operated two divisions of its Parochial School in Cheyenne in 1885. The *Sun*, cataloguing a list of supposed Mercer sins, said that he had swindled "several" Catholic seminaries out of board and tuition; although no location for the schools was mentioned, the context would imply they were in Wyoming. *Cheyenne Daily Sun*, September 14, 1894, and report of Governor Warren to the Secretary of the Interior, November 25, 1885.

accommodations of a different sort for a collection of young women. Mercer furnished the rented quarters from the inventory at Francis E. Warren's store, and by the middle of July 1884, his account with that establishment was over $1,000, which Mercer was obliged to sign a note for.[12]

As we have noted, the arrangement between the partners assigned Marney to outside solicitation and left Mercer with the management of the office in Cheyenne. Since the *Journal* included the entire western cattle region in its circulating region, Marney's travel took him far from Cheyenne, and the *Journal* gave scant public notice to him or his work.[13]

Marney soon became disenchanted with his role, which he rightly supposed to be less important than that of Mercer, who had received the unanimous praise of the Association in a resolution that made no mention at all of Marney. According to Mercer, Marney now proposed that he should stay home and "drive on the boulevard." He also began interfering with office operations, and Mercer said that at one point Marney fired all the workers. Since the bookkeeper for the enterprise was Frank J. Burton, Marney's brother-in-law, Marney presumably had inside knowledge of the Cheyenne operation, even when he was away on his frequent trips out of town.[14]

In July 1884, Marney returned from a trip to Nebraska to learn that Mercer had fired Burton, and given the job to one Trimble. Since Marney had not been consulted on these actions, a dispute at once arose, in the course of which Marney called Mercer a "damned liar," and Mercer responded by striking Marney in the face. Despite his lack of central rotundity, Mercer was apparently out of condition, and soon Marney had him on the floor.

Although the struggle in the office was witnessed by a number of men—the *Sun* said a dozen—none had thus far intervened, and but for a chance intervention from another source, one can only imagine what might then have ensued. As it happened, Annie Mer-

[12] *The Cheyenne Daily Sun*, July 23, 1884.

[13] In the spring of 1884 the *Journal* made a rare reference to Marney, saying he had taken a swing on the Santa Fe through the Arkansas valley. *Northwestern Live Stock Journal*, April 4, 1884.

[14] *The Cheyenne Daily Sun*, July 22, 1884.

cer, with son Ralph and one of her daughters in tow, was at that moment passing on the street, and the Mercer family promptly pitched in to aid the fallen patriarch. Mrs. Mercer selected as a weapon a paperweight shaped like "a fine Devon bull," which had been given to Mercer only the month before by the Warren company, but she was only able to strike Marney once. H. W. Moore, the foreman of the printing operation, then restrained her, and took the paperweight from her.[15]

Annie then picked up a large majolica spittoon, but this time it was Burton who restrained her. By this time Ralph, who was twelve, and his sister, had both armed themselves with rocks, and prepared to join the fray, causing Burton to release Annie, so that he could deflect the childrens' attack. This diversion afforded Annie the opening she needed, and she recovered the spittoon and struck Marney on the back of the head with it, causing it to shatter and leaving an ugly gash in Marney's head.[16]

Marney was carried senseless from the field of battle, and his wounds were attended back at his rooms. Although the *Sun* quoted Dr. J. J. Hunt as saying the wound was "superficial," Dr. Hunt obligingly appeared in court with the prosecuting attorney and testified that Marney's wounds could prove fatal. Complaints were served on Mercer for assault and battery, and on Annie Mercer for assault with a deadly weapon, with intent to kill. Mercer appeared in court and pleaded guilty, receiving a small fine, while Annie was released on $1,000 bail, her case to go before the grand jury.[17]

Marney did not die, and when he had recovered sufficiently to speak to the press, he pointed to the fact that he still owned half interest in the newspaper, and said he would not sell out for $30,000. Burton carried on the war by stopping payment at the bank on a check to Mercer, and Mercer reciprocated by stopping payments to Marney and Burton. But these were mere annoyances, for

[15]The bull paperweight was given to Mercer by J. P. Crossen of the Warren Mercantile Company, *Northwestern Live Stock Journal*, June 6, 1884. Also, *Cheyenne Daily Leader*, July 22, 1884 and *The Cheyenne Daily Sun*, July 22, 1884.

[16]We do not know which of the Mercer girls was involved in the incident, as both were then older than the age given in the newspapers.

[17]*The Cheyenne Daily Sun*, July 22, 1884.

it soon became apparent that Mercer had the upper hand, and Trimble told the press that Burton was no longer an employee.

The partners' dispute then spread beyond their business relationship, as creditors rushed to collect the sums they were owed. The day after the fracas, the sheriff served an attachment for $457.90 on Marney's interest in the partnership, which was sworn out by Francis E. Warren and covered the amount Marney owed for furniture he had purchased from Warren Mercantile. The sheriff also issued an attachment of $60 against Mercer, on behalf of J. E. Tuttle, for painting at Mercer's residence. Actually, this was a minor concern, for Mercer had a number of larger debts, including the mortgage of $1,064 to Warren Mercantile, and a bill from Craig, Davis & Co., for $347 of "fancy" furniture. Warren's attachment on Marney's interest in the partnership made it impossible to print the newspaper, and Mercer suspended publication of the *Journal* on July 23, not to resume until August 1.[18]

Mercer needed good legal advice, and he hired Judge Charles W. Wright to represent him. Wright was a man to be reckoned with, for he was not only the Association attorney, but he was also on retainer to oversee the Association's new detective bureau. Wright told the *Sun* the partners' difficulties arose because Marney was jealous of the attention Mercer had received, and he further stated that the *Journal* property was not worth over $2,500, before offsetting liabilities. He declared that when the debts were paid, there would not be enough left to pay Marney's debts, but he also said that Mercer would buy out his partner, if a sale could be arranged.[19]

Wright did not say where Asa would get the money to buy out his partner, but it was now clear that the *Journal's* relationship was worth more than just moral support. The Association now advanced Mercer more than $600, including $135 for the type used to print the new brand book. Moreover, it soon appeared that

[18]The stockgrowers association paid a draft by St. Louis Type Foundry for $355.94, and Mercer & Marney note for $143.30 and $135.10 for the brand book type, all on July 22, 1884. *The Democratic Leader* (Cheyenne), August 2, 1884, and check stubs, Wyoming Stock Growers Association, American Heritage Center, University of Wyoming.

[19]*The Cheyenne Daily Sun*, July 26, August 2, 3, 1884.

Annie Mercer's legal troubles were not really serious, for the grand jury, under the leadership of the noted cattleman, R. S. Van Tassell, as foreman, refused to hand up an indictment thus ending the matter.[20]

Early in August Marney decamped for Denver, where the *Denver News* reported that he was considering opening another stock paper in Cheyenne, but this was only bluff. In short order Marney accepted $3,000 for his interest in the *Journal*, and the partnership of Mercer & Marney was dissolved. By October the word was out that Marney had gone to Miles City to start his own newspaper, and soon the *Stockgrowers Journal* appeared in that city, with R. M. Hathaway as editor, and Marney as publisher and proprietor; this paper followed the same format as the Cheyenne journal. The Wyoming Stock Growers Association even gave Marney six dollars for a two-year subscription to his newspaper, perhaps signifying that its devotion to Mercer was not total.[21]

Mercer resumed publication of the *Journal* with the issue of August 1, and there was little outward evidence of the upheaval just past. Ownership by "A. S. Mercer, Proprietor," replaced the former reference to "Mercer & Marney," and the name on the masthead had changed to *The North American Live Stock Journal*, but no explanation was given for either change. Also at this time, perhaps as an indication of the growing complexity of the enterprise, Mercer made a key addition to staff by hiring Harry C. Leech as assistant editor, a post Leech would hold until his failing health forced him to leave.[22]

Just how strained relationships had become among the Cheyenne editors soon became apparent when Mercer twitted the *Leader* for a typographical error in one of its articles. This unleashed an attack by the *Leader*, the mildest part of which noted that Mercer seemed

[20] *The Democratic Leader*, November 14, 1884.

[21] The first issue of the *Stockgrowers Journal* (Miles City, Montana) appeared October 25, 1884. By the summer of 1889, Marney had sold the paper to Messrs Merrill, Butler, and Potter. *Big Horn Sentinel* (Buffalo, Wyo.), October 11, 25, 1884.

[22] Leech died in Pennsylvania in the spring of 1889. *Northwestern Live Stock Journal*, December 25, 1885, May 10, 1889. Also, *Cheyenne Daily Leader*, August 2, 1884.

to have difficulty settling on what to call his paper, calling it the *North American*, the *Journal*, and the *Stock Journal*, as well as the full masthead title, all in a single article.[23]

Then, the *Leader* editor denigrated Mercer's knowledge of the livestock industry. Recalling Mercer's address before the Wyoming Stock Growers Association convention, the *Leader* said that Mercer's lecture "deserves to rank with Josh Billings' lecture on milk, in which the lacteal fluid was not mentioned from beginning to end." According to the *Leader*, Mercer spoke about the scenery, the beauty of the city, the thrift of its citizens, the invigorating atmosphere, and the far-off "indefiniteness" of Long's Peak, but "[w]ith heroic self control, however, he never even inferentially referred to live stock."[24]

These editorial sticks and stones did not damage Asa's love affair with the Association. In the fall of 1884 Mercer went to the Chicago and St. Louis livestock conventions, with the delegation from Wyoming, traveling in the special car made available by the railroad. He was gone nearly three weeks, and at the St. Louis convention he demonstrated how far afield the *Journal* reached, by donating the gavel for the proceedings.[25]

Nevertheless, there *were* limits to how far the Association would go in its sponsorship of Mercer and his newspaper. Mercer wanted to write a monograph for the U. S. Department of Agriculture, and when he asked Sturgis to intervene with the Commissioner of Agriculture on his behalf, Sturgis demurred, saying he could comment only if his opinion was asked. Apparently, the commissioner did bring up the subject (perhaps at Asa's urging), for Mercer did write such a monograph. Moreover, although the *Journal* was effectively the house organ of the Association, that organization could not afford to abandon other newspapers, and

[23]The new name for the paper soon disappeared, to be replaced once more by the old one, and again, Mercer gave no explanation for the change.

[24]*Cheyenne Daily Leader*, August 3, 1884.

[25]W. Turrentine Jackson, "The Wyoming Stock Growers' Association: Political Power in Wyoming Territory, 1873-1890," *Annals of Wyoming*, XX, No. 1 (January, 1948), 78n, and *Northwestern Live Stock Journal*, December 4, 1885, April 9, 1886.

it continued to advertise in other papers, both in Cheyenne and elsewhere in Wyoming.[26]

For a time, things were at least quiet for Mercer and the *Journal*, and although cash flow from the *Journal* would soon prove unequal to the demands Mercer placed on it, he continued to travel and spend as though there was plenty of money. In the fall of 1886, the territorial fair was held in Cheyenne, and A. S. Mercer offered a fifty dollar silver cup for the best beef animal of any age or breed, and twenty-five dollars for the best and fastest walking horse. The *Sun* declared the silver cup "a thing of beauty."[27]

In the fall of 1886, Mercer got into a dispute with his landlady, Margaret Henne. The city of Cheyenne was then extending its sewers along the streets, and in the fall of 1886 this work reached the property on Evans Street which Mercer was renting from Mrs. Henne. Mercer had dug a well and moved a water closet—presumably in preparation for the sewer connection; this work may have been conducted in some unsatisfactory way—at least Mrs. Henne thought so. In any event, Margaret Henne hired workers to make repairs, and she also contracted for cleaning the well, digging out "a pit of manure 22 feet deep," and hauling six loads of manure to the dump. The latter detritus seems to have been accumulated under the former sanitary system, but the record does not reveal such facts.[28]

When Maggie sued Mercer in justice court to recover damages, Asa found himself facing a worthy opponent, who made up in color what she lacked in grammatical eloquence. At first Maggie was represented by a lawyer, but she soon took over the case, even to the point of cross examining herself on the stand, if we are to believe the *Leader*. Mercer, who was also represented by a lawyer, counterclaimed for the cost of digging the well, and the judge offset the

[26]Thomas W. Sturgis to A. S. Mercer, June 26, 1885, and Thomas B. Adams to I. J. Wynn, April 14, 1890, Wyoming Stock Growers Association collection, American Heritage Center, University of Wyoming, and *The Cheyenne Daily Sun*, November 7, 26, 1884.

[27]*The Cheyenne Daily Sun*, August 26, September 5, 1886.

[28]Mercer's rental was twenty-five dollars per month, a modest sum, even for that period. *The Democratic Leader*, November 19, 1886, and Mercer account book, September 25, 1886, Wyoming State Archives.

two claims, letting the landlady recover only her court costs. Maggie then gave public notice that she would appeal, saying, "I'll carry this up to the supreme court of the United States, but I'll make 'em pay that $46; do you moind [*sic*] that, now." Fortunately, Maggie did not carry out the threat, and the action ended with the justice court decision.[29]

We have noted that the *Journal* pitched its offering squarely on the side of the cattlemen and their industry, so that sometimes even the weather, when reported in the Journal, was made to be more favorable to the cattlemen. At the beginning of February 1887, when the West was still in the grips of the awful winter of 1886-87, Mercer declared that "all parts" of the range country, from Texas to Montana and from Nebraska to California, "are of the most flattering character, taken as a whole." He then added, "There is no cause for alarm as to winter losses." This, of course, was nonsense, as the events of the spring and summer would soon demonstrate.[30]

But Mercer reserved his most florid prose for the confrontations of the cattlemen with those who were accused of stealing livestock. In 1889, when James Averell and Ella Watson were lynched by a group of cattlemen, Mercer backed the rancher faction, saying, "There is but one remedy, and that is a freer use of the hanging noose." He went on to advocate "ornamenting" the trees of the territory with a hundred rustlers.[31]

These sentiments were by no means confined to the lynching incident, for Mercer had long advocated lynch law against those he called "depredators." Whenever the law seemed unable to rid the country of them, he advocated that the cattlemen should make "good Indians" of them, using a "higher court" to make "about fifty

[29]Docket No. 4-312, appeal from justice court in the case of *Margaret Henne vs. A. S. Mercer* was the case involving the landlady. *The Democratic Leader*, December 15, 1886. In the fall of 1887, Margaret Henne was back in court, charged with being a "procuress," and on this occasion she conducted her own defense, "cross examined witnesses . . . and read law from a German cook book," according to the *Leader*. *Cheyenne Daily Leader*, September 17, 1887.

[30]*Northwestern Live Stock Journal*, February 4, 1887. Mercer also came down on the side of the Big Four packers in Chicago, saying flatly that "more big fours" were wanted.

[31]*Cheyenne Daily Leader*, November 25, 1883, and *Northwestern Live Stock Journal*, quoted in the Laramie *Boomerang* (August 31, 1889). Also, *Northwestern Live Stock Journal*, June 7, 1889.

sacrificial offerings" to the goddess of Justice. In the spring of 1889 Mercer ran the story of the killing of Jack Cooper in Sweetwater County under the headline "A Good Rustler" and he encouraged those who knew of thieving on the ranges to come forward and betray the rustlers to the law. Otherwise, he warned, the thieves would find their carcasses hanging from a tree, and their souls "frying on the red-hot prongs of the devil's pitch fork." He declared that the only reason the rustlers in Wyoming enjoyed relative "immunity" was because the cattlemen there were "mostly capitalists," not men "who take hold with their hands."[32]

Notwithstanding these examples of his work, Mercer was fond of saying that he avoided commercial or political influence. Thus, in the spring of 1884 he intoned that the *Journal* was not a "boomer:" "It neither bulls nor bears the market. . . . Its mission is to give facts as they exist." The following year, he declared that the *Journal* had "no politics—surely a redeeming feature." So pure was his message, that he claimed he would not even discuss the profitability of the cattle business.[33]

When he did decide to take a stand on what was clearly a political issue, he had a curious explanation for his position. Thus, at the beginning of 1886, when it was obvious that the 1884 Maverick law was not working, Mercer backed reform of the law. He continued to protest that the *Journal* was not in politics, and said that he wanted the legislature to meet to deal with the matter, "not from a political standpoint, but as a necessity to the stock interests of the territory." Similarly, when prominent stockman Francis E. Warren was being considered for appointment as governor to replace the cattlemen's enemy, Thomas Moonlight, Mercer declared himself "proud," although he again insisted the *Journal* was not in politics.[34]

As we have noted, Mercer attended the cattlemen's conventions, and he often spoke from the floor. In the spring of 1885 he was present at the convention in Miles City (where his ex-partner had started

[32] *Northwestern Live Stock Journal,* August 21, 1885, March 1, April 19, June 14, 1889.
[33] *Northwestern Live Stock Journal,* May 16, 1884, November 20, December 25, 1885.
[34] *Northwestern Live Stock Journal,* January 1, 1886, March 1, 1889.

his own stock journal the year before), and he took the floor to berate the eastern and west coast press for their attacks on the cattlemen, which he blamed for Cleveland's anti-fencing order. The following year, at the Rich County Utah Stock Association annual meeting, he was again invited to speak, and the *Journal* printed a verbatim transcript of these proceedings in which part of four columns were taken up by the remarks of A. S. Mercer. This performance was repeated in Denver a week later, where Mercer spoke "in response to loud calls" from the assembly, and applause followed his remarks.[35]

These promotional efforts brought recognition to Asa Mercer, and also, on occasion, business for the *Journal*. The *Journal* was selected by the White River Stock Growers Association in Meeker, Colorado, to print its brand book and bylaws, and he boasted that he received a letter from England addressed simply, "Northwestern Live Stock Journal, America." As late as the end of 1887, he was insisting that he was editor of "the biggest cow paper in the world."[36]

Billy Irvine estimated that Mercer's ties to the Wyoming Stock Growers Association was worth $15,000 per year, a figure which would have included cattlemen's brand advertising. About half of the $1,300 the Association paid Mercer in 1884 was to rescue him from the split with Marney, but there was also Association revenue for printing, including the annual brand books and the list of estrays, which ran for thirty days in the newspaper. But the chief source of income for the paper was the brand ads, which the Association encouraged its members to pay for.

Although Mercer was busy with the *Journal* and with all his traveling to industry meetings, he still made time to reach back to his roots in the Midwest and in the Pacific Northwest. In the fall of 1886 he went back to Ohio, and two years later he spent a month in Seattle. In the latter city, he found that his troubles of past years had been largely forgotten, for he received a warm reception, and

[35]*Northwestern Live Stock Journal*, January 22, 29, 1886.

[36]*Northwestern Live Stock Journal*, June 11, October 29, 1886, November 4, 1887, April 19, 1889.

press coverage for his reminiscences was favorable. For the rest of his life Asa solicited opportunities to return to Seattle, so that he could retell his version of that earlier history.[37]

Mercer reached the high point in the growth of the *Journal* and its prestige in the fall of 1885, when the *Journal* moved into new quarters on Ferguson Street in the building formerly occupied by the *Sun*, and Mercer apparently bought a new press from the Campbell Printing Press company. Mercer bragged that he had spent $20,000 on the newspaper, although there is no way to determine what that sum entailed. Early in 1886 his payroll was running nearly $160 a week for ten employees, and two commission salesmen were selling ads and subscriptions. Unfortunately, from this high point, the road would be downhill.[38]

---

[37]"Proceedings, Eastern Montana Stockgrowers Association convention held at Miles City, April 3, 1885," Montana State Historical Society, Helena, *Cheyenne Daily Leader*, April 4, 1888, and *Seattle Post-Intelligencer*, September 15, 16, 1888.

[38]The Campbell Printing Press and Manufacturing Company held a mortgage on Mercer's assets which was dated January 22, 1886, and coincides with the move to new quarters at the end of 1885. The note for $1,785.70 was due in installments over a period of twenty-four months. Laramie County chattel mortgages, Box 29, p. 482. One of the employees who appeared briefly on Mercer's payroll was O. Thomas Gebhardt, who later published newspapers in the Big Horn Basin. The payroll for February 20 and 27, 1886, is found in Mercer's account book, on microfilm at the Wyoming State Archives. Mercer did not draw a salary, but paid his living expenses from the business accounts.

Chapter XV

Hard Times

Hard times were looming, both for the cattle industry, and for Mercer personally. In the fall of 1886 Annie moved to Denver, and although the move occurred about the time of the lawsuit with Margaret Henne, there is no evidence this action was a factor in her decision. The *Sun* said the Mercer family were planning to live in Denver, and that Asa would thereafter come to Cheyenne frequently to oversee the newspaper, but Mercer denied this story, saying that Annie's health had failed from some cause which he did not disclose.[1]

We do not know whether Annie remained in Denver during the entire period from October 1886, until the spring of 1888, when she was definitely back in Cheyenne. From Mercer's account book, it appears that at least one of the girls was now enrolled in a Catholic academy in the East, for he sent more than $700 to the Visitation Academy, presumably for tuition. A number of the Catholic schools with this name were located in the East, mostly clustered around Baltimore. Since Anita would have been sixteen in 1887, she would have been a logical candidate for the school.[2]

In any case, Asa was now saddled with the cost of maintaining two households, plus at least one girl in parochial school. He rented a room in Cheyenne for himself and bought meal tickets, but these

[1]Mercer said in the October 29 issue that Annie had moved to Denver a few weeks before; he was sued by Margaret Henne on November 23, 1886. Also, *The Cheyenne Daily Sun*, September 28, 1886, and Mercer financial accounts, on microfilm at the Wyoming State Archives, Cheyenne.

[2]The Archdiocese of Baltimore had five Visitation academies in 1887, of which three were in Baltimore or elsewhere in Maryland, and two in Washington, D. C. *Hoffmann's Catholic Directory and Clergy List Quarterly*, II, No. 1 (Milwaukee, 1887), *passim*. Since there is the notation "De Sallar" next to the tuition payment for April, 1888, it is likely that the academy attended by the Mercer girls was Mt. De Sales, west of Baltimore, near Catonsville.

economies did not overcome the fact that the house he rented for Annie in Denver cost forty dollars per month, a substantial increase over the twenty-five dollars he had been paying Margaret Henne. Emma Grimes, who apparently worked for Annie in Cheyenne, also traveled to Denver, and may have remained there with her.[3]

Asa may have received some outside income at this time, for the Commissioner of Agriculture had agreed to let him write a monograph on the cattle industry of California, for inclusion in the 1886 annual report of the Bureau of Animal Industry. Mercer went to California in October to research the subject, which resulted in a monograph of some fifteen pages. We must assume he at least received expenses for this work, which was undertaken pursuant to the "instructions" of the commissioner.

The paper on California was a good example of Mercer prose, and the reader was told that before the farmer came to California, the state's "ideal" cattle range stretched from the head of the Sacramento River to the boundary with Mexico—a landscape "more entrancing than artist's imagination could paint." Nevertheless, the end of the open range in the state drove much of the cattle industry away, and those that remained prospered only in the spring and summer. We are told that in the California winter, the damp climate destroyed the animals' appetite, with the result that the cattle to be fattened were "as dainty as spoiled children." In short, California was no better suited to the raising of cattle than the high plains east of the continental divide.[4]

Annie apparently remained away from Cheyenne throughout 1887, either in Denver, or elsewhere; the available evidence implies that she moved back to Cheyenne only in May 1888, when a personal tragedy overtook her. At some point, Annie's mother, Mary Stephens, had come to live with Annie, for she was ill for some

[3]Emma Grimes went to Denver about September 1, 1886, which may have been the date when the Mercer family moved. Mercer's first payment to R. B. Horrie for house rent was made on May 23, 1888. Mercer accounts, Wyoming State Archives.

[4]Asa S. Mercer, "The Cattle Industry of California," *Third Annual Report of the Bureau of Animal Industry, for the Year 1886* (Washington, D. C., 1887), 239-53. The paper was dated at Cheyenne, December 7, 1886.

time before her death at the end of May 1888, in her 87th year. The funeral was held in the Catholic cathedral, in Cheyenne, with the bishop himself presiding.[5]

Meanwhile, conditions in the cattle industry were also grim, although Asa tried to put a good face on the situation. When he went to the International Range Association meeting in Denver at the beginning of 1887, Mercer bravely intoned, "I want it distinctly understood we are not here to preach the funeral sermon of the plains cattle industry." These remarks brought applause from the audience, even though most of those cattlemen knew that the industry, although certainly not dead, had been seriously wounded by the devastating winter of 1886-87. After that winter, the industry no longer had the resources to spend freely, and there were some spectacular failures, including the bankruptcy of the Swan Brothers, followed in October by the failure of the Morton E. Post banks.[6]

If the ranchers were in financial straits, their Association suffered even more, and for a time, the work of the Wyoming Stock Growers Association, if not its very existence, was in serious question. In the fall of 1887 Thomas B. Adams, secretary of the Association, wrote to John Clay, saying that most of the members wanted to keep the organization alive, "even if our operations for some months are purely nominal." The Association assessed its members to continue the operation of its detective bureau which was formerly financed from sales of mavericks. The assessment was 2¢ per head, double that of the previous year, when a larger number of cattle were still alive on the range. In this fashion, the Association did survive, although as a mere shadow of its former powerful self.[7]

During the years of heady growth, Mercer had done little to liquidate his debts, which included the old balance on the Warren Mercantile mortgage, and the mortgage for the Campbell press. Incredibly, and despite the financial carnage around him in the cattle

---

[5] *The Cheyenne Daily Sun*, May 30, 1888.

[6] *Northwestern Live Stock Journal*, February 18, 1887.

[7] T. B. Adams to John Clay, Jr., September 19, 1887. Wyoming Stock Growers Association collection, American Heritage Center, University of Wyoming.

Thomas B. Adams, who succeeded Thomas Sturgis as secretary of the Wyoming Stock Growers Association 1888-90, and played a key role in the survival of Mercer's newspaper during that period.
Courtesy of Wyoming Division of Cultural Resources.

industry, he kept spending. In the spring of 1887 he moved the *Journal* again, this time into larger quarters on Ferguson Street, paying seventy dollars a month, and later seventy-five dollars, which was an increase over the rent Slack had been collecting. Mercer also acquired a large amount of new type for the paper.[8]

Although the industry and the Association were reeling from the losses of the previous winter, in 1887 the Association paid Mercer nearly $600 for printing. That was to be the last good year of revenues from that source. At the annual Association meeting in April, Mercer pleaded for some relief from the cost of free ads he had grandly promised to run for stray horses, and by October the *Journal* was trying to bolster sagging circulation by cutting its eight-

[8]*Northwestern Live Stock Journal*, April 29, May 6, 20, September 16, October 14, 1887. Warren Mercantile ran a display ad in the *Journal*, and payment for this was credited against Mercer's old account. The move to Jeffrey's building was made on May 1, 1887. *The Cheyenne Daily Sun*, April 21, 1887. The Ferguson street property was owned by John K. Jeffrey, Laramie County clerk.

dollar annual rate to only three dollars. By the end of the year, a large number of subscribers had still not paid their subscriptions which had left the *Journal* cramped for cash. Mercer declared that henceforth, delinquents would not receive the paper, and new subscriptions would have to be paid in advance.[9]

Warren Mercantile began pressing Mercer for payment of his old balances, and he was forced to go to Denver to borrow $1,500 from his friend Mahlon "Doc" Harrold to liquidate the balance, which was then over $1,200. Harrold had bought George L. Hutton's Laramie Plains ranch near Chimney Rock in the spring of 1887, and when he traveled to and from the ranch, it was his custom to stop in Cheyenne to see Mercer.[10]

In the middle of September 1887, Mercer incorporated the *Journal*, saying that "some new forces have been added," which was just vague enough to imply that he was getting new financing; he insisted that editorial control had not changed. The capitalization of the new corporation was $50,000, although clearly that amount of money was not paid into the corporation. Mercer was president of the new organization, and Thomas B. Adams, secretary of the Association, was secretary and treasurer, while John K. Jeffrey, Laramie County Clerk, was vice president. The other directors were the local editor, Harry C. Leech and another employee, George H. Marsh.[11]

It appears that the only new money resulting from the incorporation was from borrowing, for regular payments to the Stock Growers National Bank now appeared in the accounts. The old creditors were not paid, and almost immediately after the incorporation was announced there was a spate of justice court lawsuits against Mercer himself, undoubtedly to protect creditor's rights against the new corporation.

---

[9]In 1888, the Association paid the *Journal* a mere $31.25. *Northwestern Live Stock Journal*, October 7, December 2, 1887.

[10]The Laramie *Boomerang*, quoted in *Northwestern Live Stock Journal*, March 4, 1887. We do not know whether Mercer knew Mahlon Harrold before he left Texas, but it is possible they became acquainted when Harrold, who was in the livestock business in Texas, was still living in Fort Worth. Harrold's son, A. D. Harrold, managed the Chimney Rock ranch.

[11]The North Western Live Stock Journal Publishing Company was incorporated September 16, 1887. Its corporate life was fifty years, but the charter was revoked in 1927 for failure to file reports.

In November and December 1887, seven lawsuits resulted in judgments against him totaling more than $1,200, and Mercer had to borrow $1,100 from Frederic S. Hebard to pay the judgments from these lawsuits. On the same day as the Hebard note was signed, Mercer also borrowed $355 from Jeffrey, giving him a mortgage which was junior in priority behind those of Mahlon Harrold and the Campbell company. Although the Hebard note was paid after only a month, Jeffrey had to sue Mercer in the spring of 1888 to collect the unpaid balance of seventy dollars on his note.[12]

Mercer cut the workforce after the *Journal* was incorporated, and by the beginning of 1888 the payroll was less than seventy-one dollars per week. Leech and Marsh seem to have suffered the privileges of ownership, for their salaries were now often in arrears. Harry Leech, who was the local editor for the *Journal*, went to El Paso for his health in 1887 and again near the end of 1888, and this time he would not return. While Leech's illness was real, his departure from the paper relieved Mercer of twenty-five dollars per week, which had not always been paid when due. After Leech left, Mercer brought William E. Edwards, his old editor at Mobeetie, to Cheyenne to be local editor, which proved to be a good choice, for Edwards was as forgiving about late pay checks as Leech had been.[13]

Mercer's note with Harrold was extended and increased at the beginning of 1888, to permit payment of the installments due on the Campbell Press mortgage. The Harrold borrowings were not finally paid until the end of 1889, when Mercer was able to secure the endorsement of five sureties to guarantee a note with the Cheyenne National Bank.[14]

---

[12]The seven justice court cases were filed by J. M. Carey & Brother, James L. Beebel, *Sun* editor Edward Slack (two cases), Peter S. Cook, banker Thomas A. Kent, and Louis G. Jenks. By August, 1891, Asa Mercer once again owned the printing equipment. *Annie Mercer vs. Albert D. Kelley, et. al.*, Docket No. 5-329, Laramie County District Court.

[13]*Northwestern Live Stock Journal*, February 10, November 16, 1888. Leech died soon after leaving Cheyenne.

[14]The borrowings from Harrold were on two notes, of June 18, 1887, and February 20, 1888, for $1,770 and $2,855.50, respectively; the former note was apparently paid by the latter, which was due in twelve months. The first borrowing from the Cheyenne National was dated April 16, 1889, for $1,500, and this note was subsequently renewed until February 20, 1892, when it was assigned to Annie Mercer, as explained below. Laramie County chattel mortgages.

In the fall of 1887 Mercer got involved with a scheme to improve the finances of the range cattle industry. The ranchers, reeling from the losses sustained in the winter of 1886-87, were casting about for ways to increase prices and cut their costs, and the first idea which came to the fore was that of a trust, patterned after the successful Standard Oil Trust. Early in 1887, Edward M. McGillin, a dry-goods entrepreneur from Cleveland who had heavy investments in the cattle business, proposed to the International Range Association meeting in Denver that a cattle trust be organized, which would own the herds and market directly to the packers. He proposed a capitalization of $100 million for the Trust.[15]

Although McGillin's formula was not the one adopted in the final organization, plans went forward to create a trust; the promoters even secured a copy of the Standard Oil Trust to use as a model. At the beginning of July 1887, ex-governor John L. Routt of Colorado was in Cheyenne to talk with Wyoming cattlemen about the American Cattle Trust, which the Cheyenne newspapers understood to be designed to control markets and eliminate the commission men. Thomas Sturgis became the manager of the Trust, located in offices in New York City, at the phenomenal salary of $20,000 per year.

Sturgis committed his Union Cattle Company herds to the Trust, and he also sold his huge Nebraska feeding operation to the Trust. Other ranchers would follow, until over 210,000 head of cattle were in the Trust by the spring of 1888. The cattlemen were to contribute their herds, paid for 25 percent in cash, and 75 percent in stock of the Trust. The Trust selected the Nelson Morris packing house as its partner in the operation, and purchased Morris' Chicago plant for $2 million; it was planned that the Trust would have its own commission houses in the major cities.[16]

Mercer observed these developments, and ignoring his own ear-

---

[15]McGillin sent his proposal to the *Journal* in a letter dated November 30, 1886, but he delivered a speech to the Association meeting the following February, at which he outlined it again. *Northwestern Live Stock Journal,* December 10, 1886, February 18, 1887.

[16]*The Democratic Leader*, July 1, 2, 1887.

lier advice to the industry to avoid "schemes," he was soon in the forefront of one of his own, which soon was known as the American Beef Pool. The idea for the Pool, which was advanced as a counter to the American Cattle Trust, originated with Henry H. Metcalf, secretary of the Colorado Cattle Growers Association. It was a grand scheme to marshal three-quarters of the beef herds in the West. Mercer declared that the Pool would add three to five dollars per head in value to every animal on the range, but to do this, the Pool needed the participation of a packer to process and market the meat, and—not incidentally—to give up part of the packer's margin to the Pool. The packer selected for this honor was Armour & Company, and Mercer took on the task of presenting this key element of the scheme to Phil Armour.[17]

In September Mercer went to Chicago, where he asked Armour & Company to accept a flat payment of $2.50 per head for killing and marketing cattle for the ranchers, with the remaining net proceeds to be turned back to the selling ranchers. The Pool expected to charge 50¢ a head for its services, which was by coincidence the usual charge by the commission houses who would disappear under the Pool scheme. In this regard, the Pool had the same object as the Trust, which hoped to have its own commission houses, and market directly through its own packer connection. It is obvious that nearly all of the $3-5 added value to the ranchers, which Mercer was touting, was to come from the revenues of the packers, themselves. It is therefore not surprising that Phil Armour did not give a ringing endorsement of the idea, although conversations continued for a time.[18]

In September, Mercer chaired the organizational meeting for an American Beef Pool at the Windsor Hotel in Denver. Asa denied that the Pool would compete with the idea of the American Cattle Trust, but since the Trust would be unlikely to pay 50¢ a head to the Pool to sell its cattle, no other conclusion seemed possible. While

[17]Metcalf was president of the Elbert County Live Stock Company, and he had 200,000 acres of government land under fence along the Bijou, in Elbert County, Colorado. Robert McCaffree, *Century in the Saddle*, (Denver, 1967), 117, 120, and *Northwestern Live Stock Journal*, February 4, 1887.

[18]*Northwestern Live Stock Journal*, September 16, 1887.

the Pool would not own the ranches it represented, and in that sense was a more modest proposal than the Trust, it also could not hope to achieve the operating savings from economies of scale, which the Trust was looking for. Mercer also lamely denied that the scheme was aimed at the commission houses, noting that the Pool could not expect to include all of the cattle, thus leaving some business for the old houses. Nevertheless, his object to corner two-thirds of the herds would have left little for the established houses.[19]

The organizers of the Pool agreed to set up a corporation to administer the scheme, with headquarters in Kansas City, but the idea never got off the ground. Those who were expected to participate made polite comments, and chose to wait and see. It was not obvious that the payment of $2.50 to Armour and 50¢ to the Pool would create the necessary incentives for this untried idea to prosper. Mercer's negotiating tactics began to receive press attention. Armour's representative quoted Mercer as saying the ranchers thought dealers and commission men were robbing them, although he personally knew better, but couldn't convince his clients in the West. The idea of an American Beef Pool failed, but Mercer's involvement in the scheme undoubtedly cost him the enmity of some powerful men who would be unlikely to react favorably when he next got into trouble.

Although the American Cattle Trust staggered on for a number of years through two corporate reorganizations, it, too, failed to marshal the support necessary to accomplish its objectives, and the ranches it purchased were a collection of "financial cripples," as one editor noted. When these attempts at cattle industry consolidation passed off the scene, the established livestock commission merchants and the meat packers were as firmly entrenched as ever.[20]

Back at the *Journal* Mercer had to cope with the continuing fallout from the disastrous winter. Many ranches went bankrupt, and even the strongest cut costs, including the Swan company. Although the Swan company itself never faced bankruptcy, Alex Swan was fired as manager after his own Swan Brothers partnership failed,

[19]*Northwestern Live Stock Journal*, September 23, 1887.

[20]Gene M. Gressley, *Bankers and Cattlemen* (New York, 1966), 263ff, and *Northwestern Live Stock Journal*, September 16, 1887.

and the Scottish directors brought in hard-nosed John Clay to replace him. Clay's chief source of income was his commission house, and if Mercer's Beef Pool activities left him with ill will toward the editor, he could perhaps be forgiven for that feeling. The Swan company had been one of the largest advertisers in the *Journal*, paying $200 per year for brand ads, and after Clay took over the management the company sent a check for $73.33 to pay off its advertising contract with the *Journal*. Although there would be smaller Swan company ads in the future, the old lush days were gone forever.[21]

At the end of 1888, Mercer changed the *Journal* from a sixteen-page broad sheet to a twenty-four-page tabloid format, saying it would then be a "handier" paper, and not mentioning that the change concealed the shrinkage in size, which was equivalent to four broad sheet pages. The year-end issue was also omitted—ostensibly because of the holidays—although an issue dated December 25 had been published the previous year. By the beginning of 1890 the *Journal* had shrunk again, from twenty-four to sixteen pages in tabloid, and by the end of that year it was back to an eight-page broad sheet. At the end of 1889 Mercer's cash problems were so tight he asked Adams at the Association for the use of sixty dollars against a check he would provide. Adams did so, but when he left the secretary's post at the end of 1890, Mercer thereby lost a source of much help.[22]

Mercer found himself so surrounded by financial troubles that he now contemplated returning to Texas, where he had owned a newspaper as late as 1885, but this idea also was doomed. He ordered more newspaper equipment, but the shipment was destroyed in transit and he did not pay for it. The St. Louis Type Foundry filed suit against him, and on August 28, 1891, while this action was pending, Mercer and his wife went to the Cheyenne National Bank,

---

[21]Mercer financial accounts, March 3, 1888, Wyoming State Archives.

[22]Check stubs, Wyoming Stock Growers Association collection, American Heritage Center, University of Wyoming, *Northwestern Live Stock Journal*, January 10, October 3, 1890; John Rolfe Burroughs, *Guardian of the Grasslands: The First Hundred Years of the Wyoming Stock Growers Association* (Cheyenne, 1971), 189; Lewis L. Gould, "A. S. Mercer and the Johnson County War: A Reappraisal," *Arizona and the West* VII, No. 1 (Spring, 1965), 8; and Francis E. Warren to A. S. Mercer, June 2, 1890, Warren Collection, American Heritage Center, University of Wyoming.

where he still owed $1,500, and executed a new note for $1,800, secured by the printing equipment of the *Journal.* The $1,439.80 judgment in the St. Louis Type Foundry case was handed down the next day, but for a time no effort was made to collect on it.[23]

In the summer of 1888 Mercer also fell behind in his payments for printing paper purchased from the State Journal Company, and the unpaid balance on this account was over $500 by the summer of the following year. Another paper supplier sued him for $273.25 in the summer of 1889 and obtained a judgment, which was paid in the fall of that year. Unfortunately, there was not enough money to go around so the State Journal Company was also forced to sue him to collect its account, receiving a judgment for $673.33 at the beginning of February, 1892.[24]

On February 20, 1892, the sheriff was sent to execute the judgment in the Type Foundry case, and also the one in the State Journal Company printing paper case, neither of which had been paid. On the same day, Mercer and his wife again went to the Cheyenne National Bank, and signed another note with the receiver of the bank (the bank had failed in December, 1891) this time secured by property Annie Mercer still owned in the state of Washington. In exchange for this note Annie then took assignment of the $1,800 note and mortgage from the bank.[25]

At the time of the attempted execution in February 1892, the sheriff found there was a prior mortgage on the property, and he returned both executions, with the comment that no property could be found. No further action was taken to levy on either of these judgments until the fall of 1892 when other events made it a worthwhile to take further action in the St. Louis Type case.[26]

In the spring of 1890 Mercer was looking for additional sources of income, and he asked Governor Francis E. Warren to appoint

[23]*St. Louis Type Foundry vs. Asa S. Mercer*, Docket 5-130, and *Annie Mercer vs. Albert D. Kelley, et. al.*, Docket 5-329, Laramie County District Court.

[24]*State Journal Company vs. Asa S. Mercer*, Docket 5-196, Laramie County District Court and *J. W. Butler Paper Company vs. Asa S. Mercer*, Cheyenne justice court, Civil Docket No. 5.

[25]Apparently, this last note to the Cheyenne National Bank was finally paid in the fall of 1892.

[26]*The Cheyenne Daily Leader*, October 18, 1892.

him as a commissioner to the Chicago Exposition of 1893. Although Warren gave the appointment to A. C. Beckwith, he named Mercer as an alternate. When Beckwith did not attend the Exposition, Mercer took his place. This fortunate windfall would shore up the Mercer family finances for a time, and also give him yet another opportunity to be controversial. The *Journal* quoted with satisfaction the comment in the Omaha *Bee* that Mercer had led a "great fight" to have the Columbian Exposition at a single site in Chicago. Mercer chortled, "The one point in ye editor's character that has always been the most prominent is that he has the courage of his conviction, and yelping option buyers cannot frighten him."[27]

This moment of boasting was a fleeting one, for Asa's financial condition was deteriorating, and the events of the next few months would only make matters worse.

[27]Mercer said he had received a communication from one of the real estate "speculators" around Jackson Park, in Chicago, who opposed his position. *Northwestern Live Stock Journal*, October 3, 1890.

Chapter XVI

The Johnson County War

After the winter of 1886-87 the cattle industry in Wyoming never fully recovered its former vigor, and although the cattlemen knew that their heavy losses were caused in large part by weather and overcrowding on the ranges, they also increasingly focused on another cause. No comprehensive estimates of losses from theft were ever proposed, but there was a fair amount of anecdotal evidence of losses from cattle rustling, particularly in central and northeastern Wyoming. We have seen that Mercer not only accepted this point of view on the part of the big cattlemen, but preached it, using his best dramatic prose style.

The war of words over cattle rustling turned into a real war at the beginning of April, 1892 when a number of the big cattlemen and their hired Texas gunmen set off for Johnson County, in northern Wyoming, to eliminate the "rustler" faction in that area. This ill-conceived invasion turned into a fiasco that left the leadership of the industry in a loose sort of incarceration, under the protection of the United States Army at Fort D. A. Russell, north of Cheyenne.

From the safe sanctuary of his office in Cheyenne, Mercer did not at once react to this catastrophe and he did not interrupt his usual routines. He was at the Inter-Mountain Stock Growers Convention in Ogden at the end of April, and there he occupied his usual prominent place in the proceedings. When the convention turned to consideration of the events in northern Wyoming, its resolution supported "legitimate cattle owners, whether they be large or small," and called for an end to the troubles, on the basis of "equal and full protection of life and property to all honest men." This pronouncement could be read to favor both sides in the conflict, and Asa voted for it.[1]

Nevertheless, it was soon very apparent that Asa was in the midst of rethinking his position. A somewhat subtle sign came in the middle of May when Mercer abruptly abandoned his former advocacy of the "freer use of the noose." While he said the *Journal* would continue to uphold the cattlemen "in every legitimate effort to protect their herds," he added piously, "it will not pronounce in favor of an illegal and purely unnecessary plan to aid the few at the expense of the many."[2]

An interesting sidelight on this turn of events is the assertion of Billy Irvine, who later said that Mercer came to him when the cattlemen were interned at Fort D. A. Russell and asked for $500, which Irvine refused to pay. Although we cannot doubt that Mercer badly needed money at this time, we cannot say whether there was such a rebuff by the cattlemen. In any case, Mercer was by stages casting his lot with the other side of this hot controversy.

Another sign of a changing political climate in the *Journal* editorial office appeared in the paper's coverage of the approaching national elections. In June Mercer was asked about the nomination of Harrison on the Republican ticket, and he responded, ". . . as you insist on an opinion, I will say the nomination of Harrison foreshadows republican defeat in November." While this could be read as merely the considered judgment of a friend of the party then in power, the ambiguity disappeared two weeks later when there was a meeting in Cheyenne to ratify the nomination of Grover Cleveland and Adlai Stevenson for the Democratic ticket.

At this meeting, Mercer, the former mouthpiece for the largely Republican Stockgrowers' Association, was now on the stage, and delivered a speech to the gathering which he concluded by saying, "This country will not be turned over to the Medes and Persians,

[1]The convention convened in Ogden on April 29, and Mercer spoke on a number of issues. Although the *Sun* claimed that the resolution was introduced by Mercer, in fact it was introduced by E. P. Savage; it was adopted unanimously. *Ogden Semi-Weekly Standard*, May 4, 1892, and *Cheyenne Daily Sun*, April 30, August 24, 1892.

[2]*Northwestern Live Stock Journal*, quoted in *The Cheyenne Daily Leader*, May 14, 1892.

but to the democratic part. . . ." These sentiments by their former paid publicist must have been read with considerable interest by the incarcerated cattlemen, who were still taking their ease out at Fort D. A. Russell.[3]

Mercer's next move was surprising, not only because it further strained his nearly nonexistent financial resources, but also because it placed him on the side of a man who had been a bitter critic of Mercer's editorial policies at the *Journal.* Col. Emerson H. Kimball, editor of the Douglas *Graphic*, had accused Senator Carey of contributing two horses to the Johnson County invasion, and he followed this up with the accusation that George Baxter was contemplating another invasion of the north. The cattlemen had Kimball arrested for criminal libel and brought to Cheyenne, where bail was set at $2,500 (later reduced to $500, when it was paid).

Kimball was immediately arrested again, this time for libeling one of the cattlemen confined at Fort D. A. Russell, and bail was again set at $500. The bail bond had to be signed by a resident of Laramie County, and Asa Mercer offered to do so, although it was said he never even met Kimball. When news of Mercer's offer reached the cattlemen at Fort Russell, their reaction was entirely predictable, and the *Leader* said that nearly every ad for a stock brand was withdrawn from his paper the very next day.[4]

This action by the cattlemen has been much criticized, but in fairness to them, it must be remembered that the 1886 resolution of the Association had urged them to support the *Journal* as an organ run "strictly in the interest of the range cattle business." Now they could only suppose that their former public relations man was cheek by jowl with their enemies, and they could see no reason to continue to support him. In short, the *Journal*, had been hired to provide a service to the cattlemen, and it was no longer performing that service; they therefore declined to pay.[5]

The *Leader* report on the brand ad cancellations was actually exag-

[3]*The Cheyenne Daily Leader*, June 11, 26, 1892.

[4]The Carey charge was promptly denied by Carey's foreman and brother-in-law, Edward T. David. *Cheyenne Daily Sun*, April 26, 1892 and *The Cheyenne Daily Leader*, June 8, 1892.

[5]*Northwestern Live Stock Journal*, April 9, 1886.

gerated, but Mercer conceded that he had received five letters of cancellation from Fort Russell. He removed those ads, and proudly ran twenty blank spaces with the caption "Boycotted for Opinion's Sake," in the spaces where the cattlemen and the banks friendly to them had previously advertised. In a four-column editorial in the *Journal* of July 8, 1892, Mercer called on the Democrats, who were to meet in convention at Rock Springs later in the month, to put forward a ticket of men "who are in touch with the masses." He predicted that such a ticket would sweep the state "as a cyclone."[6]

Mercer now turned his invective on the powerful president of the Wyoming Stock Growers Association, John Clay, Jr. We do not know what Mercer's early relationship with John Clay, Jr., was, although we do know that Clay sharply reduced the Swan company advertising after he became manager of the company, and the other companies that Clay managed in Wyoming did not advertise their brands in the *Journal*. Nevertheless, after Clay was elected president of the Association in 1890, Mercer's close relationship with that organization did not at first appear to weaken significantly.

Clay had been in Scotland when the invasion of Johnson County took place, and although he came to Cheyenne to spearhead the legal defense of the cattlemen, he always tried to distance himself from any suggestion that he had participated in the planning for the invasion. He may not have planned the event, but there can be little doubt that he knew that Charles A. Campbell, his close associate, would be in the invasion party. The *Sun* took pains to deny that this was so, most likely after talking with Clay. Moreover, Clay's trusted lieutenant in Johnson County, James T. Craig, brought a key warning to the invaders, as the result of which, the invading force retreated to the TA Ranch, where they successfully withstood

[6]Four of the letters from cattlemen at Fort D. A. Russell were dated July 2, while the fourth, signed by H. E. Teschemacher, was dated July 6. *The Cheyenne Daily Leader*, July 3, 6, 1892. Francis E. Warren, whose Warren Mercantile Co. ran regular ads in the *Journal*, told his secretary that he would prefer to continue to pay the $7.70 per month for three or four months, so as to get past the election, and avoid "boycott talk," then "cut out." Francis E. Warren to S. B. Tuttle, August 2, 1892, Warren collection, American Heritage Center, University of Wyoming.

the siege led by Johnson County Sheriff Angus, until the Army could arrive to rescue them.[7]

Mercer was eager to connect Clay to these events, and when Clay reported in his own house organ that the cattlemen involved in the Invasion had been released from custody, Mercer used this comment as an excuse for a caustic editorial in the *Journal.* He said:

> The anarchy that exists is the direct result of the work of John Clay, Jr. and his boon companions. . . . Too great a coward himself to shoulder musket and fight, he sent one of his hired men and contributed to the extermination fund in cheap talk if not in shining shekels. Deliberately making a list of men to be killed and houses to be burned, this man and his coworkers plotted treason to the state with powers that be and went forth to murder and burn.

This was strong stuff. Clay was already a very powerful man, and Mercer could not have been unaware that attacking him was risky.[8]

Mercer's attack on Clay soon called forth a response. Charles A. Campbell, who had been buying cattle for Clay before the invasion, and was one of the invaders, reckoned that he was the "hired" man Mercer referred to in his editorial. As soon as he was released from confinement at Fort D. A. Russell, Campbell went to Mercer's office in Cheyenne, in the company of H. B. Ijams, secretary of the Wyoming Stock Growers Association.[9]

According to Mercer's account of the incident, Campbell said that he did not object to anything Mercer said about Clay, but didn't want his own name "bandied about." When Mercer replied that "a couple" of Clay's men were in the invasion party, Campbell struck Mercer, causing the frame of his glasses to cut his eyebrow. Campbell then immediately went before a justice of the peace and paid a fine for disturbing the peace.

[7]The *Sun* pointed out that Clay had been abroad when the Invasion occurred, and did not return until late in April. It admitted that Clay had sent instructions to Campbell from London, to sell some Johnson County cattle, but claimed he was not aware that Campbell would be in the invasion party. *Cheyenne Daily Sun*, August 24, 1892.

[8]*Cheyenne Daily Sun*, August 24, 1892.

[9]A Scot from Canada, Campbell was born about 1852, came down from Montreal, went into the cattle business and was ruined in the winter of 1886-87. He then worked on an irrigation project, and, beginning in 1890, bought cattle for John Clay, Jr. He died in January 1896. *Live Stock Report* (Chicago), January 10, 1896.

Clay, as a writer of some accomplishment, was no stranger to colorful language, and even thirty years later, memory of the incident still angered the Scotsman. Clay said that "gentle, lovable, sympathetic Charlie...took the change out of [Mercer] with his fists." Then, he fairly roared that Campbell had been goaded to this violence by "harlots" who incited cowboys to steal, by persecution in courts where lawyers "milked you," and even judges were "not above suspicion."[10]

An important element in Mercer's change of allegiance was his plunge into Democratic party politics. He placed his name for delegate to the state convention in Rock Springs, but failed in that effort, although he was permitted to go to the convention as proxy when another delegate fell ill. After the convention, where John E. Osborne was nominated for governor, Mercer stumped the state on behalf of the Democratic ticket.[11]

Mercer did receive some immediate pecuniary benefit from his decision to change sides. Joel J. Hurt, a wealthy Casper sheepman who was a contender for the Democratic nomination for governor, came forward and paid the note the Mercers had given the receiver of the Cheyenne National Bank, taking as security for this loan a mortgage on Annie Mercer's property in Washington State.[12]

Late in September, Mercer was in Buffalo stumping for the Democratic ticket. There he was warmly received by Oscar H. Flagg of the so-called "rustler" faction, who was now editor of the *People's Voice* in Buffalo, saying that Mercer was now rising "grandly above pecuniary considerations." At a crowded rally at the courthouse in Buffalo on September 24, Mercer explained his conversion to the Democratic cause.[13]

Mercer told the assembled crowd that he was like the thirsty man who drinks from a beautiful stream, then sickens and dies because

[10]*Live Stock Markets*, October 19, 1922.

[11]*Cheyenne Daily Sun*, July 24, 1892, and *The Cheyenne Daily Leader*, July 26, 1892.

[12]The Joel Hurt mortgage was filed September 10, 1892, King County Recorder, Book 95 Mortgages, 185, and John Rolfe Burroughs, *Guardian of the Grasslands: The First Hundred Years of the Wyoming Stock Growers Association* (Cheyenne, 1971), 189.

[13]Flagg had purchased the assets of the Buffalo *Echo*, and renamed it. *The People's Voice* (Buffalo), September 24, 1892.

the source of the stream was poisoned. After ten years he had discovered "at the last minute" that the cattlemen had lied to him. Now, however, he declared, "I have taken an antidote and been saved." With this as an introduction, Mercer set forth his view of the real reason for the invasion, which was he said was a nefarious conspiracy, designed to bring off a land grab of monumental proportions.

The target of Mercer's comments was Senator Warren's Arid Land Bill, which was a measure to transfer federal land to the states for development. Earlier in September Mercer had attacked the bill as threatening taxation "beyond possible endurance," creation of a "statehouse land ring," a "vast corruption fund used against the common people," and ultimate ownership of the state by a "landed plutocracy." Once under state control, capitalists could grab the federal land, and use it for grazing.

Thus far, his attack on the Warren bill was not new, but a reflection of the Populist platform on the subject. Mercer, however, carried the argument a step further, and saw behind the bill the real motive behind the Johnson County Invasion. The invasion was intended to drive the settlers off the land, and he claimed that sixteen corporations had already been organized in the east, ready to pounce on the land as soon as the invasion had succeeded.[14]

The circumstantial evidence would indicate that the idea for Mercer's next attack on the cattlemen came during this trip to Buffalo, and it was timed for maximum effect on the November elections. At the time Mercer came to town, George Dunning, who had been hired to take part in the raid on Johnson County, was languishing in the Buffalo jail, the only member of the Invasion force to be arrested by the Johnson County sheriff. Although there is no proof that Mercer met Dunning, subsequent events were consistent with such a meeting.[15]

On October 6 Dunning signed a so-called "confession," which he swore was written by him "without solicitation, fear or threats

[14]*Northwestern Live Stock Journal*, September 2, 1892.

[15]Dunning was hired in Idaho by Ijams, and when the cattlemen surrendered to the Army at the TA Ranch, Dunning hid in the loft of the house, and walked away from the scene afterward. Unfortunately, he took the wrong road, and was arrested by Sheriff Angus and lodged in the Buffalo jail.

from any party." This oath was notarized by Gustave E. A. Moeller, deputy county clerk and a leading member of the Johnson County Democratic party. The document, which implicated in detail a number of men among the leading cattle interests in the state, obviously was intended to explain Dunning's motive for participating in the invasion, other than purely mercenary considerations.

Dunning's confession would have the reader believe that he had betrayed the plans of the cattlemen on two separate occasions before he headed north with the invasion party, in the hopes that the people in Johnson County would be forewarned of their peril. For him to have done this, and then proceeded to ride off to the north with the heavily armed invasion party challenges credulity. Notwithstanding these logical problems in the document, Mercer was apparently satisfied with it, for he took it to Cheyenne and published it verbatim in the October 14 issue of the *Journal*, which was heavily subsidized by Mercer's new friends, the Democratic party.

Two days later Mercer left for Chicago to meet with the commissioners of the World's Fair as an alternate commissioner from Wyoming. Why he did not wait in Cheyenne to see the effect of the bombshell he was dropping on the state is nowhere stated, although he may well have been concerned for his own personal safety. If he thought he could not be reached in Chicago, he was mistaken, for now that Mercer was in Clay's home town the latter filed a libel action against him in Chicago. Clay even succeeded in having the editor jailed briefly in that city, although he was soon released when the suit failed on procedural grounds.[16]

Back in Cheyenne, repercussions of the *Journal's* October 14 issue were not long in coming. The 1891 judgment of the St. Louis Type Foundry had lain in abeyance for a year, because the property was already mortgaged, but now it was levied on again, and this time the sheriff ignored the existing mortgage and seized the property of the *Journal*. The property thus levied upon included all of the

[16]Since there was no evidence that the Mercer editorial had been published in Cook County, Illinois, where Clay filed the suit, the action would not be pursued against Mercer in that jurisdiction.

extra copies of the October 14 issue, but 1,400 copies already sent to subscribers escaped the sheriff's levy.

Annie Mercer responded to the levy on the *Journal* by suing the sheriff and the type foundry for recovery of the property, claiming the chattel mortgage which Asa Mercer had executed to the bank, and had been assigned to her, and was a senior lien. For their part, the defendants argued that Annie had not actually paid Asa's note, but merely substituted one of her own in order to receive assignment of the mortgage. Annie Mercer's argument eventually prevailed in court, but not until the beginning of 1897, and by that time it is doubtful whether any of the parties cared about the outcome.[17]

As one would expect, the Johnson County Invasion had a profound effect on the Wyoming election of 1892, in part because the Republican Party leadership included many who participated in the invasion. The election was also confused by the emergence of the Populists, in the form of the Wyoming People's Party, even though they did not command a large number of votes. Populism was a force in much of the West, but the small number of farmers in Wyoming and the absence of a large silver mining industry made the state a poor recruiting ground for the movement. The first local Farmers' Alliance was organized in 1890 and seven Alliance clubs were eventually established, but they were of little political importance.[18]

The Wyoming People's Party can be traced to the beginning of 1891, but the platform drawn up in Laramie in that year concentrated on national issues, and did not criticize the Wyoming Stock Growers Association or the Board of Live Stock Commissioners. This situation changed the following June, when the Laramie platform of the party included a sharp denunciation of the Johnson County Invasion. The Populists also condemned Warren's Arid Land Bill.

---

[17]Annie E. Mercer vs. Albert D. Kelly, *et. al.*, Docket 5-329, Laramie County District Court. Annie Mercer had previously given bond for return of the property, so that the judgment did not affect possession of it, and we do not know if any copies of the October 14 *Journal* were thereby recovered and distributed, but it is possible that this happened.

[18]The history of Populism in Wyoming is traced in Robert W. Larson, *Populism in the Mountain West* (Albuquerque, 1986), 44ff.

At this point there were important defections to the Populists from both of the national parties, most notably in Johnson County where unrest was at a high pitch. The entire county Republican committee resigned, and its chairman joined the Populist Party. The Democratic Party was especially eager to reach an agreement on fusion with the Populists, and after some initial opposition among the Populists was overcome, the two parties agreed to support the Democratic nominees for governor, and for Wyoming's representative in Congress.

The 1892 election was hard-fought, but the Democrats early sensed that victory was within reach. Mercer allied himself with the efforts of the chairman of the Democratic Party in Wyoming, Albert L. New, and when the New faction of the party broke with the older elements before the election, Mercer found himself at odds with John Carroll's Cheyenne *Leader*, which had a powerful voice in the state.[19]

The Democratic victory in the fall of 1892 gave Mercer his greatest—and last—taste of the public adulation he so craved. He did not occupy center stage at the victory rally in Cheyenne, where he had enemies in both parties, but the situation changed in Laramie. There, he was greeted with "rapturous applause," according to the *Boomerang*, which gave him the title "Mercer, the Martyr," and gushed, "His prose is poetry, his words are wisdom."[20]

Mercer could hope that the Democratic successes might point the way to bail out his own shaky finances, and in the fall of 1892 he began negotiating with the Democratic leaders to bring out a new Democratic newspaper in Cheyenne. He proposed that the new paper would purchase the equipment of the nearly defunct *Journal*, and of course, A. S. Mercer was to be editor. Early in 1893 the *Leader* said that the paper was to be capitalized at $10,000, and its backers included C. P. Hill, who was Governor Osborne's private secretary, A. C. Beckwith, Dr. Barkwell, C. D. Kelley and Gustave

[19]Albert L. New was from Indiana, and had been appointed register of the land office in Evanston.

[20]*The Daily Boomerang* (Laramie), November 8, 14, 1892. The fusion ticket gained control of the Wyoming house of representatives, but the Republicans continued in control of the senate.

E. A. Moeller. Nevertheless, this last Mercer newspaper venture was not to be, for the *Boomerang* soon reported that the scheme was "up in the air," and by mid-March, the *Sun* said the new daily was "out of sight."[21]

Now that the Democrats had won the Wyoming statehouse, they wanted to lay claim to Warren's Senate seat, which was to be filled by the new legislature at the beginning of 1893. Mercer immediately set out to champion the cause of Albert L. New, chairman of the Wyoming Democratic party. He launched this effort on February 6, with an extra edition of the *Journal*, in which he said that he had hoped to be out of politics, but was forced to speak out because there was no Democratic paper in the city.

Of course, there was a Democratic paper in the city. John Carroll's *Leader* had supported Mercer when he first defected from the Republicans, but the *Leader* was now estranged from the New faction of the party. The *Sun* reminded its readers, "Time was when [Mercer] and the *Leader* (and that not so long ago) were good as pie," and called attention to the fact that Mercer, who was, as always, strapped for money, had actually printed the *Journal* extra on paper he borrowed from Carroll's *Leader*. Carroll responded by calling Mercer's efforts on New's behalf, "a Texas steer stagger into politics."[22]

Mercer's support of the New candidacy was aided by the heavy-handed support of Thomas McDonald Patterson of the *Rocky Mountain News* in Denver, who has been called Colorado's first successful Democrat. Patterson had been at the Democratic national convention in Chicago in June 1892, and bolted when an anti-silver plank was adopted. He then led a Populist revolt that delivered Colorado to James B. Weaver, the first time Colorado had not been carried by a Republican presidential candidate. A colorful Irish lawyer, Patterson came to Denver in 1872, served one term as Col-

[21]The *Sun* said the new daily was backed by A. L. New and Beckwith, and would be the organ of the Democratic State Committee. *The Cheyenne Daily Leader*, February 26, 1893, *Cheyenne Daily Sun*, February 22, March 15, 1893.

[22]*Cheyenne Daily Sun,* February 7, 1893.

orado territorial delegate to Congress, and afterward practiced law in Denver, where his practice brought him in contact with Wyoming politics. In 1886-87, he represented the city council of Cheyenne in its efforts to oust the city treasurer.[23]

Patterson's dabbling in Wyoming politics may not have helped the New candidacy, and it was severely criticized by the Republican press; the *Leader* at once complained that the *News* was trying to dictate Wyoming politics. For whatever combination of reasons, Albert New did not become U. S. senator from Wyoming, and the legislature adjourned without electing a senator. Governor Osborne appointed A. C. Beckwith to the position, but the U. S. Senate refused to seat him, and he resigned after five months, leaving the state with only one senator.[24]

Nevertheless, New's devotion to the administration in Washington was rewarded in the summer of 1893 with a consolation prize, as Collector of Internal Revenue for the Colorado district, which included Wyoming. In the meantime, Asa Mercer, who had sacrificed much to support New, waited anxiously for his own reward. While he waited Mercer tried, without much success, to help others among his new-found (Democratic) friends, as when he advocated the candidacy of Elias U. Snider, a member of the so-called "rustler" faction in the TA fight, for United States Marshal from Wyoming.[25]

Finally, Mercer did receive a political appointment, as state statistical agent for the U. S. Agriculture Department, a post that paid $600 per year. This sum, together with the stipend for his work at the World's Fair, helped shore up his declining finances. But that

[23]Patterson was born in County Carlow, Ireland, November 4, 1840, and died July 23, 1916. He bought control of the *News* in 1892. *The Cheyenne Daily Sun*, January 19, 1887. Patterson's dabbling in Wyoming politics earned him severe criticism from the Republican press. *The Buffalo Bulletin*, October 31, 1895, and Robert L. Perkin, *The First Hundred Years: An Informal History of Denver and the Rocky Mountain News* (New York, 1959), 385-87.

[24]A. C. Beckwith died at Evanston, February 5, 1896. *The Buffalo Bulletin*, February 6, 1896.

[25]Snider did not get the appointment.

[26]E. U. Snider was born at Mansfield, Ohio, March 6, 1842, and died at Buffalo, January 23, 1896. *The Buffalo Bulletin*, January 23, 30, 1896.

welcome respite was brief, for the state statistician position was eliminated in June 1895.[26]

The *Journal* had not found a constituency to replace its former patrons, and the financial condition of the paper was becoming increasingly desperate. To make ends meet, the Mercers tried to sell some of the land they still owned in Washington, but the title to the property suffered from some defect. Annie wrote morosely to Daniel Bagley in the spring of 1893 that there was "just a hope" that the *Journal* could be sold, but that hope proved vain, and the paper closed down in the summer of 1893, "without any preliminary convulsions," according to the *Leader*.[27]

Mercer leased the *Journal's* equipment to J. D. Hurd, who had been with the Evanston *Register*, and Hurd told the *Leader* he intended to continue the *Journal* as a stock paper for a time, and also to advocate the cause of silver. Apparently neither of these objectives materialized, although Hurd did publish a Democratic newspaper in Cheyenne. The first issue of the *Wyoming Bee* did not reach the public until the spring of the following year, and its life could not have been long, for no copies seem to have survived.[28]

In its heyday, the *Journal* had enjoyed considerable success as an advocate for the range cattle industry, and it did not deserve an ignominious end just short of its tenth birthday in 1893. Perhaps Asa sensed that injustice to the memory of his paper when he traced its history in an interview he gave in 1911. He said not a word about the Johnson County invasion and its aftermath, and instead claimed that when he left Cheyenne, he sold the paper to J. M. Carey, who then merged it with the Cheyenne *Tribune*, which Asa called the "leading state paper of Wyoming." This would, indeed, have been a prettier ending.[29]

---

[27] *The Buffalo Bulletin* said the World's Fair job had paid Mercer six dollars per day during the six months he spent in Chicago. *The Buffalo Bulletin*, October 11, 1894, and Annie E. Mercer to Rev. Daniel Bagley, March 8, 1893, Clarence B. Bagley collection, University of Washington.

[28] The *Leader's* July 20, 1893, edition noted that the last *Journal* issue had been published a "few weeks" previously. *Northwestern Live Stock Journal*, September 2, 1892. Two of the twenty blank ads were those where the cards of banks had appeared. Also, *The People's Voice*, (Buffalo), May 19, 1894.

[29] *The Big Horn County Rustler*, September 15, 1911.

Asa had not entirely abandoned hopes of influencing political events in Wyoming, and he now turned to a project which he expected to turn the tide in another direction. While it did not achieve the results he expected, this, his most important publication, claimed for Asa Mercer a lasting prominence in the history of the Johnson County War.

Chapter XVII

THE BANDITTI OF THE PLAINS

Mercer had decided to write his version of the story of the Johnson County affray, and while he was working on this book, he had time to act as Cheyenne correspondent for Patterson's *Rocky Mountain News*. The income from this post could not have been significant, but was undoubtedly of some help to his beleaguered finances while the book was in preparation, and after that, he could expect to benefit from the proceeds from the sale of books.

The manuscript was finished before the end of February, 1894 and the book with the ungainly title, *The Banditti of the Plains, or The Cattlemen's Invasion of Wyoming in 1892:* [*The Crowning Infamy of the Ages*], came off the presses in Denver and was sent to the bindery early in August 1894. By the third week in August, copies were in Cheyenne, where the *Sun* declared that the printing and binding were of superior quality, indicating that no expense had been spared in the production of the slim volume.[1]

This "quiet looking" book consisted of 130 pages, bound in black boards, with no outside lettering, and the title page indicated that the book could be purchased for one dollar, or $1.10 if delivered by mail. Sales may also have been made at a discount, for the Douglas *Budget* sneered that a copy could be had for fifty cents cash, and if one were willing to wait, the Democratic state committee would provide one free.

Mercer wanted the book published before the Republican convention convened in August 1894, apparently in the vain hope of

[1]The preface of the book carries the date of February 20, 1894. The *Sun* claimed Albert New, whose new position had taken him to Denver, had supervised the preparation of the book. *Cheyenne Daily Sun*, August 12, 1894.

generating another fusion ticket between Democrats and Populists. When the election campaign opened in September, Asa and his son Ralph began a tour of northern Wyoming in support of the Democratic candidates, selling copies of *The Banditti of the Plains.* They went first to Buffalo, and from there, Asa went over the mountains to the Big Horn Basin, while Ralph went to Lander to sell books there. Ralph later recalled he sold 150 copies in a month.[2]

It has been alleged that the cattlemen seized and burned many copies of the *Banditti*, and although such a story lacks foundation, the original printing of the book is now scarce, and it is interesting to speculate on what happened to copies. We are not certain how many copies of the book were issued, but Mercer's son and daughter both said 1,000 copies were printed, although they thought several thousand more were burned in Denver.

Feelings toward the book ran high, and Ralph said that sometimes he was "cussed out and thrown out" with the book, while Mercer's daughter claimed copies were being purchased for thirty, and then burned. Although it is unlikely that people would have had to pay so much for a copy, it is easy to assume that some purchases were made for the purpose of burning them. Although such purchases would still have given Mercer the financial fruits of his literary effort, they would help to account for the fact so few copies seem to have survived.[3]

The Republicans were at first concerned that the book would revive interest in the invasion, and the *Sun* deplored the attention given to that "unfortunate strife," saying that even the people in Johnson County were willing to "forgive and forget." The *Sun* also suggested that the newspapers of the state should simply ignore the book, but soon its own concern over the potential political damage forced it to print a review and rebuttal.[4]

---

[2] *Cheyenne Daily Sun*, August 22, September 2, 1894.

[3] Nixon Orwin Rush visited Mrs. Louis Webb (Janet Mercer Webb) in the spring of 1951, and eight years later he saw Ralph; their recollections are reported in Rush's book, Mercer's *Banditti of the Plains* (Tallahassee, 1961), passim. Also, Mrs. Noel Morgan, "Memories of a War," *The Billings Gazette*, January 6, 1963.

[4] *Cheyenne Daily Sun*, August 16, 1894.

The title for the book was apparently taken from *The Banditti of the Prairies*, a book written in 1881 by Edward Bonney, about a gang of thieves operating in the Midwest in the 1840s. We can gain some insight into the reason for Mercer's choice of a similar title for his work, if we consider a quote from Bonney's first chapter:

> Organized bands, trampling upon right, and defying all law human or divine, have so annoyed the peaceful and quiet citizens of this great valley, that in the absence of a sufficient judicial power the aid of 'Judge Lynch' has been but too frequently called in, and a neighboring tree proved a gallows and 'a short shrift and strong cord' been the doom of those who have ever plead [*sic*] vainly for mercy at his bar.[5]

This reminds us of Mercer's style of rhetoric, although in Mercer's mind, those who were trampling on human and divine law were the cattlemen.

Mercer's book is a remarkable work, when considered as an exposition of Asa Shinn Mercer. Although the subtitle declares that the work is concerned with the Johnson County Invasion, the first chapter is devoted to the lynching of Jim Averell and Ella Watson. Mercer was not concerned with rehabilitating the reputations of the victims in this incident, for he repeated all the canards about Ella Watson, calling her a "lewd" woman, and using the nickname "Cattle Kate," which in all likelihood was never applied to her during her lifetime. He loftily accused the perpetrators of the lynching of arrogating to themselves the "power over life," and, of course, he omitted any reference to his own "freer use of the hanging noose" recommendation which was written in 1889, at the time of the lynching.[6]

Reviews by the Wyoming newspapers generally reflected the side of the conflict they had chosen to support, but even Mercer's friend, Thomas M. Patterson, at the *Rocky Mountain News*, said that Mer-

[5]Edward Bonney, *The Banditti of the Prairies: A Tale of the Mississippi Valley* (Chicago, 1881), 7. The book was also published as *The Prairie Bandits: A Tale of the Rock River Valley*.

[6]The edition of the Mercer book cited herein is that of the University of Oklahoma reprint of 1954, with foreword by William H. Kittrell, because it is much more accessible than the original edition, even though the foreword contains errors. A. S. Mercer, *The Banditti of the Plains, or The Cattlemen's Invasion of Wyoming in 1892: [The Crowning Infamy of the Ages]* (Norman, Oklahoma, 1954), 18.

cer's pen was "dipped in gall," although he praised the "free, flowing journalistic style" of the work. Patterson particularly applauded Mercer's claims that the cattlemen had tried to muzzle the press, and darkly commented that there had been visits to his offices in Denver by "several prominent Wyoming gentlemen," on a similar mission.[7]

Among the spurious claims in the *Banditti* was the assertion that Dr. Charles B. Penrose had joined the invasion party carrying a case of surgical instruments belonging to Governor Barber, and the *Sun* was at pains to point out that the instruments in question were in a case with Penrose's own name engraved on them. The *Sun* also denied that Penrose had been a college classmate of George Baxter, as Mercer claimed, although it is not clear why that point mattered to anyone.

But the most blatant lie in the book had to do with the murder of George Wellman, foreman of Henry A. Blair's Hoe Ranch, an act that Mercer incredibly attributed to the cattlemen. Wellman, a well-liked young man, had just returned from Wisconsin where he had married, and was shot from ambush on the day after his return to the ranch. Thomas Hathaway, another Hoe hand, was with Wellman when he was killed, and after some hesitation he admitted that he had seen members of the Red Sash gang at the time, one of whom stopped to examine Wellman's body. This gang, which was headed by Charles Taylor, had been terrorizing Johnson County in the anarchic aftermath of the invasion, looting ranches and even trying to burn down the barracks at Fort McKinney.[8]

Mercer's reading of the Wellman case involved yet another conspiracy theory, wherein the cattlemen killed Wellman to force the governor to declare martial law in northern Wyoming. The true facts in the case, as briefly stated above, were well known before the *Banditti* appeared, and no responsible journalist could have believed Mercer's conspiracy theory.

[7] *Rocky Mountain News*, August 26, 1894.

[8] A good analysis of the Wellman case is in Helena Huntington Smith, *The War on the Powder River: The History of an Insurrection,* (New York, 1966), 252ff.

Unfortunately for Mercer, it soon became apparent that these theories had lost their appeal to the public, and when the Republicans perceived that they need not fear him, they turned to the attack. At a monster Republican rally held in Cheyenne just before the 1894 election, Francis E. Warren, who had been timorous in 1892, now waxed wrathful, and lumped Mercer with other Democratic enemies, including, "the sneaking Hurd, the dago Mercer, the windy John Charles and the chameleon A. L. New."

Mercer's image fared somewhat better in northern Wyoming, and when he went to Buffalo in October to sell books and to stump for Democratic candidates, he contributed an attack on Henry G. Hay for Flagg's *People's Voice*. Of course, the Buffalo *Bulletin* castigated him, but that was to be expected from a newspaper that had just switched to the Republican colors.[9]

When Wyoming went to the polls in November of 1894, the Republicans carried every county in the state, and any thought that Asa Mercer was a power in Wyoming politics could safely be discarded. The *Sun* declared, "The people have . . . said to the Mercers, Hurds and Flaggs: 'Get thee behind us, or seek a more congenial clime.'" As a crowning indignity for poor Asa, Joel Hurt had to sue the Mercers on the 1892 note in the Washington courts, where he recovered a judgment that permitted him to sell Annie's Washington land.[10]

The *Banditti*, which was motivated by political considerations, and his anger with his former patrons, was the largest of Asa's several books and pamphlets, and one of the few that was not intended to be a promotional vehicle. The first printing of the book—which most likely was for 1,000 copies—sold out, and in 1916 Asa asked for a quotation to reprint 2,000 copies. Although the bid for the

[9]The *Bulletin* had announced its new affiliation on September 27. *The Buffalo Bulletin*, October 4, 11, 1894, and *The Fremont Clipper*, September 14, 1894, as well as Mrs. Noel Morgan, "Memories of a War."

[10]The judgment was handed down August 28, 1894, and the sheriff's sale was held in 1896, when Hurd bid the land in for the amount of the judgment, \$3,902.65. *The Cheyenne Daily Leader*, November 4, 1894, *Cheyenne Daily Sun*, November 9, 1894, and King County Washington Recorder, Book 205 Deeds, 83.

reprint was only $655, apparently this amount exceeded his resources, and no reprint of the book was issued during his lifetime.

Although the little book was not a financial or political success for Asa, it ultimately was the most significant of his several books and pamphlets. Much later, after his death, and after his copyright had expired, the *Banditti* was reprinted more than once, placing far more copies in the hands of readers than Asa had been able to do, but alas, he and his family did not realize any benefit from that later publishing success.[11]

At this time, Annie's health once again was cause for serious concern, as she found she was suffering from cancer and had a hysterectomy. In the spring of 1895, she went to Galveston to recover from the operation. While Asa waited for her return, he was also contemplating another change of scenery. Writing and selling the *Banditti* had occupied him during the period after the demise of the *Journal*, but with the conclusion of that work, he was ready for new challenges. This time he was not looking back toward Texas, but instead he turned north, to the west slope of the Big Horn Mountains, where he would add ranching to the long list of occupations he had tried.[12]

[11]Omaha Printing Company to Asa S. Mercer, July 12, 1916. Weintz collection.

[12]Asa S. Mercer to Clarence Bagley, March 17, 1895. Mercer later said he took the family to the Big Horn Basin at the beginning of May 1895, which may suggest that Annie was still in Galveston when the family moved.

Chapter XVIII

The Big Horn Basin

Mercer knew a great deal about ranching, and the place he chose to enter the business was still dominated by the cattle interests. Indeed, the Big Horn Basin, surrounded on three sides by mountains, and without any access to railroads, was one of the more isolated parts of Wyoming, and when the Mercers moved there the Basin had no local government at all within its boundaries. Big Horn County had not yet been organized, and that part of the Basin east of the Big Horn River was still administered by Johnson and Sheridan counties, from Buffalo and Sheridan, while all of the Basin west of the river was in Fremont County, with its seat at Lander. The Basin was still primarily a stock-raising region, although there was a Mormon settlement at Burlington, and a small German colony down on the Big Horn.[1]

The only reasonably convenient access to the Basin was from Montana, to the north, where the final treaty with the Crow Indians had opened a path to Billings. But reaching the rest of Wyoming involved a journey over mountains. The nearest shipping point was on the Northern Pacific at Billings, and most of the cattle in the Basin were shipped over that line, although some were still trailed south over the mountains to the Union Pacific. In the next ten years, this picture would change dramatically, and the expectation of such a change might well have furnished the impetus for Asa's choice of the Basin for his new home.

In a 1963 interview, Ralph Mercer remembered that he and his father had visited the Big Horn Basin "often" before the family

[1]Big Horn County was created in 1890, but not organized until 1897.

moved there in the spring of 1895, and we know he was there selling books and campaigning for Democrats in October 1894. On one such occasion, Mercer met Samuel Washington Hyatt, who had laid out the town of Hyattville some years before. Hyatt showed him 1,000 acres of bench land, still owned by the government, lying along Paintrock Creek near Hyattville.

In 1911 Asa said that he had brought his family to Hyattville on May 3, 1895, and their trip north was interrupted by a spring storm which stranded them on the divide between the Laramie and North Platte rivers, making it necessary for him to shovel three miles of snow. Once in the Basin, Asa laid out what was to be the Mercer Ranch on the land Sam Hyatt had pointed out to him, and in the fall of 1895 Asa and his four children filed homesteads on 800 acres; he also bought another 160 acres. The irrigation ditch to serve this land, which had the priority of the spring of 1896, was named for his daughter Anita. Hay was planted on this land to serve the cattle herd they were to assemble, and although the herd was only large enough to produce thirty-five calves in 1898, the future was bright for the operation, which was the largest on Paintrock Creek by the summer of 1916.[2]

These holdings were later transferred to the Mercer Brothers Land and Livestock Company, a Wyoming corporation organized in 1909, with a capitalization of $100,000. A sign of the declining position of old Asa was the fact he only received 80 of the 1,000 shares, the balance being equally divided between his sons, Asa, Jr., and Ralph.[3]

The family soon established other ties to the community, and both of Asa's daughters married after the family moved to Hyattville, Anita in 1896 to John Weintz, a neighboring rancher, and two years

[2]Homesteads were filed by Asa, Asa, Jr., Bowman, Ralph, and Janet, and the patents issued in 1903 and 1904, after an unsuccessful contest to the filings in the fall of 1895. *The Buffalo Bulletin*, September 12, 1895. Asa's account of the 1895 journey may well have been exaggerated, as the interview in which it appears contains other obvious errors; he was then an old man, nearly blind. *The Big Horn County Rustler*, September 18, 1891.

[3]Mrs. Noel Morgan, "Memories of a War," *The Billings Gazette*, January 6, 1963, and *The Big Horn County Rustler*, July 7, 1916.

later, Janet married Louis A. Webb. Webb was born in Louisiana in 1865, and in 1886 he brought 254 horses up the trail from Texas, through Kansas to Buffalo. The following year he went to work for the Bar C ranch.

In later life, Webb apparently enjoyed the trust and friendship of his neighbors, but during his early years in Johnson County he unquestionably fell in with a group who had a bad reputation. Two years after starting with the Bar C, Webb turned his back on the big cattle outfits, and bought an interest in the Hat brand, which O. H. (Jack) Flagg had purchased from W. R. Hathaway in 1886, and was then owned by Flagg and three others. When Flagg purchased the brand, there were then about ten head of cattle branded with it, and in the summer of 1887, he purchased ten mavericks. It is said that these were the only cattle purchased under the brand, but by 1889, the Hat brand had enough cattle to run its own wagon on the roundup, and when the partnership was dissolved, there were about 500 head of cattle available to be disposed of.[4]

This was a period when there were few convictions for livestock theft in Johnson County, and when Lou Webb and three other men were charged with horse stealing in 1889, they were acquitted after trial, although Judge Saufley stated publicly that they were guilty. In June of that year, the grand jury at Buffalo indicted Webb and five others for cattle theft, but after the four men were acquitted on the earlier charge, the prosecuting attorney, after consulting with Judge Saufley, concluded further prosecution of these men would be a waste of public money. The following year, the Hat brand partnership was dissolved, and most of the cattle sold in small bunches to people in the neighborhood, although Fred G. S. Hesse said that Webb and Gardner kept a remnant of the herd.

That there was bad blood between Webb and the big cattle outfits is easy to document. In the spring of 1892, when the breakaway

[4]The account of the ownership and operation of the Hat brand is taken in large part from an account written by Fred G. S. Hesse for Major Frank Wolcott, and sent to Wolcott under cover of January 25, 1893. Fred G. S. Hesse collection at the American Heritage Center, University of Wyoming.

Northern Wyoming Farmers and Stockgrowers Association scheduled its own roundups in advance of the official roundups, Webb was a member of their roundup committee. After the Johnson County Invasion, Charles Carter, foreman for the TA Ranch, swore that Lou Webb told him he must leave the area, or die. Later Webb was accused of plotting to kill Frank Canton when Canton finally returned to Buffalo in 1899.[5]

Nevertheless, after the Hat brand partnership was dissolved, Webb was apparently a respected member of the community, ranching on the eastern slope of the Big Horns. This example of the rehabilitation of those involved in the Johnson County conflict is more than trivial testimony to the contemporary community views on the subject. Rabid partisans on the subject abounded, on both sides—and still do—and significant numbers clearly saw justification for some of the so-called "rustlers'" actions, while others merely discounted the truth of published accounts.

Certainly, Webb's new father-in-law saw nothing wrong with his character, and the fact that Webb was an active member of the Democratic party certainly did not hurt his standing with Asa. Moreover, Webb was running 2,000 head of cattle on the Powder River, and was "prosperous"—a rare adjective in the Mercer family— and after the couple married, Asa proudly pointed out that the young man could afford to take his bride to spend the winter in the South and in Mexico.[6]

Ink was still in Asa's blood, and just two years after settling on Paintrock Creek Mercer was representing yet another newspaper, the Basin City *Herald*, in a cause that, for a change, was universally popular. The Billings *Gazette*, hailing him as "an old time news paper man," said Asa was in Billings to rally support of merchants to urge

[5]Affidavit of Charles Carter, dated June 10, 1892, Carey collection, American Heritage Center, University of Wyoming. The story of the proposed attempt on Canton's life, which was to avenge the murder of John Tisdale, was passed down in the Tisdale family. Robert K. DeArment, *Alias Frank Canton*, (Norman, Oklahoma, 1996), 241–42.

[6]The Hat brand was still owned by Webb & Hill in 1897. *The People's Voice* (Buffalo), March 20, 1897; also *Cheyenne Sun*, April 5, 1892, and Asa S. Mercer to Clarence B. Bagley, May 2, 1899. Weintz collection.

the post office department to improve the notoriously unreliable mail service to the Big Horn Basin, by increasing delivery from tri-weekly to daily. Mercer, confident, as usual, predicted he could enlist both the Montana and Wyoming congressional delegations in this cause.[7]

In 1896 Mercer honed his promotional skills, and traveled to the East to lecture on the beauties of Yellowstone Park, to promote tourism, and—not incidentally—to feed another Mercer business venture. Asa picked up tourists at the railroad station in Sheridan, and conducted them on a thirty-day itinerary. From Sheridan they were taken through the Big Horn Basin to Yellowstone National Park, and then south to Jackson's Hole, and back by way of Lander and Thermopolis to Sheridan. The journey was conducted using a fine four-horse team, at the not inconsiderable charge of $350 per passenger. Although this venture did not last long, it did not fail immediately, and struggled on for a couple of years.[8]

Mercer could not avoid commenting on political matters, and when there was another proposal to cede the public lands to the states where they could be leased, he rose up to oppose the idea, although for a different reason than he had used in 1892. This time, he said that leasing would "wipe out the real population" of the State, and bankrupt most.[9]

Annie's health did not improve, and in the spring of 1899 Asa told Clarence Bagley that she had been sick most of the winter. In the fall of the following year, she died while living with her daughter, Janet Webb. Of her eight children, four had preceded her in death, three in infancy and one as a teenager. It had been thirty-four years since Annie, the pious Catholic, threw in her lot with the twenty-seven-year-old redheaded Methodist. She had endured all of the insults and suffering that befell the Mercer family, and if she complained, no complaint ever received public attention. As

[7] *The Billings Gazette*, October 5, 1897.

[8] Document VII, in Charles W. Smith, "Asa Shinn Mercer," 361-63, and *The Big Horn Rustler*, quoted in *The People's Voice* (Buffalo), July 3, 1897.

[9] *Wyoming Derrick*, March 1, 1900 and John Rolfe Burroughs, *Guardian of the Grasslands: The First Hundred Years of the Wyoming Stock Growers Association* (Cheyenne, 1971), 219.

for Asa, certainly many people were eager to attribute all sorts of failings to him—true, and untrue—but none ever accused him of being unfaithful to Annie. After Annie's death, Asa spent most of his time with his daughter Janet, although he spent the winter of 1905-06 in Chicago.[10]

Despite all the financial reverses he had suffered, Asa still managed to hold on to small parcels of land in Washington, and he continued to try to realize on them. There was some waterfront land on Whidby Island, some on Camano Island and some north of the mouth of the Snohomish River.

Asa was always eager to make public appearances, and he did not cavil if the audience was small. He delivered his paper "The Pioneer," at the Opera House in Basin in the fall of 1905, which the *Republican* declared was a "masterly" performance, and he spoke at the literary club meeting in Manderson in the fall of 1910. When the farmers in Worland held a meeting to consider signing contracts with the Billings sugar factory to grow sugar beets, Asa gave a talk on beet raising. Perhaps his short stint with the Department of Agriculture had prepared him to speak on a subject about which he had had no previous experience. His thirst for speaking opportunities even contributed to a softening of the old battle lines, and he was on the program of the 1914 meeting of the Wyoming Stock Growers Association, speaking on the subject, "Baby Beef." He thus officially ended his estrangement from that group, although there were doubtless individual members who still nursed a grudge against him.[11]

Asa became obsessed with the desire to return to Seattle, where he had been so warmly received in the fall of 1888. Specifically, he wanted to deliver a Fourth of July oration in Seattle, since he claimed that he had delivered the first Fourth of July oration in that city in 1861. He volunteered to do this in 1902, and he repeated his request at intervals in the years that followed. His 1906 request emphasized

[10]Annie Mercer died October 16, 1900. Asa S. Mercer to Clarence B. Bagley, May 2, 1899, November 12, 1901, April 30, 1906. Weintz collection.

[11]*Basin Republican*, August 16, 31, 1905.

that he would have to be paid transportation and hotel costs for both himself and a companion, since the boys would no longer permit him to travel alone.

While the Seattle opportunity continued to be tantalizingly out of reach, a particularly nostalgic opportunity to speak did arise when Franklin College, Asa's old alma mater in Pennsylvania, invited him to deliver the graduation address in the spring of 1908. The next year the Memorial Day observance at Basin featured reminiscences from veterans of the Civil War, and Asa delivered an "eloquent" tribute to the living and dead of that conflict, doubtless avoiding the subject of his own whereabouts during the war.

It was also in 1909 that Asa's Fourth of July dream for Seattle was finally realized. He spent ten days in Seattle, where he attended the Alaska-Yukon-Pacific Exposition, held on the campus of the University of Washington, and delivered the principal address for the Fourth of July celebration, where the Washington governor also spoke.[12]

Asa celebrated his sixty-first birthday in 1900. He could look back over many different ventures in the years past, none of them particularly successful, but all of them exciting. Although he had settled in the relative remoteness of the Big Horn Basin, he still had the vision that the right promotion could bring settlement and economic growth, and he was prepared to devote his energies to that vision.

[12]Asa S. Mercer to Clarence B. Bagley, March 3, 1902 (written from Omaha), April 30, 1906, Weintz collection, *Seattle Post-Intelligencer,* September 15, 16, 1888, *The Big Horn County Rustler*, June 5, 1908, June 4, July 19, 1909, and *Basin Republican*, June 18, 1909.

Chapter XIX

THE LAST PROMOTION

When Mercer arrived in Big Horn County in 1895, he found conditions that in some respects were reminiscent of his experiences in west Texas more than a decade earlier. By the turn of the century, Big Horn County had been organized, after a bruising contest to decide the location for the county seat, but it still only had 4,300 people, and there were no incorporated towns within its boundaries; Basin, the county seat, would not be incorporated until 1902. Of course, the sparse pattern of settlement reflected the difficulties of communication and transportation, and in the first decade of the new century, transportation would be dramatically improved.[1]

As Mercer knew from his Texas experiences, the coming of the railroads would bring rapid growth, and he expected this scenario would be repeated in Wyoming. By 1905 the Burlington railroad had built its Toluca spur to Cody, in the northwest corner of the Big Horn Basin, and rumors soon flew that the railroad would build south into the heart of the Basin. Indeed, in the fall of 1905, the railroad gave official notice that it would build south from Frannie, but even before they had done so, the people began to arrive.

In the first five years of the new century, population in the county more than doubled, to nearly 9,000, and farmers had arrived in some numbers. They had already taken up 174,000 acres of land, of which nearly 54,000 were cultivated, and the census of 1905 counted more than 15,000 acres of grain, 21,000 acres of alfalfa and more than

[1]At the end of the nineteenth century one of its population centers actually left Big Horn county, when the merchants at Thermopolis moved their operations south to the so-called "new town," after the hot springs there were purchased from the Indians in the spring of 1896. This new location was now located in Fremont County. *The Thermopolis Record*, undated, but 1901.

20,000 fruit trees. Although more than 3,000 people lived in towns, these settlements were mostly small, and only seven could count more than fifty people. Cody, with 1,200 people, was the only town larger boast than 500, and there were only 206 in Hyattville, next door to the Mercer ranch.[2]

It was a young society, with nearly 4,000 people under age twenty-one, and there was a bad imbalance of the sexes among those of marriageable age. The county had 1,262 single males over twenty-one, but only 118 single females of that age, a ratio reminiscent of Mercer's days in Washington Territory. Soon the media were calling attention to the disparity, much as they had in that earlier instance. At the end of the year, the *Big Horn County News* in Meeteetse noted that the Grey Bull Club of Meeteetse had raised a fund to advertise in the East, offering "profitable employment" to young women who would make the journey to the Basin.

Responses from this advertising were soon coming in, and young ladies were offering to correspond with "some nice bachelor, with a view to mutual benefit;" the *News* offered to distribute these letters to those "suited to the case," without stating the editor's suitability standards. While these efforts were undoubtedly serious, the *Thermopolis Record* saw the chance to have some fun, saying that the region could offer "anything from an unbusted cow puncher to a dude drug clerk, or a corpulent mine owner," all eager to become the "worser half" of a marriage. Early the following spring, the *Record*, commenting on the dozen divorce cases then pending in Basin, returned to the subject of the mail order brides, saying, "the men of [Big Horn County] will do well to keep what wives they have."[3]

Asa Mercer undoubtedly read these stories, and we would suppose the subject was discussed at family dinners, but Asa did not step forward to lead an expedition of single women to Wyoming. Nevertheless, the shortage of marriageable women was real, and if

[2] *Census of Wyoming*, 1905 (Cheyenne, 1905), and *Basin Republican*, July 12, 1905.

[3] *Basin Republican*, June 12, December 28, 1905, and *The Thermopolis Record*, December 30, 1905, March 31, 1906. When Asa moved to the Basin in 1895, there were only 704 inhabitants of that portion of Johnson County west of the Big Horn Mountains, and there were 2.4 adult males for every adult female. *The Buffalo Bulletin*, June 27, 1895.

old Asa made no public statement on the subject, his son, Asa, Jr., did. Early in 1906, the younger Asa complained to the *Republican* that there were upwards of thirty bachelors on Paintrock Creek, and not a single marriageable woman. "Even a few old maids would look good to us," he said.[4]

If Asa did not devote his energies to attract single women to the Basin, he did see the opportunity to do the sort of promotional work he had often done before. We have already mentioned his Yellowstone Park venture, which he started soon after his arrival in the Basin. In 1897 he went back east again, on the first of several journeys to bring investors and settlers to the Basin. This time he was nominally the representative of the Basin City *Herald*, and such sponsorship usually meant that the sponsor was paying expenses.

Unfortunately, Mercer's timing for this promotional trip was bad, although this time his nemesis was a Western Indian, rather than a young feminist. While he was collecting his prospective investors for a fact-finding tour to the Basin, a Northern Cheyenne Indian killed a sheepherder on the reservation in Montana, just north of the Wyoming border. This incident caused Asa's would-be investors to bolt from his expedition, leaving Asa with only an anti-Indian editorial in the Buffalo *Bulletin* to show for his labors.[5]

Nevertheless, as we have repeatedly seen, Asa was not easily discouraged, and at the end of 1905, he was back in Basin, where he raised the money to spend four months in Chicago, laying the groundwork for another promotional expedition to the Big Horn Basin. He was touting all the opportunities in the Basin, and on his return to the East, he sent along some hard evidence of the riches to be found to back up his enthusiastic claims. He went to Bald Mountain and picked up 100 pounds of gravel, which he said was

[4]*Basin Republican*, March 8, 1906. Also in 1905, D. Clem Deaver, who worked for the Burlington railroad, mentioned to a newspaper reporter in Omaha that there were 3,000 bachelors in the West who needed wives, and he was overwhelmed by letters in response.

[5]In April of 1897, Whirlwind (also known as David Stanley) killed John Hoover, setting off a panic among neighboring ranchers; it was to be the last major conflict between Cheyennes and settlers in this region. Tom Weist, *A History of the Cheyenne People* (Billings, Montana, 1977), 142. Also, *The People's Voice* (Buffalo), July 3, 1897, and *The Buffalo Bulletin*, July 22, 1897.

rich in "float gold," and shipped it to Chicago, to be viewed by prospective immigrants.[6]

One of the key developments Mercer was touting was the coming of the railroad to the Basin, and when the Burlington built south to the county seat by the middle of June, Asa had his promotional materials ready. The first train arrived in Basin on June 19, 1906, and the following week Mercer delivered copies of his newest book to subscribers. The title of the book was *Big Horn County, Wyoming: Gem of the Rockies*. In this slim volume Mercer promoted the Big Horn Basin in exactly the same format as he used in the promotions he had written years before for Washington Territory and Marion County, Oregon.

In an interview with the *Republican*, Asa was his old optimistic self, asserting that the Basin would soon be the beet sugar producing center of the United States, and declaring that Wyoming apples could be shipped to eastern markets, paying all transportation and leaving "a margin of velvet." The editor was caught up in Asa's enthusiasm, and urged "every man" in the county to buy a copy of Mercer's book, the cost of which was fifty cents.[7]

Mercer spared no hyperbole in his description of the region. He confidently predicted that 50,000 settlers would locate in the Basin in 1906 alone, and warned that in twenty-five years those who had failed to buy land there would not be able to afford it, because the price would be beyond reach. He correctly saw the sugar beet as a major crop for the Basin, but then his imagination took over again, as he predicted there would be more than a dozen sugar factories in the county before 1920.[8]

Although the *Republican* did not say so, an important reason for Mercer's book sales efforts was undoubtedly to help raise money for his travels to the Midwest. He also asked merchants to contribute to his travel expenses for the trip, and the Worland *Grit* noted that a number of towns in the Basin responded favorably. Confirming

[6] *Basin Republican*, July 19, 1906, and *The Worland Grit*, August 23, 1906.

[7] Asa S. Mercer, *Big Horn County Wyoming: The Gem of the Rockies* (Hyattville, Wyoming, 1906). Also, *Basin Republican*, June 21, 28, July 19, September 6, 1906.

[8] Mercer, *Big Horn County*, 4, 5, 18.

this success, the Thermopolis *Record* said that Mercer raised a "good sized subscription" in Thermopolis, which was apparently the last on his circuit of the Basin, before he set out for the east early in December. Asa said he only wanted to raise travel expenses, as he would contribute his time, but without knowing the size of the purse he collected, we have no basis on which to assess that promise.[9]

By the first of February 1907, Asa was reporting back to editors in the Basin on his lectures in the Midwest. He delivered one such lecture in the opera house in Hamburg, Iowa, a place that had already sent a "large crowd" of people to buy land near Worland, and on this occasion he was joined by others from Worland, including the mayor and the editor of the *Worland Grit*. Although the temperature was 10 degrees below zero, the crowd was estimated at 300, and Mercer spoke for more than an hour.[10]

The *Grit* assured its readers that despite the presence of the Worland delegation, Asa's long address did not favor any specific locality in the Basin, but instead "confined his talk to the wonderful resources of Big Horn County." In particular, he called attention to opportunities in farming provided by several new irrigation canals, opportunities in oil, and the tourism possibilities afforded by the hot springs at Thermopolis. After the lecture, the Wyoming contingent gave prospective settlers further information on specific investment opportunities.[11]

The next month Asa was in Illinois, drawing "large and interested" audiences to lectures, which he illustrated with stereopticon views of the Basin country. Mercer's supporters back home got their money's worth in progress reports, if not actual immigration results.

In July 1907, Asa, by then familiarly styled as the "bald headed prophet," escorted James C. Dahlman, the mayor of Omaha, to a banquet hosted (and paid for) by the Basin Commercial Club. Dahlman, who had earned the nickname "cowboy mayor," was no stranger to Wyoming, for he had crossed Wyoming Territory more

[9]The Thermopolis *Record* of December 8, 1906, said that Asa would begin his eastern tour that morning. Also, *The Worland Grit*, December 13, 1906.

[10]Charles Fremont Robertson, the Worland mayor, an important promoter of the town and the nearby Hanover canals, was present for the lecture. *The Worland Grit*, February 14, 1907.

[11]*The Worland Grit*, February 14, 1907.

than once when he was only twenty-five, trailing Oregon cattle to northern Wyoming and Nebraska in the service of the Newman brothers, of western Nebraska. The banquet was intended to inform Dahlman of business opportunities in the Basin, so that this information could be passed on to "capitalists" in Omaha.[12]

In April 1908, Asa returned from another eastern fundraising trip, and he now sat down and wrote a long letter, which the Basin *Rustler* published, setting forth his credentials to be a booster for the Big Horn Basin. He claimed to have visited "practically every part" of the United States, Mexico, Central and South America," and by comparison with those places, the Big Horn Basin was "a more diversified resource" than in "any other part" of the two Americas.

Mercer said that farming under irrigation, rather than natural rainfall, meant that the farmer, by his own work, could be sure to harvest an abundant crop: "No work—no crop." For those seeking other riches, the surrounding mountains were so laden with minerals, including oil and coal, that the mining population the valley would attract gave promise of profit opportunities for "thousands of years."[13]

His clients in the Basin must have continued to open their purses to him, for Mercer did not stay long in the Basin, but went back east where he spent the entire summer of 1908. Although we do not know his full itinerary, the Worland *Grit* noted that he was in Pennsylvania near the end of June. He stayed in the Basin during the fall election campaign, but after the election he went back to Chicago, spending a few days in Omaha, ostensibly boosting the Big Horn Basin, but undoubtedly also promoting his own oil speculations, of which we will say more presently.[14]

Increasingly interested in the mineral wealth of the Basin, Asa returned to the subject of coal deposits in a speech given before the

[12]The *Basin Republican* noted that Mercer was back in town in June 1907. *Basin Republican*, March 8, June 21, July 19, 1907. Dahlman was employed as brand inspector at Valentine, Nebraska, for the Wyoming Stock Growers Association in the years 1883-84. Alfred Sorenson, *The Story of Omaha*, (Omaha, 1923), 613, and *The Worland Grit*, July 18, 1907.

[13]The *Republican* said Asa had been five months in the east, which would leave some months unaccounted for. *Basin Republican*, August 2, 1907, April 10, 1908, and *The Big Horn County Rustler*, April 10, 1908, April 16, 1909.

[14]*The Big Horn County Rustler*, November 13, 1908.

Commercial Club in Basin in the spring of 1909. He declared that there were three million acres of coal lands in the Basin, underlain by a vein averaging ten feet, representing a calculated resource of 47 billion tons, and that was only the *known* resource; "What there is below, no one knows," he said.

Mercer's promotional work earned him a place on the fifteen-man Wyoming delegation to the National Irrigation Congress, which met in Albuquerque at the end of September 1908. The Wyoming delegation, appointed by Governor Brooks, included such men as the state engineer, the state treasurer, and a number of prominent men involved in various aspects of irrigation, including J. M. Carey and Solon L. Wiley.[15]

This public prominence once more induced Asa to seek public office, and he ran for the state house of representatives on the Democratic ticket in both the 1906 and 1908 elections in Big Horn County, and he was also a delegate to the state Democratic convention in 1908. After his return from the east in September 1908, he confided to the *Rustler* that he would also do "a few stunts" in support of William Jennings Bryan's election campaign in the fall of the year.[16]

Asa was actually in Chicago in 1906 when the county convention placed his name in nomination for the legislature, and he claimed that it was done "without my knowledge, consent, or solicitation." This normally Republican county was not friendly to Democrats, and there were also campaign glitches, as when a speech in Hyattville had to be postponed because announcements were not sent out, and a late train forced rescheduling of the Worland rally. Mercer lost both elections for the legislature, finishing last among those running for the Big Horn County seats in 1906, when he did not even carry the nearby precincts of Hyattville or Bonanza. In 1908 he ran sixth in a field of eight, and he also failed to carry either Hyattville or Bonanza. In 1908 Asa explained away the result by saying he was too busy promoting Big Horn County to do any campaigning.[17]

---

[15] *The Worland Grit*, August 20, 1908.

[16] *The Big Horn County Rustler*, September 4, and *The Worland Grit*, June 25, 1908.

[17] *Basin Republican*, October 25, 1906, *The Worland Grit*, November 1, 1906, and *The Big Horn County Rustler*, May 8, October 23, 1908.

His son Ralph briefly entered Democratic politics, serving as precinct chairman in the fall of 1908, but it was Asa, Jr., who became the winning Mercer at the polls. The younger Asa had been mentioned as a possible Republican candidate as early as 1908, and when he decided to enter politics, he opted for the winning side, running for the legislature on the Republican ticket. Asa, Jr., represented the county in the state house in six sessions, 1914–22, and he was elected to the state senate in 1926, after his father's death.[18]

When J. R. Burns of the *Basin Republican* visited the Paintrock Creek valley in January 1907, he commented that the Mercer Brothers were running over a thousand head of cattle, and putting up hundreds of tons of hay. He complimented Ralph and Asa, Jr., (Bowman had already left the family ranch), but there was no mention of the patriarch of the family, although he still held a small interest in the operation.

We have no way to judge the value of Mercer's promotional work for the Big Horn Basin, although the mere fact that he began this work back in 1897, and beginning in 1905 spent a good part of four years in this effort must count for something. While there were booster clubs within the Basin, and the railroad maintained a paid immigration organization, Mercer was the only person who traveled so far afield, promoting the advantages of this region.

Even though the newspapers did not frequently notice him anymore, Asa Mercer was still very much alive, and he was not short on enthusiasm. In the section of his Big Horn Basin book where he described Hyattville, Asa said, "The citizens still have hopes that the great mountains, forming the background of the magnificent view as they greet the morning sun, has something good in store for them." Undoubtedly one of the citizens harboring such hopes was Asa Shinn Mercer.[19]

[18]In 1906, the Republican candidates each polled about 1,600 votes each, while the Democrat candidates were 1,000 or less; Asa Mercer received 945 votes, the poorest showing for the six candidates. In 1908, when four seats were available, the Republicans each polled at least 2,600 votes, and the Democrats received at least 1,600; Mercer received 1,630 votes, placing second among the Democrat candidates. *Basin Republican*, November 15, 1906, and *The Worland Grit*, September 24, 1908.

[19]Asa S. Mercer, *Big Horn County, Wyoming: The Gem of the Rockies* (Hyattville, Wyoming, 1906), 91.

Chapter XX

RANGE WARS *DÉJÀ VU*

Much as the Johnson County invasion in the spring of 1892 was a shocking interruption of the orderly growth and development of society in northeastern Wyoming, the Spring Creek raid of 1909 was a rude interruption and awakening to society of the Big Horn Basin. Aside from being a traumatic event in the Basin, the raid and its aftermath attracted much unfavorable attention from outside the immediate area, and even from outside the State of Wyoming, just as the Johnson County affair had done seventeen years earlier. Once again, Asa Mercer entered the controversy, although less forcefully than in the nineties.

Conflict between cattlemen and sheepmen probably arose with the beginnings of the herding of cattle and sheep, but it was not a problem during the early history of Wyoming because the livestock industry tended to be dominated by cattleman. Indeed, in 1870 there were only 800 sheep in Wyoming. After the turn of the twentieth century, sheep raising in Wyoming became a much larger industry. By 1908 there were 4.6 million sheep, and the following year the total would be 5.1 million, making Wyoming the "banner" sheep state in the Union. It was thus inevitable that conflict would arise over the use of the range, which still consisted largely of public land.

Recognizing the inevitability of arguments over access to grass, the sheep and cattle men in the ceded portion of the Wind River Reservation agreed at the end of 1906 to formally divide the range between sheep and cattle interests, but such a negotiated settlement was the distinct exception. More usual was the unilateral declaration of so-called "dead lines," marking someone's idea of the limits between the two industries. Consequently, tensions continued to build up all over northern Wyoming.

At the end of 1907, in a raid by eight masked men on a band of sheep in Crook county, 600 head of sheep were shot and several hundred others wounded. Late in January 1908, two sheep outfits were burned on the upper Powder River, and in April, three masked men burned a sheep wagon on Crystal Creek, in Big Horn County. This was followed in May by a raid on a sheep camp in the Crowheart Butte area of Fremont County.

These were only preliminary skirmishes, but they were followed by an event that captured the attention of everyone in the Big Horn Basin, and many people beyond. Late one night in February 1909, several masked men raided a camp at the mouth of Spring Creek, in Big Horn County, burned two sheep wagons, killed a number of sheep, and killed sheepmen Joe Emge, Joseph Alleman, and their herder, Joseph Lazier.[1]

Two men were soon arrested and charged with murder, and a grand jury was impaneled to question fifty witnesses, including virtually every person who could have known about the raid. One man who testified was later found shot to death, and a hastily summoned coroner's jury pronounced the death a suicide, although some expressed doubts at this conclusion. The use of the grand jury proved an effective instrument of investigation, for it soon became apparent that the participants in the Spring Creek raid had not been particularly quiet about their actions, and before long there was a dramatic break in the case. On May 6, five cattlemen were arrested in Basin and charged with the murder of the three men on Spring Creek.

While all this was going on, Asa was apparently in Chicago, for he returned to the Basin at the end of May. Soon, he took up his pen to enter this new controversy, and in October the *Republican* reproduced an article which Asa had written for the Omaha *World-Herald*. Interestingly enough, Asa's article was intended to counter the impact of the Spring Creek raid on his own promotional efforts

[1] *Basin Republican*, February 26, April 9, 1909.

in the east. He started off by accusing the media of exaggerating incidents between cattlemen and sheepmen. This accusation must certainly have amused his old enemies who could remember editor Mercer's outpourings in the nineties.

On the general subject of lawlessness, Mercer asserted that people in the West committed only one-tenth the crimes committed by those east of the 98th meridian, although he did not say whether this statistic reflected any adjustment for the relative populations of the two groups. When he turned to the conflict with sheepmen, Asa seemed now to have abandoned his hatred for the cattlemen, and was once more back on their side—perhaps he could not be anywhere else, considering the thriving cattle operation of Mercer Brothers.[2]

In a strange passage, he talked of a poor farmer on a 160-acre homestead, who grazed his few cattle in the surrounding hills, and looked on helplessly as sheepmen "from Utah or some other outlying place" brought in thousands of sheep to eat the grass. When the poor farmer saw his cattle starving, thus taking bread from his family, Asa said that "human nature" broke out, for self-preservation is the "first law of nature." In the abstract, such an argument might have been emotionally appealing, but the Spring Creek raid was not about a farmer killing a sheepman from Utah, or any other "outlying place." Indeed, the two sheepmen who were killed had just paid $15,000 to buy a ranch on Ten Sleep Creek.

Mercer blamed the federal government for failing to protect settlers by leasing grazing land to them, and he understandably neglected to mention that he had bitterly opposed the bills designed to grant the public lands to the states for leasing to users. He ended by calling for action by Congress, saying, "Each and every member is responsible for any crime committed by reason of inadequate laws to protect the people."[3]

After a tense period, during which soldiers guarded the courthouse in Basin, the perpetrators of the Spring Creek raid were ulti-

[2]*Basin Republican*, May 28, 1909.

[3]*Basin Republican*, October 4, 1909.

mately convicted and sentenced, and we hear no more from Asa Mercer on the subject. The incident involved a strange echo from Asa's own past, which he did not mention, for the wife of one of the men convicted of the killings was descended from a prominent cattleman back in Henrietta, Mercer's old Texas headquarters town.[4]

The Spring Creek raid may have discouraged some from moving to the Big Horn Basin, but the interruption in immigration was brief, and the pace of settlement continued to be rapid. The region no longer had need of a promoter, and Asa's promotional work had come to an end. Now, he turned his attention to an opportunity that really promised to make him rich for the very first time.

[4]Bertha Amanda Whaley was the granddaughter of Col. Henry A. Whaley, a veteran of the Mexican and Civil Wars, who came to Clay County, Texas, from Tennessee before the county was organized, and established a ranch on the Red River. J. P. Earle, *History of Clay County and Northwest Texas,* (Austin, 1963), 3ff. Bertha's father drove a herd of cattle from Henrietta to Wyoming about 1888, and then settled in the Big Horn Basin. In 1898, Bertha married George Saban, who walked away from a prison work gang after his incarceration for his role in the Spring Creek raid, and was never officially located thereafter.

Chapter XXI

THE LAST SPECULATION

When Mercer brought his family to settle on Paintrock Creek, just below the town of Hyattville, he was only a few miles upstream from the old town of Bonanza. Named for efforts to exploit nearby oil seeps, this town had enjoyed enough life to support the Basin's first newspaper, if only for a brief time. At the Bonanza oil seeps, located half a mile from the town of Bonanza, the early settlers could gather three to five gallons of oil every day to use in their lamps. In 1890 a Nebraska investment group hauled heavy machinery 400 miles over the mountains to drill near the seeps, in the hopes of finding the oil deposits. After drilling down 800 feet, the company ran out of money.

For a time the Bonanza prospect was idle, but in 1902 another company was organized to work a large number of claims near Bonanza, and they drilled a 1,200-foot well, which may have struck some oil. Later, an Omaha company drilled just 100 feet from the oil seeps, and struck a high grade of oil at 70 feet, which flowed one or two barrels per day. From a formation 200-300 feet lower, they obtained a high grade of oil, which was exhibited and won a prize at the 1904 World's Fair in St. Louis. After drilling to a total depth of 800 feet, the shareholders refused to advance further funds, and the effort was abandoned.[1]

Oil excitement in the Basin was revived in 1905, although not in the Bonanza area, when Philip Minor brought in a small gas well east of Byron, in the northern part of the Basin. The following year a Montana company struck oil in commercial quantities near the

[1] *The Big Horn County Rustler*, June 3, 1910.

same town. In the summer of 1908 Alford Brothers and Lamb drilled a successful oil well and a gas well east of Greybull, and a company that took over these operations subsequently developed a number of wells; they also secured the franchise to supply natural gas to Basin and Greybull.

The significance of these events was not lost on Asa, up at Hyattville, particularly since the apparent riches of Bonanza were almost in his back yard. He could not avoid being bitten by the oil speculation bug, and in the summer of 1902 he and the members of his family filed a number of mining claims in the area near the Mercer ranch.

When he wrote his Big Horn County promotional book in 1906, Asa devoted a fair amount of space to potential oil developments, including those at Bonanza. He described the oil seeps at Bonanza, and he related these occurrences of petroleum to those further north in the Basin, so that the oil zone, as he saw it, extended in a band from near Hyattville, northward seventy miles, to a point in the badlands north of Cowley. In his curious view of the chemistry of petroleum, he supposed that there were separate geological accumulations of the different oil products, such as illuminating oil, lubricating oil, and fuel oil, rather than differing qualities of crude oil, from which these products could be refined.

Asa also had an interesting concept for transporting the oil to markets, arising from reflection on the fact that all of the prospective areas were located at elevations above the route the Burlington railroad was expected to select for its line. He proposed that oil would flow by gravity from the wells to the railroad, from whence it could be transported by rail to refineries, without the need to install pumps on the oil pipeline.[2]

The next notice of oil activity near Bonanza was contained in a November 1907, story in the *Worland Grit*, which noted that "wealthy stockmen" in the Bonanza area were organizing a stock company to drill for oil there. While the paper did not identify the

[2]Mercer, *Big Horn County*, 41ff.

corporation or the shareholders, it is likely that this was a Mercer promotion.[3]

In the fall of 1908, the Mercer Oil Company was incorporated, with a capital of $17,640, and although its principal office was Basin, the articles of incorporation explicitly noted that it was to carry on part of its business outside the state of Wyoming. The *Rustler* said that this company was the successor to Ashton Oil Company, of Ashton, Illinois, which probably refers to the Wyoming Land & Development Company of Ashton, Illinois, which had a number of the same directors as the new Mercer Oil Company.

Mercer was not one of the directors of the Mercer Oil Company, although he wanted the public to believe that he directed its operations, and he was actively trying to raise money to explore the Bonanza field. A second company interested in the Bonanza field was the Halcyon Oil Company, involving capital from Chicago and from South Dakota, which was organized in the spring of 1908; Mercer held 12,000 shares in this corporation.[4]

Mercer was again traveling east to promote investment opportunities in the Basin, but this time he clearly expected to benefit directly from the fundraising. At the end of May 1909, he appeared in the Basin with an oil man from Chicago, and the following month the *Republican* reported that oil drilling equipment was rigging up, just five miles north of the Mercer ranch on Paintrock Creek. The newspaper reported that the drillers expected to reach the oil sand

[3] *The Worland Grit*, November 7, 1907.

[4] The first directors of Mercer Oil Company were [Dr.] Henry A. Bremmer, George A. Over, Samuel T. Zeller, William H. Kugler (probably Kuelger), W. Brown Garret, and Ralph J. Dean. *Basin Republican*, October 9, 1908. Also, *The Big Horn County Rustler*, January 22, 1909, and Weintz collection. The Wyoming Land & Development Company was organized in Ashton, Illinois in the summer of 1907; its directors were Dr. Henry A. Bremmer, Samuel T. Zeller, A. E. Hutchinson, W. Brown Garrett, George A. Over, and William H. Kuelger. It was to purchase 2,720 acres, giving it a total of 7,840 acres (the first tract cost $800). A number of men from Ashton were to go to Wyoming on July 2. *The Worland Grit*, June 20, 1907. The first directors of the Halcyon Oil Company were Charles A. Hallam, Horace B. Goodwin, William V. Smith, Philip Lawrence, and M. H. Lawrence; the first three were from Chicago, while the last two were from Huron, South Dakota. This South Dakota corporation was chartered April 17, 1908, with a capitalization of $1.5 million. When Charles A. Hallam died at the beginning of 1916, the *Rustler* carried the story, noting that he had long been interested in Wyoming oil matters.

"in a few days," and readers were assured that there was not "the slightest doubt" that either oil or gas would be encountered. Asa was too busy to wait for the results so confidently expected, and he went back to Chicago on "important business."[5]

In the fall of 1908 Alford Brothers & Lamb received a franchise to provide natural gas to the town of Basin, and Asa was determined that the Greybull producing area should not shut him out of that market for the gas he was certain he would find. The following week he was able to persuade the town council of Basin to grant him the same sort of franchise as had been granted to Alford Brothers & Lamb. He told the council that he had leases on several thousand acres of land, and that the money to bring the gas to Basin was "in sight." After securing a thirty-year franchise, Mercer set off once again for Chicago, perhaps to firm up the promises he had already made. Unfortunately for Asa, near the end of 1908 Alford Brothers & Lamb did strike the gas necessary to supply their franchise, and he did not.[6]

This competitive setback was only temporary, for in the spring of 1909 there was more evidence of real activity surrounding Mercer's oil speculations. He was hiring a man and team to haul water, and a man and team to haul coal for his oil drilling outfit. In May, the drilling rig arrived from Chicago and was unloaded from the train in Basin, and Asa, who could no longer contain his enthusiasm, told the *Worland Grit* he expected soon to be "one of the western oil kings." At the end of the month, he was showing the Basin oil lands to a party of eastern investors.[7]

Drilling commenced in the summer of 1909 at a point six miles north of the Mercer ranch, but it was not undertaken by either of the two corporations Mercer had previously been involved with.

---

[5] *Basin Republican*, May 28, June 18, 1909.

[6] Mercer was given the right to charge 25¢ per MCF (thousand cubic feet) during the first two years of the contract, and 30¢ per MCF for the balance of the contract term. *The Big Horn County Rustler*, September 25, November 6, 1908. The Alford Brothers & Lamb partnership, which consisted of Thomas Alford, George L. Alford, and Homer T. Lamb, later changed its name to the Big Horn Oil and Gas Company. *The Big Horn County Rustler*, June 4, 1909.

[7] *The Big Horn County Rustler*, April 30, May 21, 1909, and *The Worland Grit*, May 13, 27, 1909.

The new company was Valley Development Company, a South Dakota corporation, and its president was Asa Mercer, who was to have offices both in Basin, Wyoming, and in Chicago; Asa held 395 shares in this corporation. At the end of 1909 Mercer filed 125 mining locations on 20,000 acres of land, which he then conveyed to Valley Development, and that company was supposed to pay him $1.25 per acre for these claims. At the same time, he signed up a large number of oil and gas leases from other landowners in the area, on a term of five years, with a one-eighth royalty.[8]

In December 1909, the *Rustler* announced that Valley Development was unloading two additional carloads of machinery and pipe to resume drilling, as soon as weather conditions would permit. In preparation for the next year's work, H. D. Haven, who had been in charge of the drilling during the previous summer, returned to the Basin with his assistants. Havens said that the work was being done for one of the Mercer's Illinois companies, apparently a reference to the fact that much of the capital for the operation came from Chicago, although the two corporations were organized in South Dakota. Meanwhile, Asa was back in Chicago, where he spent the winter trying to raise more money.[9]

By the middle of March 1910, Mercer was back in Basin, as optimistic as ever about economic prospects. He expected the Basin would receive thousands of visitors the coming year, and that high livestock prices would make that business very attractive. But he reserved his most expansive comments for the oil and gas business. While he avoided talking about specific development plans, he noted that when the Burlington railroad completed its line from the Puget Sound to the Gulf of Mexico, there would be even more markets for Wyoming oil, such as those in Japan. When the Wyoming Oil Producers Association was organized in Cheyenne, at the end of

[8]Weintz collection. Mining locations Valley 1 through 70 and Senior 1 through 30 were filed in Big Horn County, Wyoming, on December 10, 1909; each covered 160 acres. Leasing of the private lands took place at in the winter of 1909-1910, and again at the end of 1910. *The Worland Grit*, August 26, 1909.

[9]The company referred to by Haven would have either been Halcyon or Mercer Oil, which had Chicago backers. *The Big Horn County Rustler*, December 24, 1909.

1910, Asa Mercer joined, although he had not yet logged a barrel of commercial production. He was immediately assigned as one of the three members of the publicity committee, which was undoubtedly a wise use of his talents.[10]

During 1910 Asa made a succession of somewhat frantic trips to and from Chicago, and he was back in the Basin after the middle of May, just long enough to reassure the *Rustler* and its readers that there would be a "large" development before fall. A week later, he left again for Chicago, returning at the end of July, when he said the future of the oil fields was "never so bright as now."[11]

There was good reason for all this travel and for Asa's reluctance to talk about specific oil development plans: his money-raising operations were not going well. In June 1909, he had begun contacting companies with proposals for exploration of his claims, but he did not succeed in signing anyone up for the work. By the end of 1910 he was becoming desperate, and after there had been no response from one of the prospects, he accused them of "hawking" the papers to others in London. This outburst only served to kill any hope for a deal with the company, which responded testily that if he was not interested in making a deal, they would stop trying to sell the claims.[12]

In the spring of 1911 Asa was still hoping to raise the necessary money to do more drilling, and he set off once more for Chicago; "Won't Be a Quitter," was the headline the *Rustler* gave to the item announcing this trip. Two weeks later the paper noted that it had received two letters from subscribers, including one in Illinois, asking information about oil developments. The editor briefly summarized the only facts of importance: the Greybull field was producing, and another was producing near Cody, but the Mercer filings were still only filings.[13]

Early in July 1911 the *Rustler* carried a letter from Philip Minor,

[10] *The Big Horn County Rustler*, March 18, 1910.

[11] *The Big Horn County Rustler*, May 27, July 29, December 23, 1910.

[12] The "hawking" comment is in a letter from Mercer to W. G. Young, dated November 26, 1910, in the American Heritage Center, University of Wyoming. The response from W. G. Young, Manager of the Franco-Wyoming Oil Company, is dated June 4, 1910. Weintz collection.

[13] *The Big Horn County Rustler*, May 12, May 26, 1911.

who controlled the producing field near Cody. Minor said that shortly after he arrived in the Basin in 1901, a number of mineral claims were filed, and in 1903 a number of corporations were organized and began selling stock. He then recounted the following curious tale:

> Another promoter after locating about a township of bad lands, part of which was real oil and gas land, got up his corporation with a capital of 1.5 million shares and sold his holdings to it for 600,000 shares. He then proceeded as secretary and treasurer of the company to sell all he could of his own stock and use the money to drill a well for another company.[14]

Whatever may have happened in the past, there still seemed to be hope for the Mercer oil prospecting scheme. In the fall of 1911, the *Rustler* reported that W. T. Miller, of North Baltimore, who was in charge of development work at Bonanza for the Mercer Oil Company, told the newspaper that a large company of "capitalists" were going to begin work in the field "shortly." The prospects were fair enough for Asa to announce that he would now make his headquarters in Chicago.

Alas, Asa was home again early in November 1911. In the end, he never found an oil company willing to purchase the claims he had staked in 1909, nor could he even get them to perform the necessary annual assessment work to keep the claims alive, and they all apparently lapsed. At the beginning of 1912 Mercer listed for his son, Asa, Jr., all the money he was owed that he had heretofore not confided to any written record. These sums were all related to his oil speculations, ranging downward from the $30,000 still owed to him by the Valley Development Company. Asa, Jr., wrote back that it would take some speculative excitement to make the Valley Development lands valuable, "As it is," he said, "they are not worth a d—n."[15]

Asa Mercer's last speculation was dead.[16]

[14] *The Big Horn County Rustler*, July 7, 1911.

[15] Asa S. Mercer to Asa S. Mercer, Jr. (from Chicago), January 1, 1912. Weintz collection.

[16] *The Big Horn County Rustler*, August 18, September 1, November 11, 1911.

Chapter XXII

The Last Years

While Asa busied himself with his promotional work and with the oil speculations, his children built their own separate lives. Bowman purchased the Thomas Hotel in Thermopolis in the summer of 1905, later moved to Worland, was in Hyattville by the end of the year, and then moved back to Thermopolis in February 1906, where he leased the Fair Deal saloon. Bowman divorced his wife in the spring of 1908, and married Sadie J. Small at the beginning of 1913.[1]

Asa, Jr., was one of the musicians performing regularly for the dances in Hyattville, and when the new $4,000 opera house was dedicated, he was chairman of the affair. Ralph married Jennie Pritchard in the spring of 1909. Apparently the ranching business was going well for Ralph and Asa, Jr., for they added 160 acres to their landholding, paying $10,000 for the land and crop, raising their total to 1,300 acres, in a compact form.[2]

We wonder what the old man's feelings were when his namesake son ran for the legislature in 1916 on the Republican ticket. Clearly, Asa, Sr., did not conceal his own preference for the other side, for just before the 1916 elections, he came down from Hyattville to Basin, to hear Joseph M. Carey and J. D. Clark speak in support of the Democratic ticket. Nevertheless, Asa, Jr., did what his father had not been able to do, for he led the Republican slate to victory in 1916, and would be returned to the legislative several more times.[3]

Although his health had generally been good, old Asa fell on the

[1] *The Thermopolis Record*, June 10, 1905, February 3, 1906.

[2] *Basin Republican*, March 27, 1908, September 18, 1908, *The Worland Grit*, March 1, 1906, and *The Big Horn County Rustler*, March 27, 1908, March 19, 1909, August 12, 19, 1910, February 14, 1913. Mercer Brothers were shareholders of the opera house.

[3] *The Big Horn County Rustler*, October 20, 1916.

Asa Mercer in later years.
Courtesy of Wyoming Division of Cultural Resources.

ice in Chicago in 1900, making it necessary for him to walk with a cane, and at the time of Ralph's wedding, Asa was ill enough to rate notice of the matter in the *Rustler*. He suffered another fall in the winter of 1909-10, and fell a third time at the end of 1911.[4]

In spite of these physical limitations, new speculations still had their appeal with Mercer, and in 1912 he wrote to inquire about a story that Texas school lands were going to be sold on easy terms. He said that he wanted to buy 100,000 acres, paying 5 percent down and 3 percent interest on the balance; but fortune again evaded him.[5]

Cataracts finally affected his eyesight by 1910, and in the fall of 1915, Asa wrote Bagley, saying that he had been under treatment for his eyes for two years, and had undergone cataract surgery on both eyes. Although his vision was impaired, Asa continued to write, publishing *The Pioneer* in 1913, which consists chiefly of the lecture he had delivered some years before, and in 1916 he published his last work, *Indian Chief Washakie and the Big Horn Hot Springs*. The

[4]Asa S. Mercer to Clarence B. Bagley, April 30, 1906. Weintz collection. Also, *The Big Horn County Rustler*, March 19, 1909, February 14, 1913.

[5]Asa S. Mercer to Investor Publishing Company (from Chicago), February 9, 1912. Weintz collection.

latter pamphlet of twenty-four pages, gives a short biography of Chief Washakie, and an enthusiastic description of the hot springs at Thermopolis, including the assertion that the water would "generally" cure syphilis and rheumatism, as well as "practically all kinds of stomach, kidney and liver troubles." These last two works were far less than Asa had hoped to turn out, for he had at least two other books in mind, one of 200 pages and a second twice as long. Clearly, the infirmities of the flesh stayed that prolific hand.[6]

Incredibly, the old man still had the energy for a political fight, and at the beginning of 1912 he was determined to defeat Theodore Roosevelt's ambitions for regaining the presidency. Mercer wrote to Champ Clark, Speaker of the U. S. House of Representatives, saying that he intended to deliver 50-100 speeches in support of Democratic candidates during the campaign, and requesting certain background information for use in this effort.[7]

Despite his infirmities, Asa decided to make a nostalgic trip back to Texas, beginning at the end of 1916. He was feeble enough to require Janet and her husband to accompany him to the train at Clearmont, near Sheridan, from whence he traveled first to Henrietta, his old headquarters for the Texas newspapers, and then to Goodnight, Texas, to visit with a life-long friend. His final destination was San Antonio, where he expected to spend the winter.[8]

Although Asa did not tell the Basin editors who he expected to visit in Goodnight, Texas, that town was not a large one, and its most prominent citizen at the time was the venerable cattleman, Charles Goodnight, who was then eighty. We have no other record that would indicate that Asa had known Goodnight, but Goodnight was a good friend of the Ikards, of Henrietta, and Asa certainly knew a great deal about the famous cattleman, whose

[6]A. S. Mercer, *Indian Chief Washakie and the Big Horn Hot Springs* (Hyattville, 1916), 19. In 1913, Mercer promised he would publish *Readon and Instinct*, of more than 200 pages, and *Rythms from the Log of the Duphuny Club*, of 400 pages. He expected to have both on the market before the middle of 1914. A. S. Mercer, *The Pioneer* (Chicago, 1913), 14, 15.

[7]James Beauchamp "Champ" Clark was a leading contender for the Democratic nomination, and actually led in the first 14 ballots; Woodrow Wilson was nominated on the 46th ballot. Asa S. Mercer to Clarence B. Bagley, August 6, 30, 1915, and Asa S. Mercer to Champ Clark, February 28, 1912. Weintz collection.

[8]*The Big Horn County Rustler*, December 15, 1916.

involvement with the Goodnight-Loving trail and the JA ranch in the Panhandle was legendary.[9]

After his return from the southwest, Asa's health began to fail noticeably. Anita and Ralph were summoned to Buffalo early in May 1917, and a second summons brought all his children to his side, the *Rustler* reporting that he was "critically ill." Nevertheless, at the beginning of June, Ralph said his father was "gradually improving," but this hope was vain. On August 9, 1917, Ralph was again called to Buffalo, and the next day, Asa Shinn Mercer died, of a prolonged bout with chronic dysentery. He was seventy-eight years old.[10]

Clarence Bagley, who had married Asa's niece, had the opportunity to observe Mercer in action over most of his life, and in 1908, he responded to a request for information about the Mercers. He began by noting that all of the rest of the Mercer family were "eminently truthful," although he protested that he did not want his comments to get back to Asa and hurt his feelings. Bagley then added, "I have never been able to rid myself of a liking for him, though he has given me and so many of my relatives and friends cause for bitterness toward him."[11]

In 1929, after Mercer's death, Bagley again summed up Mercer's long and diverse experiences, saying, "He was supremely optimistic of the successful outcome of his many ventures—and in later years there were many of them—but few of them materialized." Casting about for an example from literature to describe Asa, Bagley selected Dickens' Mr. Micawber, who was always waiting for something "to turn up," and ever confident that "everything would turn out for the best." Perhaps this characterization is as apt as any other we could select.[12]

---

[9]Goodnight, who had divested himself from interests in the JA and Quitaque ranches, had a small ranch by the railroad, and lived in Goodnight, Texas, until he died, December 12, 1929.

[10]*The Big Horn County Rustler*, May 4, 18, June 1, August 10, 17, 1917, and *The Basin Republican*, August 17, 1917.

[11]Clarence B. Bagley to Julia H. Emery, January 3, 1908. Weintz collection.

[12]In 1916, Bagley wrote his *History of Seattle*, and in 1919, he brought out his *History of King County Washington*. They were both three-volume works, and the latter repeated much material from the earlier publication. In each case there was a chapter on Mercer's 1864 and 1866 expeditions, but in the 1929 work, which was published after Mercer's death, Bagley obviously felt the need to comment on Mercer's life. Clarence B. Bagley, *History of King County Washington I*, (Chicago, 1929), 230-31.

EPILOGUE

The almost incredible diversity of Asa Mercer's experiences is perhaps the most striking feature of his story. In adventures spanning the American continent, Asa was a surveyor, a teacher, an immigration promoter, collector of customs, ship salvager, manager of a shipping line, editor and publisher of books and newspapers, and finally a farmer and a rancher. The list boggles the mind, and the unlikelihood of it all mounts up when one considers that these experiences were mostly financed by others' money. It is, withal, a remarkable story, and if written as fiction, would be termed unbelievable.

It is easy to tick off the important instances where Mercer stumbled, including the smuggling case, and his ungenerous treatment of the young women from New England, which made the great "Mercer's Belles" project less noble than it might otherwise have been. Still, those who did go to Seattle with him on that amazing journey seem to have thrived, and—of more importance for our analysis—not to have borne him ill will.

Mercer had the annoying habit of rewriting his own history, even when little could be gained by the exaggeration. Thus, he claimed to have crossed the Mississippi as a small boy, when the whole region from there to the Pacific was "unpeopled save by the red man." Untrue, but not much more spectacular than the reality of the frontiers that he entered more than once in his early years.[1]

Also, Asa made himself the first president of the University of Washington, although he was only the sole teacher for a collection of students, ranging from first grade through college. Yet, the truth was important enough, for he provided the first organized instruction for many of these students in that mostly unlettered region.

[1]Asa Shinn Mercer, *Big Horn County Wyoming: The Gem of the Rockies* (Hyattville, Wyoming, 1906).

Similarly, he often repeated the inflated figure of 300 women for the emigration voyage, as though bringing 75 women to the hostile west was not enough to boast of. Finally, it was surely a considerable accomplishment to open four newspapers nearly simultaneously on the Texas frontier, without the need to assert that he owned all the newspapers from Decatur, Texas, west to the New Mexico line.

To be sure, Mercer spent money unwisely—money that often belonged in some sense to others—but much of this extravagance can be traced to the foolish exuberance that refused to wait for the results of the last week's promotion, before launching the next one. As a consequence, he had little staying power, so that, for example, his investment in the string of Texas newspapers was liquidated before the region they served could grow up to support them, and perhaps even to make him rich.

What of Mercer, the man? If we look for consistent principles that may have guided his life, or some major portion of it, we face a daunting task. A search for such principles among his writings and such spoken utterances as we have the record of, will be mostly unrewarding, and pragmatism is the word that we would use, time and again, as the explanation for his words and deeds. Does this result reveal a basic character flaw, or was he a survivor, the victim of a long run of bad luck, or the machinations of enemies, or even of some of those he counted as friends?

Certainly, in the last, and largest, of the several controversies he was involved in, the Johnson County affair, Asa Mercer was used by both sides. The cattlemen were happy enough to use him as a paid mouthpiece so long as he remained tractable, and they cut their ties with him as soon as he was not so tame. But the Democratic opposition treated him no better, and they even grudged him any political recompense for the highly risky public conversion of his sympathies. When he departed for northern Wyoming, neither side seemed to care very much.

Even so, does the boundless enthusiasm—almost phoenix-like in its persistence—count for nothing? The energy with which he pursued causes that seemed fatally damaged, sometimes achieved most of the result he sought, as when his heckling of the War Department forced the sale of the *Continental*, so that it could be used in the Mercer expedition. Without Mercer, not even 75 women would have come to Washington Territory that year, even though the total was not the 300 he loved to talk about. And finally, when the record of his life was complete, it was not dull.

Selected Bibliography

MANUSCRIPT COLLECTIONS

Clarence Bagley collection, University of Washington.
Dorothy Weintz collection, University of Washington.
Wyoming Stock Growers Association collection, American Heritage Center, University of Wyoming.

NEWSPAPERS AND JOURNALS

Mercer papers:
The Bowie Cross Timbers
Henrietta Journal
Northwestern Live Stock Journal
Oregon Granger (Albany)
The Texas Panhandle
Vernon Weekly Guard
Wichita Herald

Other papers:
The Basin Republican
The Big Horn County Rustler
The Big Horn River Pilot
The Billings Gazette
The Boston Herald
The Daily Boomerang (Laramie, Wyoming)
The Buffalo Bulletin
Daily California Alta (San Francisco)
Cheyenne Daily Leader
Cheyenne Daily Sun
The Dallas Daily Herald
Denison Daily News
Denver Times
Fort Worth Daily Democrat

The Fremont Clipper (Lander, Wyoming)
Live Stock Markets (Chicago)
The Lowell Daily Courier
Morning Oregonian
New York Herald
New York Daily Tribune
The New-York Times
Ogden Semi-Weekly Standard
The Overland Press (Olympia, Washington)
Oregon Sunday Journal
Pacific Northwest Quarterly
Pacific Tribune (Olympia, Washington)
The People's Voice (Buffalo, Wyoming)
Puget Sound Weekly
The Quarterly of the Oregon Historical Society
Reed College Bulletin
The Rocky Mountain News (Denver)
San Francisco Examiner
Seattle Post Intelligencer
Seattle Times
Seattle Weekly Gazette
Thermopolis Record
Tri-Weekly Astorian
The Washington Alumnus
The Washington Historical Quarterly
Worland Grit
The Wyoming Derrick (Casper, Wyoming)

Books

Ackerman, Kenneth D. *The Gold Ring: Jim Fisk, Jay Gould and Black Friday, 1869* (New York, 1988).

Bagley, Clarence B. *History of King County Washington* I (Chicago, 1929).

______. *History of Seattle, From the Earliest Settlement to the Present Time*, 3 vol. (Chicago, 1916).

Bancroft, Hubert Howe. *History of Oregon*, II (San Francisco, 1888).

Beauregard, Erving E. *Old Franklin: The Eternal Touch, A History of Franklin College, New Athens, Harrison County, Ohio.*

Bradsby, H. C., ed. *History of Bureau County, Illinois* (Chicago, 1885).

Bonney, Edward. *The Banditti of the Prairies: A Tale of the Mississippi Valley* (Chicago, 1881).

Bowden, Angie Burt. *Early Schools of Washington Territory* (Seattle, 1935).
Buck, Solon Justus. *The Granger Movement* (Cambridge, 1913).
Burroughs, John Rolfe. *Guardian of the Grasslands: The First Hundred Years of the Wyoming Stock Growers Association* (Cheyenne, 1971).
Chester, Giraud. *Embattled Maiden: The Life of Anna Dickinson* (New York, 1951).
Clark, Malcolm, Jr., ed. *The Diary of Judge Matthew P. Deady 1871–1892* 2 vol. (Portland, Oregon, 1975).
_____. *Eden Seekers: The Settlement of Oregon, 1818–1862* (Boston, 1981).
Cloud, Barbara. *The Business of Newspapers on the Western Frontier* (Reno, 1992).
Dary, David. *Red Blood and Black Ink: Journalism in the Old West* (New York, 1998).
DeArment. *Alias Frank Canton* (Norman, Oklahoma, 1996).
Denny, Arthur A. *Pioneer Days on Puget Sound* (Seattle, 1908).
Deutsch, Lenna A., ed. *Mercer's Belles: The Journal of a Reporter, by Roger Conant* (Seattle, 1960).
Douthitt, Lorena Katherin Charistian, ed. *Romance and Dim Trails: A History of Clay County* (Dallas, 1938).
Ellington, Charles G. *The Trial of U. S. Grant: The Pacific Coast Years, 1852–1854* (Glendale, California, 1987).
Franklin College Register: Biographical and Historical (Wheeling, 1908).
Gates, Charles M. *The First Century at the University of Washington, 1861–1961* (Seattle, 1964).
Gressley, Gene M. *Bankers and Cattlemen* (Lincoln, Nebraska, 1966).
Haley, J. Evetts. *Charles Goodnight: Cowman & Plainsman* (Norman, Oklahoma, 1936).
Harrington, George B. *Past and Present of Bureau County, Illinois* (Chicago, 1906).
Henderson, Jeff S., ed. *100 Years in Montague County, Texas* (Saint Jo, Texas, 1958).
History of the Bench and Bar of Oregon (Portland, Oregon, 1910).
House of Representatives Executive Document 337 (40th Congress, Second Session), Vessels Bought, Sold and Chartered by the United States, July 16, 1868.
Ingrisano, Michael N. *A History of Enforcement in the United States Customs Service* (Washington, D. C., 1988).
Jones, Billy M. *The Saga of Texas, 1875–1900: The Search for Maturity* (Austin, 1965).
Kemble, John Haskell. *The Panama Route, 1848–1869* (Columbia, S. C., 1990).
King, Grace Elizabeth. *Jean Baptiste le Moyne, Sieur de Bienville* (New York, 1892).
Larson, Robert W. *Populism in the Mountain West* (Albuquerque, 1986).
Lucas, Mattie Davis, and Hall, Mita Holsapple. *A History of Grayson County, Texas* (Sherman, Texas, 1936).
Marshall, Don B. *Oregon Shipwrecks* (Portland, Oregon, 1984).
McCaffree, Robert. *Century in the Saddle* (Denver, 1967).
Mercer, Asa Shinn. *The Banditti of the Plains, or The Cattlemen's Invasion of Wyoming in 1892:* [*The Crowning Infamy of the Ages*] (Denver, Colorado, 1894). Reprint edition Norman, Oklahoma, 1954.

_____. *Big Horn County Wyoming: The Gem of the Rockies* (Hyattville, Wyoming, 1906).

_____. *Indian Chief Washakie, and the Big Horn Hot Springs* (Hyattville, Wyoming, 1916).

_____. *The Material Resources of Linn County, Oregon, Embracing Detailed Descriptions and Business Directory* (Albany, Oregon, 1875).

_____. *The Material Resources of Marion County, Oregon, With a Complete Business Directory* (Salem, Oregon, 1876).

_____. *The Pioneer* (Chicago, 1913).

_____. *Washington Territory: The Great North-West, Her Material Resources, and Claims to Emigration. A Plain Statement of Things as They Exist* (Utica, N. Y., 1865).

Morgan, Jonnie R. *The History of Wichita Falls* (Oklahoma City, 1931).

Otis, F. N. *Illustrated History of the Panama Railroad* (New York, 1862).

Overton, Richard C. *Gulf to Rockies: The Heritage of the Fort Worth and Denver—Colorado and Southern Railways, 1861–1898* (Austin, Texas, 1953).

Perkin, Robert L. *The First Hundred Years: An Informal History of Denver and the Rocky Mountain News* (New York, 1959).

Potter, Mrs. W. R. *History of Montague County, Texas* (Saint Jo Texas, 1958).

Prince, Carl E., and Keller, Mollie. *The U. S. Custom Service: A Bicentennial History* (Washington, D. C., 1989).

Randall, J. G., and Donald, David. *The Civil War and Reconstruction* (Lexington, Mass., 1969).

Robertson, Pauline Durrett, and Robertson, R. L. *Panhandle Pilgrimage* (Amarillo, 1976).

Ross, Charles P., and Rouse, T. L. *Official Early-Day History of Wilbarger County* (Vernon, Texas, 1973).

Rush, Nixon Orwin. *Mercer's Banditti of the Plains* (Tallahassee, 1961).

Smith, Helena Huntington. *The War on the Powder River: The History of an Insurrection* (New York, 1966).

Sorenson, Alfred. *The Story of Omaha* (Omaha, 1923).

Stanley, F. *The Story of the Texas Panhandle Railroads* (Borger, Texas, 1976).

Taylor, William Charles. *A History of Clay County* (Austin, 1972).

Three-Quarters of a Century at Washington (Seattle, 1941).

Watt, Roberta Frye. *Four Wagons West: The Story of Seattle* (Portland, Oregon, 1931).

Weist, Tom. *A History of the Cheyenne People* (Billings, Montana, 1977).

Wright, E. W. *Lewis & Dryden's Marine History of the Pacific Northwest* (Seattle, 1967).

INDEX